Praise for *The Right Way to Win*

"Zafft writes with a sense of humor, though his mission is serious: showing readers how to run businesses better and more ethically. This book is a fun-to-read, practical guide for making business ethics work in the real world." **—Bill Canfield, serial entrepreneur and former Chairman and CEO of TALX Corporation**

"This book delivers great substance that's user friendly. Fresh, practical insights into business ethics come with a writing style that is clear, sharp, and lively. Online training/certification tools make it ideal for companies of all sizes." **—Melissa Di Donato, CEO, SUSE**

The Right Way to Win colorfully illustrates how ethics live at the center of market-leading businesses. Author Zafft brings fresh perspectives to timeless issues and also offers online materials that help translate principles into practice." **—John Schilling, MD, Partner, TPG Capital, Head of Operations, North America and EU, Co-Head, Global Healthcare Team**

"Zafft provides what might be the first managerial guidebook for making ethical business decisions. Particularly laudable is his combination of analytical depth and breadth, addressing not only key philosophical differences in defining ethical behavior, but also the relevance of these differences for managers responsible for making organizational decisions and building an ethical organization. He avoids platitudes while providing clear and actionable suggestions." —**Edward J. Zajac, James F. Beré Professor of Management and Organizations, Kellogg School of Management**

"This book is a must read for any executive or professional focusing on making business ethics work in the real world and driving and sustaining ethical decisions throughout an organization. The book focuses extensively on practical managerial techniques and individual accountability, showing the reader how to do well by doing good." —**Mark Arian, CEO, Advisory at Korn Ferry**

"Helping students bridge the gap between academia and practice is one of the most formidable challenges facing professors in professional schools—this book with its mix of theory and on-the-ground suggestions will make that task easier." —**Lisa B. Bernstein, Wilson-Dickinson Professor of Law, The University of Chicago Law School**

"In marketing, nothing beats a great reputation. Zafft persuasively links how a business behaves with how it performs. His real-world perspective and light, conversational style produce an insightful and entertaining read." —**John M. Howell, Vice President, CX & Marketing at Centene Corporation**

"Ethics and integrity have become increasingly important in the modern business world and more difficult to navigate. With his book, *The Right Way to Win*, Zafft helps light the path. And he does so both with wit and humor." —**Marcus A. McDaniel, VP & Deputy General Counsel, The ServiceMaster Company**

"Of the many books I have read about business and ethics, this is by far the best. Clear. Direct. Actionable. Zafft's insights into reputational risk and crisis management are particularly dead on." —**Amos Gelb, Executive Director, Washington Media Institute and former Senior Producer, CNN Investigative**

"Ensuring that our global enterprise operates ethically—from top to bottom—is of utmost importance. Zafft hits the nail on the head: it's easy to identify the ethical standards under which to operate; the hard part lies in implementing strict adherence through a culture of accountability. Zafft's *practical* recommendations provide business leaders the necessary tools to succeed in building, and sustaining, an ethical business in the real world." —**Mark A. Menghini, Senior Vice President & General Counsel, Aegion Corporation**

"Mixing case studies with background theory and pragmatic advice, this book offers a thoughtful and engaging framework for business leaders to develop and maintain a culture that values ethics and reputation in the increasingly challenging environment of 21st-century business." —**Mark Enyedy, CEO, ImmunoGen, Inc.**

"Trust is the currency of business, and ethics the backbone of trust. Zafft not only dissects the how-to of doing the right thing but also the why. He nimbly takes us from theory to vision to an actionable review of real-life failures of integrity, their consequences, and how to avoid repeating previously unfathomable business disasters. Spoiler alert: Doing the right thing always wins." —**Ernest Greer, co-President, Greenberg Traurig, LLP**

"Informed by Zafft's years as an attorney and management consultant in the no-holds-barred, business climate of the former Soviet Union, this book is well-researched, soundly argued and always entertaining. *The Right Way to Win* ranks up there with the best of Dale Carnegie as an indispensable management tool for the modern business executive." —**Steven Hellman, CEO (former), Credit Suisse Russia/CIS**

"The world is full of Machiavellis and, thank goodness, they generally lose in the end. Robert Zafft's book offers nuts and bolts techniques for becoming an ethical business warrior who wins in the both the short term and the long. May he and his readers be strengthened!" —**Salvador Litvak, Executive Director, AccidentalTalmudist.org**

"Who says ethics is boring? This book grabs you from the start, reads like a novel, and is totally real. I highly recommend it to those responsible for governing and managing organizations; professionals in legal, ethics and compliance; business school programs from undergraduate to executive levels; and anyone who is interested in doing the right thing and leading the right way." —**Yuen Teen MAK, Associate Professor at National University of Singapore**

"Zafft's straightforward style and conversational tone, plus real, easily understandable anecdotes, make business ethics accessible, interesting, and mainstream. A must-read book for those working in Asia, where the book's lessons learned definitely apply!" —**Mark Militello, Head of Markets and Clearance & Collateral Management, Asia Pacific, BNY Mellon**

"Zafft deals with how real people behave in the real world, offering tools and techniques for running an ethical organization. His book correctly argues that leaders should build firm cultures that align employee self-esteem with their organization's end goals." —**Dariusz Oleszczuk, former CEO, Dentons Europe**

"Ethical choices are often obvious in hindsight, this book provides a prospective roadmap for winning in the long term." —**Mark Sherman, Managing Director, Telstra Ventures**

Ethics lie at the core of business decisions and leadership. Modern business leaders seek to balance the interests of stakeholders and apply values as well as analyze data in their leadership. Robert Zafft's book, building on the author's decades of leadership experience and advising, as well as his extensive business school teaching experience, is a tour de force in modern business ethics. A must-read for aspiring and actual business executives." —**Mark P. Taylor, Dean and Donald Danforth, Jr. Distinguished Professor of Finance, John M. Olin School of Business, Washington University in St. Louis**

The Right Way to Win

Making Business Ethics Work in the Real World

■ ■ ■

Robert Zafft

ROWMAN & LITTLEFIELD
Lanham • Boulder • New York • London

Acquisitions Editor: Natalie Mandziuk
Assistant Editor: Deni Remsberg
Executive Channel Manager: Karin Cholak

Credits and acknowledgments for material borrowed from other sources, and reproduced with permission, appear on the appropriate pages within the text.

Published by Rowman & Littlefield
An imprint of The Rowman & Littlefield Publishing Group, Inc.
4501 Forbes Boulevard, Suite 200, Lanham, Maryland 20706
www.rowman.com

6 Tinworth Street, London SE11 5AL, United Kingdom

British Library Cataloguing in Publication Information Available

Library of Congress Cataloging-in-Publication Data

ISBN 978-1-5381-4070-3 (cloth : alk. paper)
ISBN 978-1-5381-4071-0 (paperback : alk. paper)
ISBN 978-1-5381-4072-7 (electronic)

∞™ The paper used in this publication meets the minimum requirements of American National Standard for Information Sciences – Permanence of Paper for Printed Library Materials, ANSI/NISO Z39.48-1992.

To my brother, Richard,
with gratitude
for his love, encouragement, and example

Contents

■ ■ ■

Acknowledgments

■ ■ ■

Writing a book is a lone pilgrimage, but not necessarily a lonely one.

Along this journey, I have enjoyed the encouragement, guidance, and help of many people. I would like to extend particular acknowledgment and thanks to: Prof. Robert C. Clark, Prof. Lisa Bernstein, Patrick Cotter, Warren Buffett, Steve Sandweiss, Dimitri Vaynblat, PhD, Prof. Hillary Elfenbein, Amos Gelb, and Dennis P. Guilliams, as well as reviewers: Julian Chu (Fortune 50 company), Assoc. Prof. Yuen Teen MAK (National University of Singapore), Marcus A. McDaniel (ServiceMaster Global Holdings, Inc.), Brian D. Ray (University of Florida), and Jessica McManus Warnell (University of Notre Dame). Any errors are my own.

To my family, I owe a debt of gratitude reaching far beyond this book. This includes my mother, Marlene, and my siblings, Susie (of blessed memory), Richard, and Nancy. The spirit and example of my late father, Gene (of blessed memory), continue to guide not only my steps but also those of so many others whose lives he touched.

Finally, I would like to acknowledge and thank my wife, Tara, and our children, Eleanor, Dietrich, and Eva, for the privilege and joy of being their husband and father, as well as for their putting up with the writing of this book. It has been a long-term and at-times-inconvenient guest in our home. The family-room table is now free . . . for the time being.

Enough Already!

■ ■ ■

"Am I the only one around here who gives a sh-t about the rules?!"

—John Goodman, as Walter Sobchak, in *The Big Lebowski*

People are angry.

On the Internet, on TV, in their daily lives, people look around and see a system that's broken.

Cheaters prosper. Officials charged with upholding the law break it without consequence.

Business leaders buy or lawyer their way out of rules the rest of us have to follow. Friendly Boards of Directors ratchet executive pay above performance.

CEOs whose companies have crashed into the ground float to safety beneath golden parachutes. Meanwhile, the companies' employees, customers, shareholders, creditors, and communities burn amid the wreckage.

This isn't how things are supposed to work.

Things are falling apart. We have to put them back together.

But how?

That's what this book is about.

WHY THIS BOOK IS FOR YOU

The ideas and examples in this book come from a business-ethics course I teach at Olin Business School, Washington University in St. Louis.

Nearly all of my students have demanding jobs in the real world. They are busy. They have mortgages to pay and families to feed. They want the fundamentals of business ethics explained in ways that are simple, straightforward, practical, and fun.

This book serves a stand-alone guide to making business ethics work in the real world. It is meant, in part, for people already in the workforce. It is also meant for students in business or nonbusiness programs who want to understand the basics of business ethics. Such students include those preparing for job interviews. Ninety-six percent of employers rate ethics as important or very important in their hiring decisions.[1] So, the nuts and bolts of business ethics are things every job seeker should be ready to discuss knowledgeably.

This book also forms the core of turnkey courses for business-school programs, leadership development and corporate training, and continuing professional education. Visit www.therightwaytowin.com to access coursework and exercises, to qualify for a certificate in Business Ethics, or to earn continuing-professional-education (CPE) credits in accounting, law, and other fields.

Business ethics, of course, should matter not just to people in the workforce and students but to all of us. So, I have written this book for them—and for you.

WHAT MAKES THIS BOOK DIFFERENT

Mine has not been a typical career. And so this is not a typical business-ethics book.

Inspired by Sailing in a Perfect Storm

My introduction to business ethics came as an American lawyer working in Russia during its wild 1990s. Bankers were getting blown up on Main Street during rush hour. Bureaucrats and gangsters were carving up the crown jewels of the most resource-rich country on Earth. Western carpetbaggers were fanning out across Mother Russia hoping to exploit the locals but typically getting ripped off themselves.

After ten years on the Russian Front, I joined the Chicago office of McKinsey & Company, the world's premier consulting firm, just in time for the Dot.Com Boom & Bust, and later traveled frequently to Asia in the aftermath of its financial crisis. I worked in the Bay Area technology and private-equity/venture-capital sectors during the U.S. mortgage meltdown, as well as the first phase of a social-media revolution that continues to this day.

A glutton for punishment, I left the Bay Area to spend three years in Central Asia, working first for retired British Prime Minister Tony Blair and then once again for McKinsey & Company. Advising governments and enterprises in Central Asia was like reliving the 1990s in Russia, only even colder.

Practical, Compact, and Implementation Oriented

Experience has taught me that business ethics must deal with how real people behave in the real world. Moralizing is for academics, politicians, and commentators who, before criticizing anyone else, should take a good look in the mirror.

This book keeps things short, simple, and to the point. It leaves out the nonessential. Compliance issues are important, of course, but real-world businesspeople will seek advice on them from compliance functions like legal, accounting, and human resources. Likewise, this book shuns the flavor-of-the-week approach of many business-ethics books. Sustainability and fair trade may seem top-of-mind today, for example, but nobody knows for sure what tomorrow's hot-button issues will be.

What really matters, then, is learning how to spot ethical issues generally and to think about them deeply and practically. Just as critically, though, readers must grasp the managerial tools and techniques for putting a chosen ethical course of action into effect. Ethics have to work on the shop floor, on the loading dock, and out in the field.

People who treat ethics as a back-office issue will fail.

Focused on Winning

This book lays out two themes uncommon for a business-ethics book. First, in the real world, deciding what is ethical is often straightforward. What is hard for any organization is getting the people in it to act in the ethical manner set out by management. This means that sound ethical practices flow from sound managerial practices. Such practices must, above all, define and enforce individual accountability. They include organizational design, setting of key performance indicators (KPIs), process control, culture building, and crisis management.

The second theme concerns the real-world importance of reputation. A businessperson's, and a business's, prime asset is reputation. Entrepreneurs, owners, and managers simply cannot afford to gamble with it—or to let their subordinates gamble with it. Typically, the greatest victim of wrongdoing by managers and employees is the business they work for. So, at the end of the day, learning the right way to win is about *winning*.

Part I of this book describes what we mean by "ethical behavior." Various ethical frameworks exist, and these can produce varying—and sometimes directly contradictory—outcomes. Sometimes, both sides can be right.

Part II looks at what it means for a company, or other organization, to be ethical. This is not a simple question. Liberals and conservatives can end up on the opposite sides of an issue from where people might expect. This part also looks at how critical business reputation is to business leaders ranging from history's "real" Godfather, Carlo Gambino, to the world's greatest investor, Warren Buffett.

Part III focuses on the managerial tools and techniques for encouraging and enforcing ethical behavior throughout an organization. These include the organizational designs and process controls that managers must put in place to define and enforce individual accountability. Part III also explores the primacy of culture, which, in Warren Buffett's view, "Determines how an organization behaves . . . more than rule books."[2]

In this regard, case examples will show how successful cultures align the interests of employees with those of the company. They make employees feel that doing a good job is about more than a paycheck; it's about expressing who they are as individuals. It's about employees building and enjoying self-esteem.

Without both individual accountability and alignment of interests, the people in an organization will not act ethically.

Finally, part III considers special situations. The first is crisis management. Crises overturn normal incentives and expectations and can trigger a shortsightedness that sees ethics of small account.

The second special situation involves cross-fires. In a cross-fire, the business finds itself caught between contending outside forces. These situations particularly arise when technologies or social mores are so new, or so fast-changing, that the nuts and bolts of ethical behavior haven't been worked out yet. One example would be the do's and don'ts of online privacy when Internet advertising was in its early stages. More recently, the ethics of restroom and changing-room policies have caught national attention, costing one major retailer over $10 billion in market value.

A colleague of Mark Twain once quipped that "everybody talks about the weather, but nobody does anything about it."[3]

So it is with business ethics. Lots of people talk about it. A lot.

But the time has come to do more than talk. This book is for people who want to *do* something about business ethics.

Let's get started!

NOTES

1. Hart Research Associates, "It Takes More Than a Major: Employer Priorities for College Learning and Student Success," *Liberal Education* 99, no. 2 (Spring 2013), accessed May 24, 2017, https://www.aacu.org/publications-research/periodicals/it-takes-more-major-employer-priorities-college-learning-and.

2. Warren Buffett, "Memorandum to Berkshire Hathaway Managers," July 26, 2010, accessed October 25, 2016, http://prosperosworld.com/warren-buffetts-memo-to-managers/2011/.

3. Charles Dudley Warner, "Everybody Talks about the Weather, but Nobody Does Anything About It," Quote Investigator, accessed May 3, 2019, https://quoteinvestigator.com/2010/04/23/everybody-talks-about-the-weather/.

Part I

WHAT IS ETHICAL BEHAVIOR?

1

CEO Follies: Beyond Greed

■ ■ ■

"Can't anybody here play this game?"

—NY Mets Manager Casey Stengel

CEO follies make great headlines. They sell newspapers. They boost ratings and drive website traffic.

Unmasking the corporate high-and-mighty for what they really are seems right and just. But is there more to the story? Is our thirst for sport and payback blinding us to things we need to see and understand to make business ethics work in the real world?

Let's look at three, high-profile CEO scandals. The basic stories—Clueless, Bootless, and Shameless—may be familiar. But the backstories are not. It is these backstories which expose the deeper challenges of business ethics. And it is these backstories which, paradoxically, show why making business ethics work in the real world requires us to look beyond greed.

CLUELESS: JOHN STUMPF, CEO, WELLS FARGO

It was time for a smackdown.

And a good one at that.

CEO John Stumpf took his place before the Senate Committee on Banking, Housing, and Urban Affairs. He knew what was coming.

Stumpf ran Wells Fargo, the world's most valuable bank. On his watch, 5,300 Wells Fargo employees had opened over two million phony accounts in the names of hundreds of thousands of customers. In most cases, customers had suffered no harm. But other customers had been hit with bogus fees and either paid them or had their credit scores dinged.

The fraud had done almost nothing to benefit Wells Fargo directly. The bogus accounts generated no commercial activity, no loans, nor credit-card payments. Wells Fargo did earn $2.6 million or so in fake fees, which bore the same relation to the bank's $86 billion in revenues as the 9,600 residents of Cody, Wyoming, to the entire population of the United States.

So why cheat?

Financial services are a cut-throat business. Wells Fargo's upper management wanted to capture all the financial-services business of each of the bank's customers: credit cards, checking accounts, mortgages, insurance, and so on. The more accounts a customer had with Wells Fargo, the more profitable that customer became and the less likely he or she was to switch to a competitor.

In consultant speak, the bank wanted to "own the customer wallet." Consequently, Stumpf and his direct reports set high goals for rank-and-file sales staff. Staff received firm targets for the average number of accounts per customer. Line managers warned these lower-level employees: hit your sales numbers, or hit the road.

Faced with difficult, if not impossible, goals, the staff kept their jobs by opening fake accounts and crediting these accounts to their sales numbers.

Managers took the good news at face value, reported it up the chain, and landed rich bonuses. With Wall Street analysts also tracking Wells Fargo's average number of accounts per customer, the bank's stock price soared. CEO Stumpf became $200 million richer.

Eventually, the wrongdoing came to light. Wells Fargo paid $190 million in fines and restitution, equal to about 0.2 percent of revenues. The bank fired the 5,300 lower-level employees caught cheating but allowed the senior manager most responsible for the fiasco to retire with a fat financial package.

So, like many disgraced CEOs before him, Stumpf was called before a Congressional committee.

At the hearing, Senator Elizabeth Warren, a razor-sharp former Harvard Law professor and Director of the U.S. Consumer Financial Protection Bureau, laid into Stumpf with a fury. "You haven't resigned. You haven't returned a single nickel of your personal earnings! You haven't fired a single senior executive," she thundered. "It's gutless leadership! . . . You should resign! You should give back the money that you took! . . . You should be criminally investigated!"

There was both more and less to Senator Warren's verbal body slam of Stumpf than met the eye. Her grilling of the disgraced CEO included the following specific accusations:

- "In your time as Chairman & CEO, Wells has been famous for cross selling. . . . Other big banks average fewer than three accounts per customer, but you set the target at eight accounts. . . [and] you squeezed your employees to the breaking point to meet cross-sell quotas."
- "Wall Street loved it."
- "Cross selling is one of the major reasons that Wells has become the most valuable bank in the world."

In other words, Warren lambasted Stumpf for doing his job! Banks are supposed to cross-sell. Private-sector firms, if they want to stay in business, must beat their competitors. Good managers drive their employees with both carrot and stick. General Electric CEO Jack Welch, for example, became a billionaire and media darling by setting nearly impossible stretch targets for managers and rank-and-file employees, the bottom 10 percent of whom he canned. Finally, shouldn't every CEO be trying to make his or her company the most valuable in its industry?

So, what gives?

By virtually all accounts, Stumpf had been an outstanding CEO. In 2013, *Fortune* magazine named him Businessperson of the Year. Stumpf also received Morningstar's 2015 CEO of the Year Award, besting Amazon's Jeff Bezos and General Electric's Jeff Immelt. Ironically, the Morningstar award praised Stumpf for "shunn[ing] activities that put profits ahead of customers."[1]

John Stumpf grew up a humble, if not poor, farm boy in Minnesota. A below-average student, he knocked around for several years after high school, working in a bakery, handling automobile repossessions. He got a job in banking in his late twenties and began a slow, steady rise through various corporate ranks, becoming Wells Fargo's CEO in 2007. Wells Fargo weathered the 2008 recession well, being forced to take, rather than seeking, $25 billion in U.S. Troubled Asset Relief Program (TARP) funds.[2] Wells Fargo repaid the funds as soon as allowed in order to free itself from TARP oversight.

Under Stumpf's leadership, from the depth of the recession to his resignation under fire in October 2016, Wells Fargo's stock price quadrupled.

Sadly, however uplifting his personal story and successful his stewardship, Stumpf will be remembered for the fraudulent account scandal that bounced him from the helm of Wells Fargo.

Before the Committee, Stumpf pointed out that the scandal involved fewer than 2 percent of bank employees. The amount of money at issue represented a rounding error in the bank's financial statements.

What Stumpf's story skipped over was that fraud involving over 5,000 employees in a single business unit shows not just a breakdown in normal rules and controls but a deeply corrupt culture. And the crux of the CEO's job is to drive the culture.

YouTube clips of Stumpf before the Senate Committee make painful watching.[3] An invitee to the Congressional woodshed knows not to fight back against Senators or Congressmen, however much they taunt, bully, or grandstand. But Stumpf's soft-spokenness came across first as indifference, then as disdain. He failed to grasp how this fraud looked from the outside, as well as how his low-key, steady-hand-on-the-tiller demeanor might goad Senators on both sides of the aisle.

The Senators wanted to see Stumpf confess the scale and seriousness of what went wrong. They wanted him to admit fault and to describe how he had—and would continue to—kick ass and take names. Instead, he matter-of-factly admitted letting the senior executive most at fault resign with her bonuses and stock options intact.[4] Pressed on how he would clean house going forward, he blandly stated that he would wait for the corporation's normal governance processes to work and then accept the outcome. In other words, he seemed to say, he would sit back and do nothing! This passivity cost him his job.[5]

A Watergate-era Senator once declared, "It's not the crime, it's the cover-up" which leads to a public figure's downfall. For Stumpf, it wasn't even the cover-up; it was the cluelessness.

BOOTLESS: MARISSA MAYER, CEO, YAHOO

Marissa Mayer—the woman who had everything—got something she never wanted: an ethics scandal.

A Stanford engineer who danced in the school's performance of *The Nutcracker Suite*, Mayer had joined Google as one of its first twenty employees. She had initiated or led core products like Google News, Desktop Search, Local Search, Google Earth, and Google Maps. At one point, Mayer was the youngest member of Google's executive operating committee.

A proven innovator and popular leader, she left Google in 2012 to become CEO of Yahoo. At the time, she was thirty-seven years old and pregnant with her first child. The sixth Yahoo CEO within the previous five years, she tried to revive the Internet icon's fortunes with a push into mobile technology.

Brilliant, accomplished, and beautiful, Mayer became an icon in her own right, as likely to appear on the cover of *Vanity Fair* as *Fortune* or *Forbes*.

But Mayer failed, notwithstanding her undeniable talent and drive. Formerly admiring employees began calling her "Evita" to mock her combined love of the limelight and her inability to get things done.

After four years as CEO, she put what was left of Yahoo on the auction block. Yahoo, which in 2008 had spurned a $45 billion offer from Microsoft, sold itself in 2016 to Verizon for $4.8 billion.[6]

Within two months of inking the Verizon deal, however, a scandal broke. Yahoo announced that in 2014, nearly 500 million Yahoo mail accounts had been hacked. Immediately after the announcement, users started closing their Yahoo accounts, and lawyers started planning class-action lawsuits for Yahoo's violation of data-breach-notification laws. The familiar American refrain of "What did she know, and when did she know it" rang out. Verizon's lawyers began wading through the deal documents to see what leverage the company had in the scandal's wake.

The Verizon-Yahoo deal ultimately closed, but in light of the hacking scandal, Verizon forced Yahoo to chop $350 million (over 7 percent) off the purchase price.[7]

Still, Mayer did not come out too badly. Her compensation and severance package, valued at $187–219 million, doubtless took some of the sting out of failure.[8]

Compared to Stumpf's case, Marissa Mayer's seems less complex, but that may be because fewer facts have as yet come to light.

Discovery of an IT-system breach starts a countdown clock. Generally, the company has a fixed amount of time before it must give notice of the breach under federal and state notification laws. In that time, the company has to overcome a host of technical and operational challenges.[9] The company has to secure the system, to plug data leaks, to identify and destroy any remaining malware, and to fix the breach itself. This means figuring out the cause of the breach, coming up with and putting in place new safeguards, and testing the new system.

Next, in order to disclose properly, the company has to understand what data has been compromised, whether it was in some way encrypted, and how likely it is that the data will be used by third parties. The company must also determine who will be adversely affected, who should be notified, and when notification should take place.

But there's a catch: breach notification may sometimes be delayed if required to restore the integrity of the system. If Yahoo had been hacked by a state intelligence service, as the company suspected, restoring system integrity might not have been simple or quick. Delay in notification might have been justified.

A second question arises about disclosure, in this case to Verizon. If Yahoo believed itself unready to disclose the breach to its own customers, what, if any, disclosure was it required or permitted to make to its potential acquirer?

Lots of lawyers bickered, and made lots of money, over what Yahoo did right, and what it did wrong, with regard to the data breach and notification.

Throughout this process, CEO Mayer no doubt had plenty of expert advice, but that did not make her decisions easy. For Yahoo's shareholders, the resulting 7 percent cut in Yahoo's sale price added insult to injury. Pressed to respond, Yahoo's Board denied Mayer a cash bonus for 2016, as well as equity awards for 2017. Her reputation as a business leader and Silicon Valley icon, however, took an ever bigger hit. Down but not out, Mayer left Yahoo post-acquisition and co-founded a technology-business incubator.[10]

SHAMELESS: RAJAT GUPTA, FORMER MANAGING DIRECTOR, MCKINSEY & COMPANY; BOARD MEMBER, THE GOLDMAN SACHS GROUP, INC.

It was October 23, 2012. Rajat Gupta and his lawyer stood up before U.S. District Court Judge Jed Rakoff.

From 1994 to 2003, Gupta had led McKinsey & Company, the world's premier consulting firm. Reaching retirement age, he harvested plum directorships at top-flight companies. The final chapter of his career, though, would feature betrayal, scandal, and jail.

Where and how did things go so wrong?

On Gupta's watch at McKinsey, the company went truly global. It opened offices in twenty-three countries, doubled the number of partners, and nearly tripled revenues.[11] No firm was more influential. None more respected. Except for General Electric and IBM, no other firm had placed so many of its senior executives as CEOs of major companies, who then hired the firm for multimillion dollar assignments.[12] Near the end of Gupta's tenure, both McKinsey's supporters and detractors began referring to the firm as "The Jesuits of Capitalism."[13]

Success had its rewards, and Gupta was no stranger to the good life. While Gupta was still McKinsey's Managing Director, a young McKinsey partner—also named Rajat Gupta—received a check from the Accounting Department. The amount of the check was so large that the young partner thought he just been given his annual bonus. What he had in fact received, by mistake, was the check reimbursing Managing Director Gupta for travel and entertainment expenses.

Wealth and poverty are relative, though. Gupta flew First Class, stayed in five-star hotels, and had a net worth in the millions of dollars. But he moved among billionaires. Such poverty rankled. As Gupta lugged his roller bag in and out of First Class airport lounges, he must have envied the Fortune 100 CEOs, Silicon Valley investors, and hedge-fund owners who, like Gordon Gekko in the movie, *Wall Street*, had already taken off in their own jets.

After retiring from McKinsey, Gupta served as a Board Director for several of the world's leading companies, including Procter & Gamble, AMR (the parent company of American Airlines), and Goldman Sachs.

Goldman Sachs was to the world of finance what McKinsey was to consulting: the sharpest, the richest, the most prestigious firm in its line of business. In any meeting, Goldman bankers were the self-proclaimed "smartest guys in the room."

Gupta betrayed their trust. According to the U.S. Securities and Exchange Commission, moments after the close of two separate Goldman Board meetings, Gupta called his friend Raj Rajaratnam, a co-founder of the Galleon Group LLC hedge fund. Gupta unlawfully tipped his friend off to Berkshire Hathaway Inc.'s pending $5 billion investment in Goldman, as well as Goldman's expected financial results. Rajaratnam bought 120,000 Goldman shares based on this inside information. He netted about $17 million, or one-quarter the cost of a Gulfstream G650 executive jet.

Cell-phone records connected Gupta's calls to Rajaratnam with Goldman's Board meetings and with Rajaratnam's trades. The federal government prosecuted them both for insider trading and won convictions. After Gupta and his lawyer rose, Judge Rakoff sentenced the former McKinsey & Company Managing Director to two years in jail, along with a $5 million fine.

Gupta was released from federal prison after sixteen months. He appealed his conviction on what to most people was a technicality. Win or lose in court, he has become an unperson. McKinsey formally states that it has no connection with him, and his name does not even appear in the alumni directory of the firm he led for nine years.

Unlike John Stumpf or Marissa Mayer, Rajat Gupta cannot try to put harm in perspective, make excuses, or cite mitigating circumstances.

His actions were inexcusable. They also remain puzzling.

To many people, the great unanswered riddle of Gupta's tragedy is, "*Why* did he do it?" He was one of the most respected business figures in the world. He sat on the Boards of the world's leading companies. He had made millions of dollars, with the likelihood of making many millions more. Perhaps he couldn't buy his own plane—but he could time-share. Why did he take the risks he did, and in such a stupid way? Any fan of the television crime show *CSI* knows not to commit a crime using your own cell phone!

The "why" of Gupta is an entertaining question. But, maybe, it's not the one we should ask. There is another take on Gupta's downfall, and it is one that neither he nor McKinsey & Company wanted people looking into.

What if the real question involving Gupta is not *why* he did it but *when* he did it?

Gupta's wealth, sway, and renown as a Director flowed directly from his nine years helming McKinsey. Arguably, it was he who had turned the firm into The Jesuits of Capitalism. As a result, his crimes more than discredited him personally. They threatened McKinsey's global mystique, power, and primacy. They also called into question the multibillion-dollar symbiosis between top-flight consulting firms and their corporate clients.

In light of these stakes, the *when* of Gupta's misdeeds takes center stage. Gupta's rise at McKinsey had been neither smooth nor certain. In that firm's up-or-out promotion system, Gupta came close to getting fired before making partner. What if trading on confidential information was not just how Rajat Gupta fell *after* he left McKinsey but how Gupta rose *during* his time there? Nothing is more valuable to companies than inside information on their competitors, the very thing Gupta had access to throughout his McKinsey career.

A follow-up question is whether Gupta truly was an ethical outlier.[14] CEOs set the tone. They drive the culture. Gupta ran McKinsey for nearly a decade. The number of partners doubled while he was in charge. So far, only one other McKinsey partner, Anil Kumar, has been convicted for passing confidential client information. Would it be unfair to speculate whether he and Gupta were just the tip of an iceberg?

Clearly, after Gupta's and Kumar's crimes came to light, quelling client doubts and fears about more widespread corruption became McKinsey's number one task.[15]

The firm succeeded.

Should it have?

THE BACKSTORIES AND CEO FOLLIES RECONSIDERED

Watching CEOs get smacked in the Senate, slammed in the media, or sentenced in federal court both enrages and delights us.

We can't stand cheaters. We love to see the proud and powerful brought low. Small wonder beheadings at the Tower of London drew such large crowds.

But as entertaining as the morality plays of Stumpf, Mayer, and Gupta are, there is more to their stories.

Knowing versus Suspecting versus Wishing to Believe

Re-telling CEO Follies makes a key point. There is what we know, what we suspect, and what we wish to believe. To get business ethics right, we cannot mix or muddle them.

Human beings like stories. We are hard-wired to remember and re-tell them. They're the most natural way to engage and persuade other people.

Senator Warren had a story to tell about John Stumpf: he's a greedy man who drove his underlings to the breaking point. He sat back while they cheated customers and now thinks he and his senior reports can just take the money and run. We have to stop them. We have to punish them. To do this, we need more severe laws and more determined prosecutors who will put these people in jail where they belong.

Warren's story was simple. It was moving. But was it the whole story? The Dodd–Frank Wall Street Reform and Consumer Protection Act passed after the 2008 recession runs 2,300 pages and has spawned 14,000 pages of regulations. That is only a single piece of financial-services legislation. All rules governing financial institutions and their operations run into the tens of thousands of pages. Is it likely that the problems at Wells Fargo sprang from a gap in this vast regulatory scheme that failed adequately to ban or penalize fraud?

Regarding firmer determination to prosecute, was there reason to think the Obama-era Justice Department had gone soft? Across numerous cases in recent years, federal prosecutors have indicted senior business executives, only to have charges tossed out by trial judges, rejected by juries, or reversed by appeals courts. If any problem with prosecutors plagues our legal system currently, it may be abuse by overzealous prosecutors, rather than unwillingness to file charges when a worthy case exists.[16] Various rationales might exist for why high-level wrongdoers at banks seem to escape individual punishment. But, according to the very judge who sentenced Rajat Gupta, the reasons cited by Senator Warren are not among them.[17]

Looking beyond Greed

Suspecting that Senator Warren's story may have been incomplete does not clear Stumpf of mistakes or wrongdoing. Far from it. But we must always beware letting our love of stories, particularly fairy tales with their stock heroes and villains, confuse what we wish to believe with what we suspect or know.

Stumpf wanted us to believe one fairy tale. Warren asked us to believe another.

So what should we do?

The first thing is to quit listening to, telling, or believing in fairy tales! In other words, if we want to grapple with making business ethics work in the real world, we should start by looking beyond greed.

That's right: look beyond greed.

Looking beyond greed doesn't mean that some, most, or all of us are not greedy at some point. But the fact is that more often than not, **one person's "greed" is another person's "ambition."** It may feel good to sit in judgment of others, but it rarely gets us anywhere in terms of creating ground rules for how we should *behave*.

Readiness to find greed in others steers us into thinking that every failure springs from a failing. This leads us to craft fixes for problems that don't exist, or to try controlling or punishing misbehavior where there was none. For example, Marissa Mayer failed to revive Yahoo's fortunes. Did she therefore mismanage? Did she disclose the data breach of accounts to her customers or to Verizon less promptly than she should have? Did Yahoo on her watch necessarily break the law, misrepresent, or breach the agreement with Verizon? Or did she and Yahoo act properly? At this point, we might suspect or even wish to believe, one way or another. But we don't know.

The flip side of focusing on entertaining failures is that we may fail to spot and attack things which do not make for good stories, but might cause or enable ethical failings. For example, did the focus on Gupta's misdeeds on Goldman's Board detract attention from potentially deep or widespread ethical problems in the consulting firm he led for so long?

A second reason to look beyond greed is that **human beings rationalize their behavior**.[18] Did Wells Fargo's lower-level employees consider themselves greedy when they cheated customers for their own gain? Did they even think of themselves as doing wrong, as opposed to having wrong done to them? Senator Warren herself painted these employees as victims. They were merely trying to keep their $14/hour jobs as they were driven to the breaking point by their corporate taskmasters. If a fake account were opened, and no activity took place, who would be hurt? In the rare case where a customer had to pay a bogus fee, or had his or her credit score hurt by not paying, the employees involved possibly shrugged it off by assuring themselves that no real harm was done, or that it was management which was truly to blame.

Because people rationalize, putting in place rules that simply condemn and punish greed will not necessarily work. If the people involved don't think of themselves as greedy, they simply won't see the rules as applying to them.

The last reason for looking beyond greed is that **human nature does not change**. Mankind's basic hopes, fears, strengths, and weaknesses remain unaltered from biblical times.

Two points follow from this premise. The first is that trying to improve business ethics by replacing less moral people with more moral people is unlikely to work across a group of any size. People are people. Real-world business ethics has to take them as they are, not as we might wish them to be.

The second point is that people live in contexts and in communities. They work within organizations, processes, and cultures. They form bonds and respond to incentives, good and bad.[19] Planning and implementing these things call for hard work and heavy lifting. Such tasks also require constant checking, tinkering, re-checking, and from time to time, complete re-building.

All of the above takes *leadership*. Leaders see what is not but should be, and bring it into being. To McKinsey's credit, in the aftermath of Gupta's disgrace, the firm put in place new structures, procedures, training, and incentives. It worked hard to define and nurture a more upright culture while also back-stopping these efforts with oversight, audit, and control of client information.

So, as strange as it may seem, to begin laying a sound foundation for real-world business ethics, we must start by clearing away the brushwood of stories based on greed.

It is to the shape and the building blocks of this foundation that we now turn.

NOTES

1. Jan Wieczner, "Wells Fargo's John Stumpf Beats Out Amazon's Jeff Bezos to Win CEO of the Year," *Fortune*, January 26, 2016, accessed October 27, 2016, http://fortune.com/2016/01/26/wells-fargo-amazon-ceo/.

2. Stan Lepro, "First Nine Banks Were Forced to Take Bailouts," *Associated Press*, accessed October 21, 2019, http://archive.boston.com/business/articles/2009/05/15/first_nine_banks_were_forced_to_take_bailouts/.

3. Senator Warren Subscriber Channel, "Senator Elizabeth Warren Questions Wells Fargo CEO John Stumpf at Banking Committee Hearing," YouTube, accessed September 23, 2019, https://www.youtube.com/watch.

4. In mid-April 2017, Wells Fargo's Board of Directors canceled $48 million of the executive's stock options. Laura J. Keller, "Wells Fargo Board Claws Back $28 Million More from Ex-CEO Stumpf," *BNA Corporate Counsel Weekly* 32, no. 15 (2017): 113–5.

5. At the time Stumpf stepped down as CEO in October 2016, he agreed to forfeit $41 million in equity awards built up over his career. In mid-April 2017, the Board clawed back an additional $28 million in pay (ibid.).

6. The offer excluded Yahoo's interest in the Chinese e-commerce firm Ali Baba.

7. Alex Spencer, "Verizon to Shutter Yahoo and AOL Brands, Combining Both to Make Oath," *Mobile Marketing*, April 4, 2017, accessed April 19, 2017, http://mobilemarketingmagazine.com/verizon-yahoo-aol-acquisiton-oath-rebrand.

8. David Goldman, "Marissa Mayer's Payday: 4 Years, $219 Million," *CNN*, July 25, 2016, accessed April 24, 2017, http://money.cnn.com/2016/07/25/technology/marissa-mayer-pay/. In March 2017, the Board announced, as a result, that Ms. Mayer would not receive a 2016 cash bonus, or equity awards for 2017. Deepa Seetharaman, "Yahoo's Marissa Mayer to Reap $187 Million after Verizon Deal," *The Wall Street Journal*, April 25, 2017, accessed April 27, 2017, https://www.wsj.com/articles/yahoos-marissa-mayer-to-make-186-million-from-verizon-deal-1493103650.

9. Weil, Gotshal & Manges LLP, "Security Breach Notification Laws Data Privacy Survey 2014," Weil.com, accessed October 27, 2016, http://www.weil.com/~/media/files/pdfs/Weils_Security_Breach_Notification_Laws_Data_Privacy_Survey_2014.pdf.

10. Sarah McBride, "Former Yahoo CEO Marissa Mayer Creates Tech Startup Incubator," *Bloomberg*, October 18, 2018, accessed October 30, 2019, https://www.bloomberg.com/news/articles/2018-04-19/former-yahoo-ceo-marissa-mayer-creates-tech-startup-incubator.

11. Walter Kiechel, "The Tempting of Rajat Gupta," *Harvard Business Review Blogs*, hbr.org, March 24, 2011, accessed October 25, 2016, https://hbr.org/2011/03/the-tempting-of-rajat-gupta.

12. Del Jones, "Some Firms' Fertile Soil Grows Crop of Future CEOs," *USA Today*, January 8, 2008, accessed October 25, 2016, http://usatoday30.usatoday.com/money/companies/management/2008-01-08-ceo-companies_N.htm.

13. Sandra Laville and Nels Pratley, "Brothers Who Sit at Blair's Right Hand: How McKinsey, the Secretive Global Consultancy Firm, Is Gaining Influence at the Heart of UK plc," *The Guardian*, June 14, 2005, accessed October 21, 2019, https://www.theguardian.com/uk/2005/jun/14/Whitehall.politics.

14. John Gapper, "McKinsey Model Springs a Leak," *Financial Times*, March 9, 2011, accessed October 27, 2016, https://www.ft.com/content/144e6728-4a87-11e0-82ab-00144feab49a.

15. Andrew Hill, "Inside McKinsey," *Financial Times*, November 25, 2011, accessed October 27, 2016, https://www.ft.com/content/0d506e0e-1583-11e1-b9b8-00144feabdc0.

16. Editorial Board, "Bringing Justice to Justice: Sen. Chuck Grassley Wants Answers from DOJ on Prosecutorial Abuse," *The Wall Street Journal*, June 5, 2016, accessed October 27, 2016, http://www.wsj.com/articles/bringing-justice-to-justice-1465167217.

17. The Hon. Jed S. Rakoff, "The Financial Crisis: Why Have No High-Level Executives Been Prosecuted?" *The New York Review of Books*, January 9, 2014, accessed October 27, 2017, http://www.nybooks.com/articles/2014/01/09/financial-crisis-why-no-executive-prosecutions/.

18. *See*, for example, Dan Ariely, *The (Honest) Truth about Dishonesty: How We Lie to Everyone—Especially Ourselves* (New York: HarperCollins, 2012).

19. *See*, for example, Max Bazerman and Ann Tenbrunsel, *Blind Spots: Why We Fail to Do What's Right and What to Do about It* (Princeton, NJ; and Oxford: Princeton University Press, 2011).

2

Finding Ethics in a Lifeboat: Decision-Making Frameworks

■ ■ ■

"We are often compelled to set up standards we cannot reach ourselves, and to lay down rules which we could not ourselves satisfy."

—Lord Coleridge, Chief Justice, in *R v. Dudley and Stephens* (involving murder and cannibalism among starving, lifeboat passengers)[1]

Gut hunches may be good enough in our personal lives. Something just feels right; or, it feels wrong. We decide and move on.

Business ethics, on the other hand, demands more.

Business by its nature involves us with other people. Whenever we buy or sell, there's someone on the other side selling or buying. Also, in addition to ourselves, in business we often act on behalf of others, be they family members, partners, or shareholders. Such actions may impact third parties, like employees or members of the surrounding community.

In short, business is interpersonal rather than personal. People have to want to trade with us, to work with us, to trust us. So, business ethics forces us to take into account not just our wants and views but those of others, too.

Here, gut hunches may no longer work. They might lead us to overlook or mistake others' interests or perspectives. Also, basing decisions on gut hunches ("Because that's how I feel") will persuade very few people on matters where their consent and cooperation are required.

What, then, must we do?

This chapter defines and describes the main frameworks used in ethical decision-making. Descriptions will include each framework's basic approach, strengths, weaknesses, and limitations. Understanding these frameworks helps us make ethical business decisions that are sound and well reasoned. These frameworks also teach us how to weigh and respond to alternative or opposing ethical arguments put forth by others.

WHAT IS ETHICS, ANYWAY?

Simply stated, ethics is "a code of conduct that allows members of a society to live constructively together and to flourish together."[2]

Various ethical systems have arisen across the world in various times and places. The more significant non-Western ethical systems include the Islamic, Hindu, Buddhist, Taoist, and Confucian.

This book focuses on various Western ethical systems, or frameworks. These frameworks include: (1) Cost/Benefit, (2) Golden Rule, (3) Blind Bargaining, and (4) Virtue.[3]

This focus does not mean that Western frameworks are inherently better than non-Western frameworks, but it does recognize that Western frameworks underlie the laws and business practices which now dominate global commerce.

From the sixteenth through the nineteenth centuries, as European empires spread, they took with them their commercial laws and practices. Although Germany did not have sizable overseas possessions, its civil code influenced a number of Asian countries, including China, Japan, and Korea. These three countries sought to modernize their legal systems. They preferred to borrow from a non-imperial power, rather than from the British or the French, who threatened them geopolitically.

With the collapse of the Soviet Union and the opening of Mainland China to the world economy in the late twentieth century, Western-style commercial and company laws effectively captured the global market. Of course, non-Western business ethics still hold sway in some areas, like moneylending in Islamic countries. But, by and large, global business is done according to Western rules, resting on Western ethical frameworks.

Most people reading this book have run across these frameworks in their daily lives. People hear them and use them, though perhaps without realizing it.

A good introduction to Cost/Benefit, Golden Rule, Blind Bargaining, and Virtue frameworks comes from playing a game which shows just how familiar and straightforward these frameworks truly are.

THE LIFEBOAT GAME

Note: This game is more fun if you play it with friends or colleagues.

Imagine that an ocean liner has hit an iceberg in the North Atlantic. Ten people have scrambled into a single lifeboat.

The winds and waves have driven this small boat far from the other boats. The ten passengers are therefore all alone. They don't know where they are, how far away land is, or when and from where help might arrive.

What's worse, this particular lifeboat can only hold six people. If four passengers don't go overboard, into the icy water and to certain death, all ten will drown. It is a matter of minutes.

You must quickly decide who stays and who goes.

Here are the passengers:

1. Annie Able: Annie is a fifty-one-year-old divorcee with two children, one autistic. She heads R&D for a pharma start-up with a potential breakthrough drug. She attends church and volunteers at a soup kitchen. She has badly sprained her wrist.
2. Billy Baker: Billy, twenty-six, is an MBA student engaged to a medical resident. He wants to work in venture philanthropy in Africa with his doctor-spouse after graduation. Billy has diabetes; in his pocket, he has a five-day supply of insulin.
3. Charles Charlie: Charles is a seventy-year-old physician Board certified in Emergency Medicine. A bachelor, he competes in sailing races and has expertise in open-boat navigation. This cruise was on his bucket list because, though robust now, he suffers from lymphoma and has no more than three to four months to live.
4. Delia Delta: Delia is a twelve-year-old girl. She is in shock, as her parents and younger brother have just drowned. Having swum to the lifeboat, she is beginning to shiver from the cold; Dr. Charlie says she is at risk for hypothermia.

5. Enrico Echo: Enrico is a thirty-five-year-old opera singer with millions of adoring fans. Twice divorced and previously convicted of mail fraud and drunk driving, he reputedly left a friend to die on the sidewalk outside a club where they were snorting cocaine. Enrico is very fit, and his singing greatly cheers the others.

6. Francine Foxtrot: Francine is a twenty-three-year-old ensign. She was supposed to be monitoring the ship's radar and sonar for icebergs but was instead watching a Game of Thrones re-run on her iPad. She supports a widowed mother ashore whose prescription drugs are not covered by insurance and also finances her disabled younger sister's therapy. She is a fair navigator and rows well.

7. Godfrey Golf: Godfrey is a six-year-old boy. He is the seventh of eight children. He was traveling with a grandparent (now drowned) and is inconsolable. He has tried to bite several passengers. Dr. Charlie warns that a bite in open-boat conditions can quickly go septic.

8. Holly Hotel: Holly, sixty-five, owns a successful mail-order party-goods business now run by her four children. A grandmother of ten, over the last five years, she has traveled the world with her spouse of forty-three years. They contribute to a number of charities. She bails well but tires quickly. She is the only passenger who can somewhat quiet Godfrey.

9. Ignatius Igloo: Ignatius, thirty-eight, is a married father of three young children. He secured his current spot on the lifeboat by asking his twenty-year-old lover to fetch from the cabin the keys to the BMW 5-Series he told the lover was a surprise gift. Neither the car nor the keys exist. Ignatius captained his college rowing team. He has begged God to forgive his past sins and now claims that he is a changed man.

10. Julia Juliet: Julia is a forty-one-year-old private-equity investor famous for stripping companies of valuable assets, firing the employees, and selling the bones. She is being sued by her partners for fraud and by her children for plundering the trust fund their father left them. Julia has sworn, if she is not thrown overboard, to donate $1 billion to charities selected by the other survivors and to give $10 million to the family of each person who goes overboard. Julia is a triathlete.

Write down your choices, with your reasons. Other players should do the same.

1.
2.
3.
4.

Figure 2.1 The Lifeboat Game

Credit: Eva Zafft. Used by permission.

As you might have guessed, there is no single answer to the Lifeboat Game. There are only various approaches yielding various choices, based upon the ethical framework chosen:

Cost/Benefit

Cost/Benefit analysis represents the most popular approach, typically chosen by 40–50 percent of players.

As its name implies, Cost/Benefit analysis requires us to identify and weigh the costs, and the benefits, of various courses of action.

When we weigh the costs and benefits together, the result is called "utility." When the benefits outweigh the costs, we say that utility is "positive." When the costs outweigh the benefits, utility is "negative."

The general goal of Cost/Benefit reasoning is to pick the option that results in the greatest positive utility. This is a fancy way of saying, "Do the most good for the most people."

Sometimes all choices have negative utility. In this case, we should pick the option which does the least harm. In everyday language, we "make the best of a bad situation."

Having to decide which passengers to throw overboard is indeed making the best of a bad situation. What becomes clear in looking over the passenger biographies, of course, is the need to determine and weigh different kinds of utility:

- **Immediate Utility**—The passenger's contribution to helping the remaining passengers survive long enough to be rescued.
- **Personal Utility**—The likelihood the passenger, if not thrown overboard, will survive long enough to be rescued; also, the benefit to the passenger of being rescued.
- **Family Utility**—The utility to the passenger's *family* of his or her surviving long enough to be rescued.
- **Societal Utility**—The utility to *society at large* of the passenger's surviving long enough to be rescued.

We can lay out these factors and the passengers' biographical information (*see* table 2.1).

Table 2.1 makes one thing evident. Even when broken out in detail, Cost/Benefit analysis does not necessarily yield a clear answer. Reasonable people can differ with regard to Negative, Neutral, Positive ratings.

In practice, for example, some players keep Charles Charlie, the physician-sailor, because of his immediate contributions to group survival; but other players toss him overboard because he has only three to four months to live. Some people think the danger Godfrey poses to the other passengers from biting outweighs the benefits he would enjoy by living perhaps another seventy plus years.

Sizing and ranking immediate and individual costs and benefits is hard enough. Ranking utility of passengers' survival for their family members with any confidence is even harder. Judging passengers' potential future contributions to society quickly becomes guesswork.

Table 2.1 Cost/Benefit analysis

No.	Name	Immediate utility	Personal utility	Family utility	Societal utility
1	Annie Able	**Negative** Badly sprained wrist prevents her from rowing or bailing	**Neutral** Healthy but middle-aged	**Positive** Divorced, but has a special-needs child who depends on her	**Positive** May create breakthrough drug; contributes to church and charity
2	Billy Baker	**Neutral** Can row and bail but only until insulin gives out	**Neutral/negative** Has prospect of long life and marriage, but only if rescued within five days	**Neutral** Has a fiancée but no dependents	**Positive** Will dedicate life to good works
3	Charles Charlie	**Very Positive** Has medical and navigational skills and can row and bail	**Negative** Senior citizen. Even if rescued, will only live three to four months	**Negative** Has no spouse or dependents	**Negative** Even if rescued, will only live three to four months and require care
4	Delia Delta	**Negative** Shock makes her unable to row or bail	**Neutral** Has nearly whole life ahead of her, but hypothermia makes her unlikely to survive until rescued	**Positive** Has no dependents or spouse, but her death would wipe out her immediate family	**Neutral** Unknown how she will contribute to society in future
5	Enrico Echo	**Positive** Fitness allows him to row and bail, and his singing raises morale	**Positive** Relatively young and enjoys stardom	**Neutral** Has no spouse or dependents (other than two ex-wives)	**Positive** Has millions of adoring fans

(Continued)

Table 2.1 Continued

No.	Name	Immediate utility	Personal utility	Family utility	Societal utility
6	Francine Foxtrot	**Positive** Is a fair navigator who rows well; as an officer, can exercise leadership	**Positive** Is a young adult with nearly her whole life ahead of her	**Positive** Has no spouse but supports both mother and sister	**Neutral** Does not materially contribute to wider society
7	Godfrey Golf	**Very negative** Too young to row or bail. His biting makes him an affirmative danger	**Very Positive** Is a child with his whole life ahead of him	**Neutral/Positive** Has no spouse or dependents; will be survived by parents and seven siblings	**Neutral** Unknown how he will contribute to society in future
8	Holly Hotel	**Negative** No navigating or rowing skills and tires quickly when bailing; ability to calm Godfrey only counts as positive if Godfrey stays on board	**Neutral** Is a senior citizen who has already led a very full life	**Neutral** Will leave behind many family members, but all are well established and provided for	**Neutral** Is retired, but contributes to charity
9	Ignatius Igloo	**Positive** Is an expert rower	**Positive** An adult with most of his life ahead of him, including a family	**Positive** Has a spouse and three young children who depend upon him	**Neutral** Unclear whether his repentance is sincere, and he will lead a better life
10	Julia Juliet	**Positive** As a triathlete, she can row and bail	**Positive** Is in early middle age with half her life ahead of her	**Negative/Neutral** Is in conflict with her family; if her promise to contribute is sincere, she might help the families of those who go overboard	**Neutral** Doubt exists that she will donate any money to charity. No estimate of the societal value of her work

The fact is that any Cost/Benefit analysis involves subjective answers to questions over which people can widely and sharply disagree. These questions are:

- Who should set the relative values of various costs and benefits?
- How will these relative values be set, including the odds of whether such costs and benefits will actually come about?
- How far out should we draw the circle of people whose costs and benefits should be taken into account?
- How do we address the fact that, for a modest benefit to many people, we might be imposing harsh costs on a few?

As we will see with real-world examples later on, these questions confront us any time Cost/Benefit analysis applies.

We also need to bear in mind that, from an ethical point of view, Cost/Benefit analysis does not care about our motives, only our results. There is no ethical credit for feeling badly about throwing someone overboard. When we apply Cost/Benefit frameworks, what matters is the accuracy of calculation and the maximization of utility. Nothing more, nothing less.

Golden Rule

If 40–50 percent of Lifeboat Game players typically use Cost/Benefit analysis, about 20–30 percent apply the Golden Rule.

People typically recite the "Golden Rule" as "Do unto others as you would have others do unto you." For the purposes of this book, though, when the term "Golden Rule" appears, it will mean one of two ways of describing ethical duties.[4]

The first way is:

1. **Act so that the principle motivating your act could become a universal law of human action in a world in which you would want to live.**

Examples include:

- "I will respect the property of others because I want to live in a world where people respect other people's property" or

- "I will give to charity because I think the world will be a better place if everybody gives to charity"

A second form of the Golden Rule reads as follows:

1. Treat others as ends in themselves rather than as means to your own ends.

Examples include:

- Don't lie to get other people to do what you want since that is using them for your own ends

or

- Disclose the full facts to someone so that he or she can make an informed and voluntary choice about whether to do what you want him or her to do

The advantages and disadvantages of the Golden Rule become clear as we play the Lifeboat Game.

First of all, one disadvantage of the Golden Rule is that it can yield more than one principle of action. In the case of the Lifeboat Game, for example, a player might easily use any of the following principles:

- **Women & children first**—I will give preference to the physically weaker, because I want to live a world where the weaker are protected. Such a world will be gentle and harmonious.
- **Sacrifice for the future**—I will favor the young over the old. If everybody does so, as people age, they will have reason to make the world more orderly, prosperous, and just.
- **What goes around comes around**—I will favor those who do good and disfavor those who do bad because a world in which people face the consequences of their actions will be more orderly and just.

Applying these three rules of action yields three very different results (*see* table 2.2).

Table 2.2 Golden Rule analysis

No.	Name	Women & children first	Sacrifice for the future	What goes around comes around
1	Annie Able	**Save** Woman	**Sacrifice** Third oldest	**Save** Nice person
2	Billy Baker	**Sacrifice** Man	**Save** Seventh oldest	**Save** Nice person
3	Charles Charlie	**Sacrifice** Man	**Sacrifice** Oldest	**Save** Nice person
4	Delia Delta	**Save** Child	**Save** Ninth oldest	**Save** Nice person
5	Enrico Echo	**Sacrifice** Man	**Save** Sixth oldest	**Sacrifice** Reputedly left a friend to die; is a convicted criminal
6	Francine Foxtrot	**Save** Woman	**Save** Eighth oldest	**Sacrifice** Her negligence caused the disaster in the first place
7	Godfrey Golf	**Save** Child	**Save** Tenth oldest	**Save** Nice person
8	Holly Hotel	**Save** Woman	**Sacrifice** Second oldest	**Save** Nice person
9	Ignatius Igloo	**Sacrifice** Man	**Save** Fifth oldest	**Sacrifice** Tricked his lover into sacrificing her life for his; adulterer
10	Julia Juliet	**Save** Woman	**Sacrifice** Fourth oldest	**Sacrifice** Appears to be a heartless, greedy cheater

As table 2.2 shows, the Golden Rule involves advantages and disadvantages. On the plus side, once a player has decided upon a principle of action, such principle is usually easier and quicker to apply than Cost/Benefit.

Usually, but not always. If five people had to go overboard, the "Women & Children First" rule would not suffice, since the boat currently holds a total of six women and children. One of them would have to go, too. With "What Goes Around Comes Around," players luckily have four bad apples to pitch from the boat. But what if players had to pick a fifth or sixth passenger to heave out? Based on current passenger biographies, players lack the information to decide rationally.

Another disadvantage of the Golden Rule, as shown in Table 2.2, is that it sometimes generates competing principles of action, which yield conflicting outcomes. This situation leads to perhaps the biggest downside of the Golden Rule framework: it doesn't guide us in ranking, or selecting among, competing principles of action.

This said, there is a corresponding upside of sorts. If we are strict followers of the Golden Rule, we don't worry about making mistakes. Golden Rule ethics focuses exclusively on our motives and intentions; actual outcomes do not matter. For example, assume a player wants to save as many women and children as possible. That player might apply the Women and Children First principle of action. As a result, the player throws overboard the only doctor and best navigator (Charlie), as well as two of the best rowers (Enrico and Ignatius). This might cause the boat to drift help-lessly until all women and children on board freeze to death, die of thirst, or starve. "Sh-t happens," shrugs the Golden Rule. The fact that, in trying to save women and children, the player has selected a principle of action which *when implemented* has killed them all does not matter. The player has followed the Golden Rule, and according to it, has acted ethically.

Readers may notice that with respect to the importance of a person's motives, Cost/Benefit and Golden Rule frameworks represent wholly opposite approaches. Cost/Benefit looks only at objective results; the Golden Rule, only at intentions.

Like Cost/Benefit, though, the Golden Rule always involves certain questions people must wrestle with in practice. Golden Rule questions include:

- Does my principle of action match a form of the Golden Rule?
- Do I know enough in the case at hand to apply the principle?
- If I can come up with more than one principle action, and they produce conflicting outcomes, which one should I pick?

Blind Bargaining

About 10–20 percent of players find themselves unable or unwilling to pick individual passengers to throw overboard. These players balk at analyzing possible costs/benefits. They refuse to craft a principle of action to pick and choose among passengers.

So what do these players do?

They draw lots, or refuse to play.

Drawing lots doesn't mean copping out. It means applying an ethical framework that has ancient roots. For example, when a unit of the Roman army disgraced itself in battle, its members would draw lots. The 10 percent who drew the unlucky lot would be killed by the other 90 percent (hence the word, "decimation").

Drawing lots values all passengers in the lifeboat equally. It is probably the method real passengers would use among themselves if they had comparable force of will and strength and knew nothing about the other passengers' biographies.

Alternatively, someone applying Blind Bargaining ethics might refuse to play. No passenger's life has greater intrinsic value than another's. So, if the passengers all find themselves in a zone of danger, neither we nor they may sacrifice someone inside (or outside) the zone to save others within it. As traditional Jewish law provides in a situation analogous to the Lifeboat Game, "Allow yourself to be killed, but you may not kill another. Who says that your blood is redder than his? Perhaps his blood is redder than yours."[5]

Modern thinking about Blind Bargaining asks us to imagine that we find ourselves behind a "veil of ignorance."[6] We don't know our race, ethnicity, or nationality. We don't know our sex or inherent strengths or weaknesses. We don't know our social or economic status.

In such a situation, so the modern theory of Blind Bargaining goes, people will only agree to rules that benefit the least well off, since that is the group in which people behind the veil of ignorance might find themselves when the veil is lifted.

So much for theory. The fact is that the Blind Bargaining framework voices itself often in the real world. One case arises whenever people draw lots. Another occurs whenever people argue for rules that produce more equal outcomes.

A famous example of Blind Bargaining reasoning is the U.S. Supreme Court's Miranda Rule.[7] Here, the U.S. Supreme Court has ruled that the U.S. Constitution requires the police to inform someone whom they have arrested that he/she has the right to remain silent, and so on. The Miranda Rule creates a more level playing field between the police and the arrestee. The Miranda Rule also produces more similar outcomes between informed arrestees (people who already knew their rights) and uninformed arrestees (who did not).

The Miranda Rule does not spring from the Golden Rule. The first form of the Golden Rule might lead us to say, "Since I do not want the police to violate my rights, I do not want them to violate the rights of others." This principle of action focuses on police misconduct.

The second form of the Golden Rule also focuses on police misconduct. The form asks whether police, by not informing an arrestee of his or her rights, are using that arrestee as a means to their own ends. The answer here is "No." Ideally, the police want an innocent arrestee to speak up so that he can clear himself, and the police can move on to other suspects. A guilty arrestee who speaks might disadvantage himself. However, since he is guilty, the police are not exploiting him by finding out the truth.

The distinction between Golden Rule and Blind Bargaining is important to bear in mind. The Golden Rule focuses on somebody willfully doing wrong, either breaching a duty of some kind, or seeking to exploit somebody who doesn't know better. Blind Bargaining, on the other hand, focuses on the fact that people with different starting points will likely have different end points. The thrust of Blind Bargaining ethics is to try to handicap the race, so to speak, in order to bring the outcomes more in line with each other.

Virtue

My classes have comprised 600 or so players. So far, only one player has suggested asking among the passengers for volunteers to jump overboard.

It is an *MBA* class, after all.

Volunteering to sacrifice oneself would be an example of Virtue Ethics. Even if these ethics have yet to play much of a role in the Lifeboat Game, they do impact real-world behavior and deserve mentioning here.

Virtue Ethics as used in this book focuses on the ethics of the ancient Greek philosopher Aristotle.[8] He argued that happiness represents the highest human goal, since it is the goal to which all other goals (wealth, status, power) tend. At the same time, happiness tends toward nothing else. People want to be happy for no other reason than to be happy.

Aristotle thought that people best pursued happiness through moral virtue/excellence. They gain moral virtue/excellence by restraining harmful desires (sloth, greed, lust, etc.) and cultivating beneficial ones (courage, wisdom, generosity, self-restraint, etc.).

Even today, appeals to virtue frequently happen in day-to-day conversation. This includes whenever a parent tells a child, "Act your age," or someone says to an errant friend or colleague, "You're better than that."

Virtue Ethics is about training one's desires, thoughts, and behaviors to become a more virtuous, excellent person. A challenge of this approach is translating its principles into everyday rules of action, or balancing competing virtues.

Appeals to virtue represent about the only non-religious ethical calls that can persuade people to sacrifice their own lives.[9] When seeking volunteers, the U.S. Army does not advertise, "Apply for a low-paying job that might get you killed," but "Be all that you can be." Likewise, the U.S. Marine Corps has lured young people with the call that the Marines "are looking for a few good men" and that a successful recruit will join "The few. The proud. The Marines." Implied in these pitches is that the recruit will become a better person, part of an elite of the excellent.

Such pitches reflect classic Virtue Ethics.

Some people may snigger at these pitches, or at Virtue Ethics generally. As chapter 11 will show, however, Virtue Ethics plays a key role in building employee self-esteem in a way that aligns with the business's end goals, which represents the bedrock of ethical business cultures.

Mixed Frameworks

For those doing the math, the final 10–20 percent of players combine frameworks when deciding which passengers to throw overboard.

Typically, these players apply Cost/Benefit or Golden Rule frameworks but find a particular passenger, or passengers (Enrico, Ignatius, Julia), so loathsome that the players make an exception to toss these passengers out of the boat.

And good riddance, too.

LESSONS LEARNED: FRAMEWORK SPOTTING FOR FUN AND PROFIT

The Lifeboat Game shows how various ethical approaches apply to the same situation. Different players often come up with differing answers, sometimes even when applying the same framework.

As quickly becomes clear, the Lifeboat Game has no one right answer. But that does not mean that anything goes or that all answers are equivalent. Understanding each framework's strengths, weaknesses, and limitations tells us what additional information or analysis might lead to a better answer.

"Better" in this case means an answer that more fully or precisely applies a given framework. "Better" also means an answer that attracts other peoples' agreement and support. In business, one rarely makes and implements decisions alone. Being able to explain one's reasoning to others, while exploring their reasoning in turn, moves a business toward ethical consensus and action.

NOTES

1. *R v. Dudley and Stephens* [1884] 14 QBD 273 DC. In this famous English case, two thirsty, starving lifeboat passengers survived by killing a third passenger in order to drink his blood and eat his flesh. The case established the common-law principle that necessity (self-preservation) is not by itself a defense to a charge of murder.

2. Rabbi Lord Jonathan Sacks, "The Relevance of the Bible for Law and Ethics in Society Today," King's College London Lecture, March 3, 2014, at 13:02–15, accessed March 7, 2020, https://www.youtube.com/watch.

3. These frameworks are more formally known, respectively, as: (1) teleological/utilitarian; (2) deontological/Kantian; (3) contractarian/Rawlsian; and (4) Aristotelian. This book will mainly use the informal names for these frameworks, which more simply describe their meanings. A second form of contractarian ethics, based on the writings of John Locke, is not discussed.

4. The "Golden Rule" as used here reflects the first two formulations of Immanuel Kant's "Categorical Imperative." Immanuel Kant, *Groundwork of the Metaphysics of Morals*, trans. Mary Gregor and Jens Timmermans (Cambridge: Cambridge University Press, 2nd ed., 2012). A third formulation combines and extends the first two, emphasizing the individual as a disinterested giver of rules rather than a follower. ("Act so that through your maxims you could be a legislator of universal laws.") An extension of this reasoning adds a social dimension in which an individual's actions should further progress toward "a systematic

union of different rational beings under common law." Stanford Encyclopedia of Philosophy, "Kant's Moral Philosophy," February 23, 2004 (revised July 7, 2016), accessed February 21, 2020, https://plato.stanford.edu/entries/kant-moral/.

5. Talmud, Sanhedrin 74a-b, Sefaria.org., accessed March 7, 2020, https://www.sefaria.org/.

6. John Rawls, *A Theory of Justice*, 2nd ed. (Cambridge, MA: Belknap Press, 1999).

7. *Miranda v. Arizona*, 384 US 436 (1966).

8. Aristotle, *Nicomachean Ethics*, 2nd ed., trans. Terence Irwin (Indianapolis, IN: Hackett, 1999).

9. Religions can offer the promise of Heaven through martyrdom, an example of Cost/Benefit calculus.

3

Machiavelli: Self-Interest and Self-Regard Posing as Ethics

■ ■ ■

"One [man] has got all the goodness, and the other [man] all the appearance of it."

—Elizabeth Bennett, in Jane Austen's *Pride and Prejudice*

The Lifeboat Game is instructive. But, in one important respect the game is unrealistic.

The game places us outside of and above the action. The reader is not asked to imagine himself or herself in the boat, as one of the passengers whose life is at stake.

Real-world, ethical decision-making rarely works that way. Even where someone does not directly bear the consequences of his or her decision, the risk of reputational blowback from a bad or unpopular decision means the decision maker has some skin in the game.

In such cases, in addition to understanding basic frameworks, both decision maker and those potentially affected by him or her need to appreciate the philosophy and advice of Niccolo Machiavelli.

MACHIAVELLI—PATRON SAINT OF POLITICAL OPERATIVES AND SPIN DOCTORS

Niccolo Machiavelli (1469–1527) holds fair claim as the father of modern political science. He advised rulers of various Italian principalities and republics during some of Italy's most bloody and disordered times.

As noted earlier, the Lifeboat Game does not involve Machiavelli's views directly because the players need not imagine themselves as passengers. Anyone who has watched Survivor or The Apprentice (regular or Celebrity), on the other hand, will quickly realize how central Machiavelli's thinking is to cases where we find ourselves not outside the drama, but in it.

And we do live in dramatic times.

We live in cynical and selfish times, too.

In part, we feel this way because we simply know more. Computerized information and the Internet strip away nearly every fig leaf of privacy or secrecy. In part, media echo chambers spin and re-cycle rumors—or even outright falsehoods—to the point where, by dint of sensory overload, people treat them as truth.

Machiavelli warrants mentioning here, but not because he devised an ethical framework like Cost/Benefit or Golden Rule. Rather, he did just the opposite. In his book, *The Prince*, written in 1513, Machiavelli set forth a non-ethical, win-at-all-costs framework now associated with the term *real-politik* and airing on any number of so-called reality shows.[1]

Non-ethical does not mean anti-ethical, however. Machiavelli counseled that to remain in power, a leader could not shrink from hard or brutal acts. At the same time, Machiavelli argued that sadism and unbridled self-interest were self-defeating. In his view, a leader should prefer being feared to being loved, but on all accounts, the leader had to avoid being despised or hated. To this degree, at least, Machiavelli believed that a shrewd leader had to take into account the morals and ethics of surrounding society, even if he did not—or could not afford to—share them on a personal level or at all times.

Machiavelli's thinking serves as a modern tonic in a couple of ways. First, anyone angry or heartsick over the lying, cheating, and stealing infesting today's politics and business can look back to Machiavelli's times and see that at least things haven't gotten worse, even if they don't appear to have gotten better.

Second, and more seriously, Machiavelli contributed greatly to modern ethics by, among other things, pointing out that, in practice, virtue and vice are not wholly distinct from each other. They are linked. Some virtues, if unbounded, turn into vices. And some vices, if properly channeled, have virtuous effects.

Three virtue-vice pairs bear particular discussion: (1) generosity & stinginess; (2) mercy & strictness; and (3) faithfulness & trickery.[2]

Generosity and Stinginess

The quickest way to win people's hearts is through generosity. How else could the previously hated miser Ebenezer Scrooge in Charles Dickens's novel *A Christmas Carol* become so beloved in less than a day?

But Machiavelli did not write fiction. He saw from history and personal experience that generous leaders enjoy early popularity. Such generosity, though, quickly empties the treasury, often with little lasting benefit.

To keep things going, the generous leader cuts corners in the common goods and services he should provide, like roads, public safety, and justice. He also comes up with ways to squeeze money from the people. The people get pinched, overtaxed, and sometimes outright expropriated. Ultimately, the people under a generous leader find themselves poorer due to their leader's generosity.

As Machiavelli saw it, a leader who is stingy, on the other hand, builds up wealth to use for common goods and services without needing to raise taxes or fees. No one gets squeezed. Over time, people with a stingy leader make and keep more money and build up wealth of their own. The leader's stinginess thus plays out in practice as a form of generosity.

Machiavelli's argument may sound familiar, if not convincing, to anyone who follows contemporary politics.

Mercy and Strictness

Another element in current political debate is the link between mercy and strictness.

Machiavelli observed that excessive mercy on the part of leaders—that is, too much leniency toward wrongdoers—encourages law-breaking. As a result, lawlessness and disorder spike, oppressing the average person, who now lives in fear for his person, his family, and his property. In Machiavelli's view, this ongoing state of oppression and fear represents a form of cruelty inflicted on the average person by his merciful leader.

Strictness, on the other hand, promotes order and security. By harshly punishing a few for wrongdoing, the strict leader ultimately exercises mercy by discouraging would-be wrongdoers from breaking the rules. The average person and his or her family, moreover, enjoy peace and safety.

Faithfulness and Trickery

Machiavelli's linkage of faithfulness and trickery reflects a very dim view of human nature and human affairs.

As Machiavelli puts it, "The lion cannot defend himself against snares, and the fox cannot defend himself against wolves." A ruler who is too faithful—too upright and predictable—will find himself betrayed and deceived. A ruler who is too obviously wily will fail to form alliances, to build loyalty, or to fool people when the interests of the state require it. As a consequence, Machiavelli wrote, "It is necessary [for a leader] to know well how to disguise this characteristic [of trickery], and to be a great pretender and dissembler. . . . It is unnecessary . . . to have all . . . good qualities, but it is necessary to appear to have them."[3]

So much for trickery. What has this to do with faithfulness?

Machiavelli argues that the ruler's primary duty is to preserve the state, and in so doing, to safeguard his subjects. Excessive personal scruples will lead to the state's ruin and betray the ruler's duty to safeguard. A ruler who exercises guile in the service of policy, however, maintains himself, the state, and his people. He thus keeps faith with what matters most.

SELF-REGARD MASQUERADING AS ETHICS

However distasteful Machiavelli's views are, he at least stands for self-awareness in making decisions and wielding power.

Just as the virtue-vice pairs discussed earlier can morph into one another, the main ethical Cost/Benefit, Golden Rule, Blind Bargaining, and Virtue frameworks can, if taken to an extreme, lead to unethical behavior.

Cost/Benefit

There is a risk when using a Cost/Benefit framework, for example, in passing over or discounting factors that cannot be readily quantified.[4] A tragic example involves the whiz-kid analysts who ran the U.S. Department of Defense during the Vietnam War. These analysts wanted to precisely measure everything they did. Over time, however, this approach created a bias in which the analysts would only do—or permit others to do—what could be precisely measured.[5] Potentially advantageous but hard-to-quantify options or results were ignored.

Since Cost/Benefit cares only about outcomes, skewed but well-intentioned thinking will not lead to ethical results.

Golden Rule

Countless examples from business and politics show leaders and organizations plowing forward with programs or efforts that appear well intentioned, but have proven ineffective or even counterproductive.

Although Golden Rule ethics should look only at motives, at some point, ignoring actual results becomes unethical. Persons or groups may persist in fruitless or harmful efforts in order to feel good *about themselves* for trying to help others. This represents a form of naïve *kitsch*.[6] *Kitsch* violates the second form of the Golden Rule because the persons/groups use others as means to their own ends, these ends being inflated self-regard and/or praise.

In other cases, so-called ethical motives simply represent Machiavellian guile. Persons or groups state a noble motive, but as a cover for gaining wealth, power, or rank.

Of course, both situations can take place at the same time. Self-interested special interests may use naïve people eager for self-esteem/praise as fronts to push through programs designed to enrich the special interests.

Blind Bargaining

As mentioned earlier, Blind Bargaining holds that behind a veil of ignorance, individuals should only agree to rules that benefit the least well off. A real-life example would be a progressive income tax. Under such a tax, people who make more increasingly more money must pay an increasingly high percentage of their income as tax. At several points in U.S. history, for every extra dollar earned, the top taxpayers paid over ninety cents in tax.[7]

One critique of Blind Bargaining points out that such a rule inevitably treats the more capable simply as means to uplifting the less capable, which can amount to unethical exploitation. The critique further argues that Blind Bargaining fails to consider and leverage the role of the community in shaping and sustaining its members. Because the community has helped protect and raise individuals, so the critique maintains, the community may make claims on the more capable without treating them simply as means. Instead, the community may balance the claims of the more capable for freedom of action with the claims of the less capable for support. As a result, the community, and not a hypothetical blind bargain, justly moderates and mediates among individuals.[8]

A second critique of Blind Bargaining states that stripping all personal characteristics from people also strips away the capacity for self-reflection necessary for meaningful choice. In a sense, no agreement can occur behind the veil of ignorance because the individuals existing behind the veil of ignorance, bereft of all identity, outlooks, and values, aren't real human beings capable of ethical decision-making.[9]

Not everyone buys into these critiques of Blind Bargaining.[10] In fact, many people find the framework inspiring. Fans might include those attracted to the world described in John Lennon's song "Imagine":

> *Imagine there's no countries . . .*
> *And no religion too . . . .*[11]

Of course, the patriotic and pious might find the world of "Imagine" dreadful. Their love of country and of God as expressed through their patriotism and faith, respectively, may represent key aspects of their personal identity and lives.

Blind Bargaining levels the top in the name of uplifting the bottom. This policy, pursued to an extreme, crushes diversity, tolerance, and free expression. Witness highly egalitarian societies like the Soviet Union, or China during the Cultural Revolution.

Even "Imagine" fans might think twice about dreaming of a world that "will be as one" on those terms.

Virtue

The pursuit of excellence comes at a price. When this price is paid by others, vices like pride and selfishness can be cultivated along with any intended virtues.

LESSONS LEARNED: MACHIAVELLI AND BUSINESS ETHICS

The Lifeboat Game introduces the basic ethical frameworks that apply to life generally and to business in particular: (1) Cost/Benefit; (2) Golden Rule; (3) Blind Bargaining; and (4) Virtue. The Game also shows the varying strengths, weaknesses, and questions each framework entails.

For quick reference, figure 3.1 lays out the principal ethical frameworks, their underlying ideas, and the challenges and questions that each framework faces in practice.

Machiavelli adds a gloss to these frameworks and their use in the real world. He teaches that virtues and vices, under certain circumstances, can morph into one another. Similarly, an ethical framework, if applied unboundedly or unthinkingly, can do harm rather than good.

Figure 3.1 Basic ethical frameworks

Basic Ethical Frameworks

Framework	Underlying Idea	Challenges/Questions
Cost/Benefit (Teleological)	Do the greatest good for the greatest number	• Who calculates cost/benefit? • How is cost/benefit calculated? • How far out do we measure? • How do we allocate cost/benefit?
Golden Rule (Deontological)	• Act consistently with a rule you would want everyone to follow • Treat people as ends in themselves, not as means to your ends	• How do we prioritize competing rules? • Does lack of concern with outcomes lead to *kitsch*?
Blind Bargaining (Contractarian)	• Rules should benefit least well off • Promote equal outcomes	• How do we assess whether starting positions are adequate? • What is "me" v "mine"? • May we exploit the talented or fortunate without end?
Virtue (Aristotelian)	Pursue happiness through excellence by cultivating good habits (e.g., courage)	How do we translate this general rule into specific action?

The limits of each framework remind us that the frameworks are just frameworks. They help us understand life, but do not explain it entirely or in all cases. Sometimes, for example, Cost/Benefit analysis will yield a cleaner and quicker answer than Golden Rule. Other times, the opposite will be true. So it may be, too, with Blind Bargaining and Virtue.

Consequently, as we turn from games and theory to actual examples from life, we should be ready to apply more than one framework, looking for that which yields the clearest answer and most persuasive approach.

We must also stay ever mindful of the human tendency, conscious or subconscious, to dress naked self-interest or self-regard in the robes of impartial ethics.

NOTES

1. Niccolo Machiavelli, *The Prince*, 2nd ed., trans. Harvey C. Mansfield (Chicago: University of Chicago Press, 1998).

2. These virtue-vice pairs are more precisely translated as: (1) liberality & meanness; (2) clemency & cruelty; and (3) faithfulness & guile (Machiavelli, *The Prince*, Mansfield translation). I have used terms more common in everyday American speech.

3. Machiavelli, *The Prince*, 70.

4. Russell L. Ackoff, *Ackoff's Best: His Classic Writings on Management* (New York: John Wiley & Sons, Inc., 1999) (Chapter 25: The Future of Operations Research Is Past), 315–30.

5. Martin van Creveld, *Command in War* (Cambridge, MA: Harvard University Press, 1987), 259.

6. "Kitsch causes two tears to flow in quick succession. The first tear says: How nice to see children running on the grass! The second tear says: How nice to be moved, together with all mankind, by children running on the grass!" Milan Kundera, *The Unbearable Lightness of Being: A Novel*, trans. Michael Henry Heim (New York: HarperCollins, 2005), 251.

7. Tax Policy Center, "Historical Highest Marginal Income Tax Rate," January 18, 2019, accessed October 28, 2019, https://www.taxpolicycenter.org/statistics/historical-highest-marginal-income-tax-rates.

8. Michael J. Sandel, *Liberalism and the Limits of Justice*, 2nd ed. (Cambridge: Cambridge University Press, 1998).

9. Ibid.

10. *See*, for example, C. Edwin Baker, "Sandel on Rawls," *University of Pennsylvania Law Review* 133 (1985): 895–928, accessed November 21, 2016, http://scholarship.law.upenn.edu/cgi/viewcontent.cgi.

11. Copyright © 1971, Apple Records.

4

The Trashing of Hilton Head: Who Sets the Ethical Baseline?

■ ■ ■

"I'll let you write the substance. You let me write the procedure, and I'll screw you every time."

—U.S. Congressman John Dingell

This chapter applies ethical frameworks and theory to a real-world situation: whether a job-creating chemical plant should be built upstream of a pristine vacation resort/nature preserve.[1]

As often happens in the real world, both sides advance sound ethical arguments. But which one should prevail? And if neither side persuades the other, how shall the deadlock be broken?

TROUBLE IN PARADISE

Hilton Head Island, in Beaufort County, South Carolina ("Hilton Head"), is one of the premier vacation and retirement spots on the U.S. Atlantic Coast. Part of South Carolina's Lowcountry region, Hilton Head features spectacular bays and beaches, a national wildlife refuge, water sports, golf courses, five-star resorts and restaurants, and entertainment.

Hilton Head did not always present itself as a playground for the wealthy, however. It was only in the 1960s that Hilton Head began its transformation

43

into a choice leisure destination.[2] At that time, Hilton Head still formed part of the Bluffton Census County Division, or "Bluffton subdivision" of Beaufort County, and, unfortunately, Hilton Head's boom had not spilled over into the rest of Bluffton subdivision, nor into greater Beaufort County.

Bluffton subdivision residents outside of Hilton Head suffered from poverty, joblessness, and poor physical and social infrastructure. Other subdivisions of Beaufort County fared better than Bluffton. Still, overall median family income among permanent residents of Beaufort County was only 44 percent of Hilton Head's estimated median.[3] This gap would widen further if Hilton Head's wealthy visitors and non-resident property owners were taken into account.

The county government was therefore delighted when, in October 1969, BASF, a global chemical company, announced plans to build and operate a plant in Bluffton subdivision, Beaufort County, on 1,800 acres the company had quietly purchased there. State officials also cheered the project, as did 80 percent of county residents. The project promised high-paying construction jobs, numerous permanent jobs at the plant, plus higher tax revenues. The income earned by construction workers and full-time plant employees would boost local demand for housing, stores, restaurants, and so on. A richer tax base would pay for better roads, schools, and other common goods and services.

BASF had chosen the site with care. Headquartered in Ludwigshafen, Germany, the company sought a base in North America from which to expand BASF's business. For a site to hold promise, several factors had to come together. The site had to be well over 1,000 acres, with a supply of at least five million gallons per day of fresh water. The site needed nearby rail and port facilities, as well as a pool of inexpensive but trainable labor. The plant would discharge some pollutants into the air and water, so local environmental standards could not be too strict. Bluffton subdivision of Beaufort County perfectly fit the bill.

Or so it seemed. The rub lay in one factor of the Bluffton subdivision site not on BASF's list. The site was three miles upstream of Hilton Head. The same river system that provided the plant's fresh water threatened to carry plant discharge into Hilton Head's bays and onto its beaches.[4]

Hilton Head residents, businesses, and developers had no desire to receive this discharge, no interest in the plant, and no intention of allowing it to be built. Environmentalists joined with Hilton Head locals to fight the project tooth and nail. Opponents did not care that the State Pollution Central Authority foresaw no environmental problems; regulators' analyses showed that the plant would stay within existing state pollution limits. While it appeared possible for BASF to install additional pollution-control equipment that would reduce discharge to near zero, the cost of such equipment would make the project unprofitable for BASF.

BASF likely found itself blindsided by this opposition. The company also saw the irony of developers vowing to safeguard "the scenic splendor of the area." Developers make their living developing. Having gotten in first, these developers well understood the value of keeping all other development out. Such concern over the environment constituted classic Not-in-My-Backyard (NIMBY) hypocrisy. Machiavelli would have applauded.

Many poor residents of the Bluffton subdivision did not cheer, however. From their perspective, opposition to the plant would keep them in poverty and choke off their and their children's futures.

The two sides found themselves at loggerheads.

Who was in the right?

DECIDING WHO WAS RIGHT DEPENDS ON THE BASELINE

In one sense, both sides were right: they could both make perfectly sound ethical arguments.

Using the Golden Rule framework, plant opponents claimed that the Beaufort County and BASF intended to use Hilton Head as a means to their own ends: polluting Hilton Head in order to generate income from plant operations. Beaufort County and BASF, meanwhile, claimed the reverse. They argued that by blocking lawful economic development upstream, Hilton Head exploited BASF and Beaufort County residents outside of Hilton Head. They would be left poorer so that Hilton Head residents and businesses could enjoy the bays and beaches undisturbed.

Applying a Cost/Benefit analysis to the dispute would also look at exploitation. In the context of the Cost/Benefit framework, exploitation particularly arises when the benefits from an activity go to one group, while the costs fall upon another. In this regard, think of a dog owner who enjoys walking his or her pet but leaves the dog's feces on a neighbor's yard or the public sidewalk. When costs from an activity are thus unilaterally pushed onto people who do not enjoy its benefits, these costs are called "externalities" (*see* figure 4.1).

Splitting the benefits of an activity from its related costs leads those people who benefit to ignore or miscalculate overall utility. Such splitting also exploits those left bearing the externality. These elements make for an unethical result.

In the present case, one could argue that Beaufort County/BASF sought to keep the benefits of the plant while pushing some of its costs—namely, pollution—downstream onto Hilton Head.

We can reverse this argument, however, by stating that Hilton Head wanted to enjoy the benefits of its "scenic splendor" while forcing some of its costs—in the form of blocked economic development and continuing poverty—onto BASF and the rest of Beaufort County.

One lesson of the Hilton Head/BASF case is that, **in a real-world dispute, both sides often put forward logically sound ethical arguments.**

Figure 4.1 Externalities: Keeping the benefits, off-loading the costs

Source: Art by Eva Zafft.

What then typically decides the issue is the baseline, or starting point. How the ethical dilemma is framed will often go a long way toward deciding its outcome. So, it is in framing the dilemma that the real fight often takes place.

In the present case, South Carolina state law and U.S. federal law set the baseline.

Generally speaking, a property owner may use his own property as he pleases. But such use may not: (1) break the law; (2) unreasonably interfere with another property owner's use and enjoyment of his own property; nor (3) unreasonably obstruct, damage, or inconvenience the rights of the community.

This rule, however, is subject to state and federal laws establishing specific limits on the types and maximum amounts of pollutants that can be discharged into the environment. So long as the plant stayed within these limits, Beaufort County and BASF could argue that plant operations met the three conditions listed previously.

(Some readers committed to environmental protection might object to this answer. I would ask them to withhold final judgment until the end of the chapter.)

So much for the substance of the dispute. Hilton Head stubbornly refused to give in. It also had the motivation and means to block or delay procedures for getting the plant permitted, built, and commissioned.

With the parties still deadlocked, was there a way forward?

THE WAY FORWARD—FOLLOW THE MONEY

In the real world, deciding between two ethical arguments may be impossible. Or the decision in favor of the party with the stronger ethical argument may be frustrated. In other words, the losing side may be able to block the winners from enjoying their victory.

The best practical outcome in such circumstances may come from compromise. But compromise becomes harder when people dig in by recasting their self-interest as morality. They mask their selfish goals behind noble-sounding motives. They lie. Where each side thinks its position is ethical and the other side's position is unethical, compromise may seem unnecessary and even wrong.

At this point, one or both parties may have to put ethics aside. In such case, they should simply follow the money. This means unearthing concretely what each side stands to gain or lose. It means understanding each side's fundamental economic interests and measuring and re-allocating any externalities.

In the present situation, Hilton Head, BASF, and Beaufort County faced three basic options:

1. Don't build the plant.
2. Build the plant with standard pollution controls.
3. Build the plant with stricter-than-mandated pollution controls.

The fundamental interests in building or not building the plant line up as shown in table 4.1.

As table 4.1 shows, BASF and Beaufort County (excluding Hilton Head) will experience only costs from cancellation of the project. Hilton Head will enjoy only benefits, and the State of South Carolina will enjoy a blend of costs and benefits.

In theory, Hilton Head and the State of South Carolina could avoid an unethical outcome by compensating BASF, Beaufort County (and the State of South Carolina) for the benefits they will miss out on. This will require the parties to agree on the amount of these foregone benefits.

Table 4.1 Cost/Benefit analysis for Option No. 1: Don't build

	BASF	Beaufort County (excluding Hilton Head)	Hilton Head	State of South Carolina (SC)	*How to adjust for externality*
Option No. 1: Don't Build the Plant	**Cost** Future profits not realized	**Cost** Economic and social benefits not enjoyed	**Benefit** Added tax and social benefits of "pristine nature"	**Cost** Taxes not received; added social costs from continued poverty **Benefit** Taxes on added benefits from pristine nature	**Compromise:** *Hilton Head and/or SC reimburse BASF, Beaufort County, and SC for lost profits, benefits, and taxes*

What quickly becomes clear from the table is how vague and speculative the various costs and benefits from the Don't Build the Plant option are. BASF no doubt developed a financial model to support its decision to build a plant in Beaufort Country. But that model included numerous assumptions, such as the cost to build the plant, the cost of labor and of various feedstock chemicals, and the prices at which BASF would sell finished products. The financial model guessed at costs and prices going out more than thirty years into the future.

BASF's financial model should have included a best-case scenario. This scenario would have made assumptions favorable to the project and represents a reasonable upper bound to what BASF might have lost out on if the project were cancelled.

The costs and benefits for other parties would likely be much larger, but are even harder to assess with any confidence.[5] To take one small example, how should the parties calculate the net value to residents of Beaufort County of better public schools due to a richer tax base?

Similar problems attend Option No. 2, which calls for operation of the plant with standard pollution controls (*see* table 4.2).

Table 4.2 Cost/Benefit analysis for Option No. 2: Build with standard pollution controls

	BASF	Beaufort County (excluding Hilton Head)	Hilton Head	State of SC	How to adjust for externality
Option No. 2 Build the plant with standard pollution controls	Benefit Net present value of profits from the project	Benefit Overall economic and social benefits of the project	Cost Reduction in value of pristine nature caused by pollution (lower property values, lower revenue from tourism, etc.)	Cost Decrease in taxes from Hilton Head because nature no longer pristine Benefit Taxes from the project and increased economic activity in Beaufort County	Compromise: BASF, Beaufort, and SC compensate Hilton Head and SC for decrease in value from damage to pristine nature and lost taxes

The situation in Option No. 2 simply represents the flip side of Option No. 1. Now, BASF, Beaufort County and the State of South Carolina have to compensate Hilton Head (and the State of South Carolina) for seemingly large—but hard to measure—costs arising from pollution flowing down the river, into the bays, and onto the beaches.

Option No. 3—build the plant with stricter-than-mandated pollution controls—however, involves very different economics, and therefore the potential for a very different outcome (*see* table 4.3).

The first thing to notice is that all costs are now allocated to one party, namely, BASF. The second thing is that the externality in this case is precisely quantifiable: the cost of stricter-than-mandated pollution controls. The externality also appears modest compared to the vague but potentially huge externalities sprouting from Option No. 1 or Option No. 2.

A well-defined and modestly sized externality can lead to a workable compromise. Through a direct grant, property tax abatement, or income-tax credit, Beaufort County, Hilton Head, and/or the State of South Carolina

Table 4.3 Cost/Benefit analysis for Option No. 3: Build with stricter-than-mandated pollution controls

	BASF	Beaufort County (excluding Hilton Head)	Hilton Head	State of SC	*How to adjust for externality*
Option No. 3 Build the plant with stricter-than-mandated pollution controls	**Cost** The cost of stricter-than-mandated pollution controls (equivalent to the amount of future profits that make the project financially attractive)	**Benefit** Overall economic and social benefits of the project	**Benefit** Added tax and social, benefits of "pristine nature"	**Benefit** Taxes from the project and increased economic activity in Beaufort County; Investment, taxes, and social benefits; from pristine nature	**Compromise:** *Beaufort County, Hilton Head, and State of South Carolina compensate BASF for the cost of added pollution controls*

could have compensated BASF for the cost of the added pollution-control equipment. In so doing, they would have linked, rather than split, costs and benefits. Overall utility would have been maximized, and no party would have been exploited.

LESSONS LEARNED: NUMBERS AND NARRATIVES

In the case of the BASF plant in the Bluffton subdivision of Beaufort County, following the money—focusing on fundamental economic interests—strips away posturing by the parties. Such focus shows where compromise might be had. The key lies in spotting and sizing the externalities and then finding a mutually acceptable way to re-allocate costs and/ or benefits.

Unfortunately for BASF and Beaufort County residents, this compromise never happened. Faced with stiff and effective opposition from Hilton Head, BASF scotched the project.

The project's death may gladden readers who prize nature dearly, or who doubt that even added pollution controls would have safeguarded Hilton Head's scenic splendor. Skeptics have a point. State and federal pollution-control regulations and enforcement can fall short. Physical pollution-control systems sometimes fail. Causes include natural disasters, accidents, equipment breakdowns, simple human error, or criminal vandalism. Any of these causes might lead to discharge of toxins downstream. Of course, BASF could have insured against a chemical spill, but some risk would always have remained. And some environmental damage might have proven non-compensable. "Better safe than sorry," a wise nature lover might say.

But there is another side to the story. In fact, there is another story.

That story unfolds when one looks at racial and other demographics of Hilton Head, Bluffton subdivision, and Beaufort County as a whole (*see* figure 4.2).

Figure 4.2 shows that at the time the project was considered, Hilton Head was much whiter, wealthier, and older than Bluffton subdivision and/or Beaufort County.[6] So, what has been presented for years

Figure 4.2 Hilton Head, Bluffton, and Beaufort County demographics

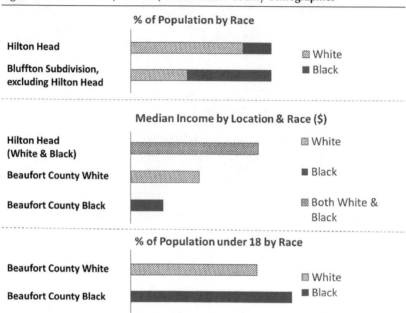

in business-school textbooks as a case in environmental ethics might in reality be no more than an exercise in wealthy, white privilege.

In this story, the privileged of Hilton Head did not worry about ethical baselines. They did not care about the poverty or stunted hopes of people upstream of their own vacation homes, resorts, and restaurants. They did not trouble themselves with externalities or compromise. The privileged of Hilton Head wanted to kill the BASF project, and kill it they did.

This story comprises all the facts of the original story. The parties and the economics remain unchanged. But, even for those who cherish the environment, the census data might tilt sympathies and cloud what seemed to be the clear and straightforward ethics of protecting nature from industry.

So, the final lesson of the story of The Trashing of Hilton Head is this: beware taking someone else's presentation of an ethical dilemma at face value. Too often, people stop investigating or thinking once the information at hand matches their view of how the world is, or should be.

Stay skeptical. Ethical behavior requires gathering and weighing all of the facts, not just the ones that make us feel good.

NOTES

1. "BASF Corporation vs. the Hilton Head Island Developers," in *Business and Society*, ed. Robert D. Hay, et al. (Cincinnati: Southwestern Publishing Co., 1984), 100–12; *see* also, "Introduction to Ethical Reasoning," Donaldson, Thomas, and Werhane, Patricia, eds., 1–12, accessed November 21, 2016, http://faculty.tuck. dartmouth.edu/images/uploads/faculty/adam-kleinbaum/introduction_to_ethical_ reasoning.pdf.

2. Horace W. Fleming, Jr., et al., "Hilton Head Government: Analysis and Alternatives," Report Prepared for the Hilton Head Island Community Association, Inc., 1974.

3. *See* Bureau of the Census, *1970 Census of the Population*, Vol. 1, Part 42 (South Carolina) (Washington, DC: U.S. Department of Commerce, 1973), Table 44, 42–132; *see* also Fleming, 110.

4. Michael N. Danielson, *Profits and Politics in Paradise: The Development of Hilton Head Island* (Columbia: University of South Carolina Press, 1995), 149–56.

5. This table only considers the parties in close proximity to the plant. If the plant were not built in Beaufort County, it might have been built somewhere else. In theory, Cost/Benefit analysis should account for the interests of people living in that other place.

6. The 1970 U.S. census did not report Hilton Head separately from Bluffton subdivision or Beaufort County. *See* Fleming et al. for estimates of Hilton Head population and median family income, as well as comments on the accuracy of the 1970 census as it related to the full-time resident population of Hilton Head. The graphic for the percentage of population under 18 years of age reflects the female population only. Census figures for the male population are skewed by the U.S. Marine Corps Recruit Depot, Parris Island, Beaufort County, SC, as well as nearby U.S. military facilities and so have been omitted.

Part II

THE ETHICAL BUSINESS AND OTHER FANTASTIC BEASTS

5

Owners, Managers, and Stakeholders: Whose Business Is It, Anyway?

■ ■ ■

"Corporations have no consciences, no beliefs, no feelings, no thoughts, no desires."

—U.S. Supreme Court Justice John Paul Stevens, dissenting in *Citizens United*[1]

Part I (chapters 1–4) of this book introduced basic ethical frameworks through the Lifeboat Game (and Machiavelli) and then applied these frameworks to BASF's actual effort build a chemical plant in Beaufort County, South Carolina.

The Lifeboat Game involved individuals. Chapter 4 discussed BASF, developers, and resorts, but did not distinguish among natural persons and legal persons/business entities like BASF.

This chapter will now dig deeper. What is the difference between a natural person and a legal person? Does this difference matter in the context of business ethics? If so, what do we mean when we say that business entities should act ethically? How do the ethical obligations of a business entity flow (or not flow) between and among the entity's shareholders, directors, officers, and employees?

We begin with the following simple question, which turns out not to be so simple: Is business ethics an oxymoron?

IS "BUSINESS ETHICS" AN OXYMORON?

Jumbo shrimp. Military intelligence. Business ethics. Reciting a list of seemingly self-contradictory phrases rarely fails to wring from listeners either grins or groans.

But the term "business ethics" raises a real question with real consequences. *Can* a business be ethical?

Legal Persons versus Natural Persons

When an individual runs a business as a sole proprietor, there is no legal or practical difference between the person and the business. The same holds true for general partnerships involving individuals. A partnership simply means that two or more persons carry on an activity for the purpose of sharing profit and loss.

In these cases, the businesses will be as ethical as the people who own and run them.

Sole proprietorships comprise over 70 percent of the businesses registered in the United States.[2] On the other hand, while numerous, sole proprietorships and general partnerships are not where the action is. Nearly 95 percent of business activity by revenue in the United States comes from corporations and other legal entities, like limited liability companies.[3] A wide range of non-profit activities, like private charity, education, and healthcare, also takes place through legal entities.

The law treats corporations, limited liability companies, and other legal entities as "legal persons." As such, they enjoy a number of the same rights as "natural persons" (i.e., individual human beings). Legal persons have the right to own and transfer property in their own names. They can make contracts. They can sue and be sued. A high-profile U.S. Supreme Court case, *Citizens United v. Federal Election Commission* (*FEC*), even held that legal persons, as associations of individuals, have Free Speech rights to advocate, and to spend money on advocating, political positions.[4]

A decade after *Citizens United* was decided, many people—including one of the justices who dissented in the case—continue to detest and contest the Court's ruling.[5] Rightly or wrongly, *Citizens United* fixed a key boundary in the mapping of rights and responsibilities of legal persons versus those of natural persons. This mapping continues to occupy the High Court, as well as the public mind.[6]

Of course, legal persons do not enjoy all of the rights of a natural person. Legal persons may not vote. They may not assert Fifth Amendment rights against self-incrimination. They do not have Second Amendment rights to keep and bear arms. As a practical matter, legal persons cannot be imprisoned, though they can be convicted of crimes and punished through fines or limits on their activities.

The boundaries between the rights and responsibilities of natural persons and those of legal entities directly impact business ethics. Justice Stevens wrote in dissent in *Citizens United* that "corporations [and other legal persons] have no consciences, no beliefs, no feelings, no thoughts, no desires."

If this is indeed so, how can we ask, let alone expect, business entities to act ethically?

Hobby Lobby: A Business Gets Religion

In a follow-on case to *Citizens United*, the U.S. Supreme Court considered whether a for-profit business entity could exercise religion in a way entitled to protection under federal law.

In 1970, David and Barbara Green founded Hobby Lobby with a $600 loan. They began working from their home, making and selling miniature picture frames. Over the next forty-five years, the Greens grew Hobby Lobby, a corporation, into the largest privately owned arts-and-crafts retailer in the world. Hobby Lobby currently employs approximately 32,000 people spread across over 700 stores in forty-seven states.[7] During all these years, the corporation has remained 100 percent owned by the Green family.

The Greens are devout Christians. Their faith compels them to operate their company in line with their understanding of biblical principles. Following these principles can require financial sacrifice. So, for example, in observance of the Christian Sabbath, no Hobby Lobby stores are open on Sundays. Partly for religious reasons, the Greens also cause Hobby Lobby to sponsor employee health-insurance plans.

The Green's principles came under threat in 2010, when the U.S. Government issued regulations to implement the Affordable Care Act ("Obamacare"). These regulations provided, among other things, that businesses like Hobby Lobby, which sponsored employee health plans, make certain contraceptive methods available to their employees free of charge.

Of the twenty contraceptive methods required by the government, four methods involved prevention of a fertilized egg from attaching to the uterine wall and developing. The Greens' faith holds that human life begins at conception. The four methods therefore constitute a form of abortion, which the Greens believe wrongfully takes an innocent human life.

The Greens' views fall well within the religious mainstream. In fact, in recognition of potential, sincere religious objections, the government had specifically exempted religious institutions, like churches, from the contraception requirement. The government had also exempted religious non-profit organizations, like Catholic hospitals, that had religious objections.

The U.S. government did not, however, exempt for-profit businesses with religious objections. Nor did it have interest in doing so. Officials therefore gave the Greens the choice of: (1) shutting down their business; (2) refusing to include the four methods in employee plans and paying a large fine; or (3) dropping company-sponsored health plans entirely and paying a smaller fine.

Unwilling to bow or bend, the Greens caused Hobby Lobby to sue the U.S. government. The company claimed that the regulations violated its rights under the federal Religious Freedom Restoration Act (RFRA). Under RFRA, the federal government may not take any action that substantially burdens a person's exercise of religion unless that action constitutes the least restrictive means of serving a compelling governmental interest.

The U.S. Supreme Court, by a 5–4 majority, found for Hobby Lobby. The Court ruled that the RFRA excused the company from having to fund contraceptive methods contravening the owners' sincerely held religious beliefs.

Hobby Lobby's Import for Business Ethics

Much ink has been shed over this decision, which sharply divided the Court. What interests us for business-ethics purposes, though, is not what divided the justices, but how close to each other their positions actually lay.

In finding for Hobby Lobby, the majority ruled, among other things, that a for-profit legal person can exercise religion. This ruling implies that the psychic components necessary for religious exercise (e.g., conscience, beliefs, feelings, thoughts, desires) of the business's owners/managers can be imputed to the company. By extension, such a company can also act ethically. This is not to say that religion and ethics are the same thing. But their exercise involves common psychic components. Absent such psychic components, neither religious exercise nor ethical deliberation can take place.

While the majority opinion held that Hobby Lobby could exercise religion, the opinion included a large caveat. Writing for the Court, Justice Samuel Alito noted that Hobby Lobby was a "closely held corporation . . . owned and controlled by members of a single family, and no one has disputed the sincerity of their religious beliefs." In other words, Hobby Lobby's exercising religion rested on the fact that its owners made up a small, discrete group of identifiably like-minded individuals. Because of these factors, the Court concluded that the company took on (or exercised) the psychic components and religious identity of its owners.

The dissent, written by Justice Ruth Bader Ginsburg, argued that a for-profit entity did not constitute a "person" under RFRA. Nor, in the dissent's view, could such a for-profit entity exercise religion.

What is interesting here is that, like Alito, Ginsburg focused on the business owners' homogeneity, or like-mindedness, as critical to a legal person's exercising of religion.

In her dissent, Ginsburg needed to walk a fine line. She did not want to argue that *non-profit* entities could not exercise religion. Such a ruling might call into question numerous accommodations federal, state, and local governments have made to churches and faith-based charities, as well as to non-profit, religiously affiliated educational and healthcare institutions.

So, Ginsburg argued that what distinguished religious organizations from non-religious entities was the identity of interest and outlook of the persons running and benefiting from these entities. Here, Ginsburg wrote, "Religious organizations exist to foster the interests of persons subscribing to the same religious faith. Not so for for-profit corporations."

As an assertion of fact, Ginsburg's statement may not quite hold up. Religious organizations foster the interests of both those who run the organizations and those who benefit from them. For example, in 1950, Saint Teresa of Calcutta founded the Missionaries of Charity. By 2012, this Roman Catholic organization consisted of over 4,500 sisters active in 133 countries. Far from "fostering the interests of persons subscribing to the same religious faith," the sisters vow to give "whole-hearted free service to the poorest of the poor" irrespective of faith. Numerous other religious organizations, and their members, dedicate themselves—in the name of their faith—to the service of mankind, rather than merely of their co-religionists. On top of this, inter-faith religious organizations routinely bring together members of various faiths and denominations. These organizations foster interests (whether from running or benefiting) which cannot, by definition, be confined to "persons subscribing to the same religious faith."

Finally, lest a cynic think that such activities are nothing more than disguised proselytizing, it should be noted that some religious organizations even commit themselves to the welfare of animals.[8]

Ginsburg may have been right on other issues in the case, but her "same religious faith" distinction seems to have missed the mark. What matters here, however, is that both her dissent and the majority opinion highlighted the key role which a shared outlook among a business's owners plays in determining the business's capacity for religious, moral, or ethical behavior. On this point, the Justices appeared unanimous.

The Ethical Business Will Always Be a Rare Beast

Recapping the *Hobby Lobby* case, a business entity can be ethical. But its capacity for ethical behavior depends upon having a small, discrete, and like-minded group of owners who transmit and infuse into the business they own their own clearly drawn, shared views and values.

Relatively few legal persons will meet this criterion. Certainly no large-scale, publicly owned enterprises will. Since corporations and limited-liability companies dominate the U.S. economy by revenue, the ethical business as defined by *Hobby Lobby* will always be a rare beast.

For the companies that make up the bulk of business activity, therefore, a different standard has to apply. And developing this standard leads us to ask what it means for senior leaders of a company to act ethically, and what a company's ultimate goal should be.

ETHICAL ACTION BY DIRECTORS AND MANAGERS—
THE SAGA OF WIDGETCO

It may be that some companies cannot be ethical. But the individuals who own and run them can.

What does it mean for an individual who sits on the Board of a company to act ethically?

What does it mean for a member of management?

To attack these questions, it's helpful to consider the hypothetical case of the Widget family and their company, WidgetCo.

Sole Ownership

Imagine that entrepreneur Bo Widget incorporates WidgetCo to manufacture widgets. Bo owns 100 percent of the shares (*see* figure 5.1).

As the sole shareholder, Bo elects all of the members of the Board of Directors. The Board appoints Bo CEO.

Over time, like Hobby Lobby, WidgetCo grows and prospers. Bo, like David and Barbara Green, gets rich.

Then, Bo goes green. He decides that, henceforth, he will draw a reasonable salary and enjoy some perks, such as a company car and business-class air travel on business trips. However, through his control of 100 percent of the shares, Bo will cause WidgetCo, after it pays its expenses and makes capital investments, to donate 100 percent of its remaining profits to The

Figure 5.1 WidgetCo—sole ownership

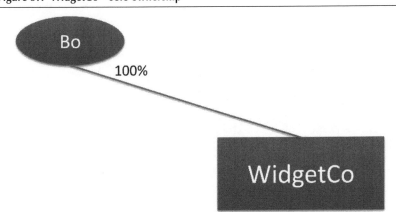

Sierra Club Foundation. The Foundation is an independent public charity that supports a variety of environmental programs and organizations.

Since Bo is the 100 percent owner, his causing WidgetCo to give away all its profits would not seem to raise any ethical concerns. After all, the company's assets and its profits effectively belong to him anyway.

Sibling "Partnership"

Now suppose, however, that Bo did not found WidgetCo by himself but with his sibling, Billie. The resulting ownership structure is shown in figure 5.2.

Figure 5.2 WidgetCo—sibling "partnership"

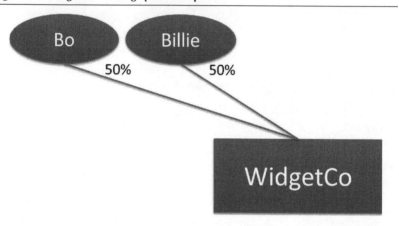

Under this new structure, let's assume that Bo and Billie are the only two people on the Board of Directors. As Directors, they appoint Bo CEO and Billie COO. They draw mutually agreed-upon salaries. They enjoy similar perks. After covering other expenses and capital investments, WidgetCo will donate 50 percent of its profits to the Sierra Club Foundation. The remaining 50 percent will go to Billie's favorite charity, the American Society for the Prevention of Cruelty to Animals (ASPCA).

Even with two owners and two charities, there still seems to be no ethical problem, as 100 percent of WidgetCo owners have agreed on how to run the company, to handle its assets, and to dole out its profits.

Cousin Consortium

Let's consider a third scenario. Bo and Billie did not found the company. They inherited 52 percent of the company's stock from their mother.

Figure 5.3 WidgetCo—cousin consortium

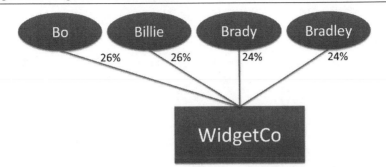

Meanwhile, their first cousins, Brady and Bradley, inherited 48 percent of the company's stock from their father, who was the brother of Bo and Billie's mother.

The ownership structure of the company is shown in figure 5.3.

Assume that Bo and Billie, as in earlier examples, built the company from a small sibling partnership. Their 52 percent ownership of WidgetCo gives them complete day-to-day control. They remain the only two people on the Board of Directors. They appoint themselves CEO and COO. As before, they draw salaries, receive perks, and give WidgetCo's profits, 50/50, to the Sierra Club Foundation and the ASPCA.

Brady and Bradley don't like this setup, however. They don't work for company and so draw no salaries. They get no perks. They also think that Bo and Billie's salaries exceed reasonable levels and resent the company paying for Bo's and Billie's cars and business-class airfare. Finally, Brady and Bradley do not want their cousins giving away the company's profits. Brady and Bradley have their own needs and favorite charities. As things stand, Brady and Bradley see no benefit from their ownership of 48 percent of company shares.

At this point, almost everybody will agree that an ethical problem exists. Bo and Billie own 52 percent of the company but are taking or redirecting some of the assets and all of the profits. If the salaries and perks are indeed excessive, they will represent a waste of assets through self-dealing. Such waste harms Brady and Bradley, who, as shareholders, have an indirect claim on some of these assets.

With regard to WidgetCo's donations, the Sierra Club Foundation and ASPCA may be worthy organizations. But Bo and Billie should not use company assets to further their personal causes when they own less than one-hundred percent of the company.

Public Company

Adding public shareholders to this mix enlarges the problem, but does not change its nature (*see* figure 5.4).

Figure 5.4 WidgetCo—publicly traded company

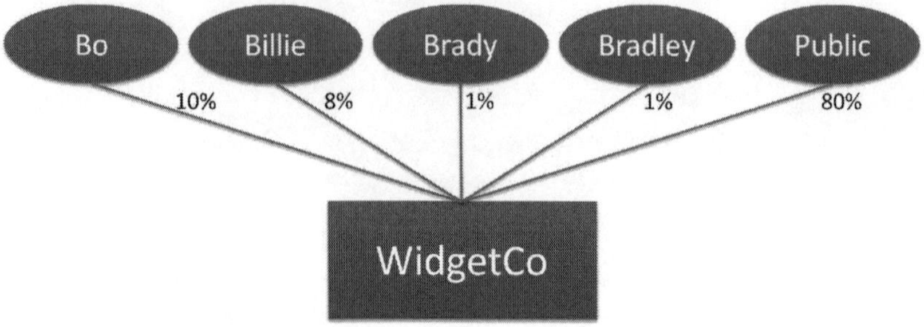

Ethics for Directors and Managers Relate to Their Duties, Not Their Personal Preferences

By law, a legal person belongs to all of its owners. The legal person's directors and senior managers ("officers") owe the legal person heightened duties of loyalty and care, among other duties. These duties are collectively called "fiduciary duties." As a rule of thumb, directors and officers must put the interests of the legal person before their own and must disclose any potential conflicts of interest they have with the legal person.

The Saga of WidgetCo shows that as a company's ownership become more diverse, the company's managers must increasingly guard against using company assets to further their own personal goals or interests, or those of a group of shareholders. It does not matter if these goals are inherently worthy ones, like protecting the environment or preventing cruelty to animals.

Use of assets to favor the personal ethical preferences of fewer than 100 percent of the shareholders exploits non-controlling shareholders (Golden Rule). It also splits costs from benefits, frustrating calculation and maximization of overall utility (Cost/Benefit).[9]

In the examples given previously, corporate law and other rules should protect Brady, Bradley, and public shareholders from abuse by Bo and

Billic. But the fact that the law may not bar, catch, or adequately punish similar behavior in all circumstances does not make it ethical.

WHAT SHOULD BE A BUSINESS'S ULTIMATE GOAL?

This chapter began by asking whether a business could be ethical.

For sole proprietorships and general partnerships, the answer is "yes" because no distinction exists between the individual owner(s)/manager(s) and the business.

For legal persons, which dominate commerce, the *Hobby Lobby* case tells us that only under rare conditions can a business entity be considered to have the psychic components (conscience, beliefs, thoughts, etc.) necessary to exercise religion, which components are also required to act ethically.

The rarity of an ethical business entity raises two questions for those entities which do not make the cut: (1) what does it mean for controlling owner(s), directors, and managers to act ethically; and (2) what should be the entity's ultimate goal?

The Saga of WidgetCo points out that business entities belong, indirectly, to *all* of their owners. Herein lies a constant challenge. The controlling owner(s), directors, and managers may be tempted to use the entity for their own purposes. These purposes might be selfish, like paying themselves excessive salaries or wasteful perks; or, these purposes might arise from good intentions, like giving to worthy charities. But these well-intentioned purposes are those of the controlling owner(s), directors and/or managers, not of the business entity itself or all of its owners. If all the owners are not on board, pursuing these purposes will be unethical.

So, if controlling owner(s), "directors," and "managers" should not serve their own purposes but only those of the company (or ownership group as a whole), how do the controlling owner(s), directors, and managers know what the company's purposes should be? In other words, what ethical guidelines tell controlling owners, directors, and managers how to direct and run the business?

Responses to this question fall into five broad clusters called: (1) Dualism; (2) Monism; (3) Modest Idealism; (4) High Idealism; and (5) Pragmatism.[10]

Not surprisingly, the experts writing about these clusters find themselves even more divided than the U.S. Supreme Court. To make business ethics work in the real world, we need to understand the basic arguments, strengths, and weakness of each of these clusters.

Dualism: The Guideline of Strict Profit Maximization

Dualism draws a stark line between private and public spheres of activity. **Dualism holds that a company's directors and managers should seek to maximize the wealth of all of the company's owners.** This duty is subject to obeying the law. It is subject to respecting the contractual commitments the company has made to others, such as employees, suppliers, and customers. Finally, it is subject to observing customary commercial practices in the company's geography and industry.[11]

Dualism offers a single, clear benchmark for judging a business's performance. This benchmark enables shareholders to hold management's feet to the fire. In so doing, Dualism encourages peak company performance, which maximizes shareholder wealth.

Dualism does not give the nod to anything goes. Rather, it argues that society will enjoy the greatest benefits if businesses focus on maximizing shareholder wealth, with social goals met by public bodies adjusting legal, background-contractual, and customary obligations in order to constrain and guide business behavior.

The principal criticism of Dualism points out that external constraints on businesses from regulation and the like often prove inadequate. In some cases, these constraints lack specificity or effective enforcement. In other cases, they cannot move fast enough to match evolving business technologies and practices. Finally, through political contributions, lobbying, and a revolving door between government and business, companies have not infrequently captured the governmental bodies charged with regulating them. What results is not constraint but favoritism.

Even if true, this criticism does not necessarily push us to drop the goal of maximizing shareholder wealth. We should only drop the goal if someone comes up with a better system which does not include it. Several better systems have been proposed and tried across the world, but no clearly better alternative has emerged in practice.

Monism: Long-Run Identity between Public and Private Interests

Monists argue that companies do well by doing good. This means that activities and expenditures for the public good which reduce shareholder wealth in the short term will maximize such wealth over the long haul.

Courts will generally defer to directors and manager in deciding what is best for a business "if the directors of a corporation act . . . on an informed basis, in good faith and in the honest belief that the action taken. . . [is] in the best interests of the company."[12] Management of the corporation must answer to the Board of Directors.

This deference is known as the Business Judgment Rule. It applies not only to corporations but to other legal persons.

Business directors and managers therefore have considerable discretion to spend company resources on public or social matters as long as they can tie the spending in some plausible way to the company's long-term interests. For example, companies might refuse to lay off unnecessary staff during a downturn in the belief that the added loyalty and staff cohesion will more than pay off once the economy improves. Managers even have discretion to donate company funds to a charity, where the managers can reasonably argue that the donation will redound to the company's benefit.

Critics of Monism point out how readily the leeway given directors and managers leads to waste and abuse. The hypothetical example of Bo and Billie Widget and their cousins pales in comparison to thousands of actual cases where directors, and/or managers self-dealt, wasted resources, or indulged their pet causes at company expense.

This said, in theory, Monism does not inherently conflict with Dualism (i.e., shareholder wealth maximization), since the stated—if not always actual—purpose of monistic expenditures is to satisfy the dualistic goal of maximizing overall shareholder wealth.

Modest Idealism: Voluntary Compliance with the Law

Modest Idealism provides that companies should comply with laws and regulations even when non-compliance would be more profitable.

This approach states that in weighing costs and benefits, managers should not discount the cost of cheating by the probability of getting caught and punished.

Modest idealism does not conflict with Dualism, since the latter makes wealth maximization subject to observance of legal and contractual obligations.

Theoretically, everybody would be better off if everyone followed the rules. In practice, some people cheat. Many more rationalize their behavior, often aided by cunning lawyers. Also, some rules are silly or unfair, or both. Having practiced law in emerging markets (and Chicago) for many years. I can state from personal experience that some corrupt and bureaucratic regimes make it impossible for a business which obeys all the laws to survive. This arrangement forces the business to bribe the officials who run the regime.

Is the business wrong to do so? The Golden Rule would say it is. But, to use a concrete metaphor, imagine that a policeman orders you to stand still. You know he intends to punch you in the face. In such case, is standing still ethical, or merely foolish?

In sum, on one level, Modest Idealism represents an excellent organizing principle; on another level, it may not be practical enough to guide behavior in a harsh and competitive world.

High Idealism: Interest-Group Accommodation and the Public Interest as Ultimate Goals

High Idealism challenges the idea that a business only belongs to its owners. The High Idealist argues that various persons interacting with, or affected by, the business also have a claim on its resources. These persons, called stakeholders, can include employees, suppliers, customers, members of the communities in which the business operates, and even current and future members of society at large.[13]

The consequence of High Idealism is that **directors and managers must seek not only to generate wealth for company owner(s) but to advance the welfare of stakeholders.**[14]

Unlike, other clusters, therefore, High Idealism is logically inconsistent with Dualism. In practice, High Idealism can be pursued in several ways. For example, the business might operate or transfer resources so as to benefit stakeholders, without expecting these actions to maximize shareholder wealth. Additionally, employee representatives might take formal roles in company decision-making. The government might own a "golden share" of company equity giving the government veto rights over major company decisions. Finally, the government might appoint officials to the Board of Directors, or representatives of company employees might have a right to sit on company Boards or councils.

High Idealism judges external controls on company behavior inadequate. These controls include not only laws and regulations (of which there is no shortage), but contracts. Presumably, the concentration of economic and political power within large-scale businesses justifies direct participation of stakeholders and governmental officials in company decision-making bodies and processes.

High Idealism's detractors make several arguments. First, pursuit of goals other than shareholder wealth maximization comes at a high cost. By tasking directors and managers with multiple goals, monitoring and measuring managerial performance become extremely hard. Lack of accountability in turn undermines economic efficiency, in part by opening avenues for large-scale managerial self-dealing and waste.

Second, over time, stakeholder demands on the business will multiply and conflict. For example, should the company give employees a raise, or keep pay where it is and donate the savings to build a public park? Squabbles among stakeholders will make the business harder to run.

Finally, inefficiency and discord will eventually threaten the business's competitiveness against firms solely focused on maximizing shareholder wealth. Protecting Highly Idealistic directors and managers from Dualistic competitors will further entrench poor management, encourage self-dealing and waste, and cripple economic efficiency.

Pragmatism: Private Capabilities Used to Implement Public Policies

Pragmatism argues that governmental bodies should make greater use of private businesses to implement public policies. Moreover, businesses should look for ways to take over delivery of goods and services currently performed by the public sector.

In line with this principle, some governments now apply a "Yellow Pages" test to their activities. If a good or service is available through a business directory, the government should not provide it.

Objections to pragmatism center on the likelihood that for-profit enterprises will cut corners to boost profits. Prisons run by for-profit entities represent an oft-cited example.

LESSONS LEARNED: SENSE AND SENSIBILITY

Promoting ethical business requires us to do more than act uprightly. We have to think clearly, too. This means understanding and respecting the roles and limitations placed on business entities, their owners, directors, managers, and stakeholders.

At a gut level, we would all like to see businesses do the right thing. The right thing, though, depends upon more than a final decision. It depends upon the *processes* by which the final decision was reached and upon the *purposes* for which the decision was made.

The academic debate over Dualism, Monism, Modest Idealism, High Idealism, and Pragmatism will go on. Supporters of these various schools of thought yet jockey for position and headlines. For example, an August 2019, blog post from the Business Roundtable proclaimed that the "Business Round-table Redefines the Purpose of a Corporation to Promote 'An Economy That Serves All Americans.'" The blog post then published a Statement signed by 181 global-company CEOs participating in the Roundtable.[15]

The new Statement replaces a previous one that was explicitly dual-istic. Does the new Statement mean game, set, and match in favor of High Idealism? Hardly. First off, the Statement has no legal force. Second, the Statement's text comprises platitudes that might fit any approach. In this regard, the Statement reads in part, "While each of our individual companies serves its own corporate purpose, we share a fundamental commitment to all of our stakeholders." This purpose is not further defined, nor is the fundamental commitment set forth in a way that neces-sarily violates Dualism.

The Statement's strategic ambiguity leads us to ask whether the CEOs who signed it intended to break new corporate-governance ground, or simply to shrink their target silhouette vis-a-vis non-dualistic critics. One clue springs from the Statement's language on serving Americans and "our country." The signing CEOs run global companies. Why would High Idealists limit the circle of stakeholders to the United States?

Roundtable CEOs have reached the business world's top rung. They have experience handling uncertainty, contradiction, and compromise. These CEOs know that even a purely dualistic company must care about its reputation among stakeholders. And highly idealistic businesses that take their eye off of their customers or their bottom line will go bankrupt, be swallowed up by dualistic competitors, or end up costing society far more than the wealth the businesses have created.

Sometimes, life gives us not one answer but several competing answers. From these we must divine a way forward. In this light, the next chapter looks from various angles at one of the most infamous and spectacular scandals in American corporate history.

NOTES

1. *Citizens United v. Federal Election Commission*, 558 U.S. 310 (2010).

2. Reference.com, accessed December 1, 2016, https://www.reference.com/business-finance/percentage-businesses-sole-proprietorships-731c60f3bd02b528#.

3. 2012 Statistical Abstract of the United States, "Table 744 (2008 Year)," accessed December 1, 2016, http://www.census.gov/library/publications/2011/compendia/statab/131ed/business-enterprise.html. In line with IRS data, $700 billion of revenues ascribed to "partnerships" was assumed to come from general or limited partnerships. The remaining $4.2 trillion ascribed to "partnerships" was assumed to come from limited liability companies electing to be taxed as partnerships. *See* Elizabeth Wasserman, "How to Structure a Partnership," *Inc.*, accessed December 1, 2016, http://www.inc.com/guides/structuring-partnerships.html.

4. *Citizens United v. FEC*, 558 U.S. 310 (2010).

5. Tara Golshan, "Ruth Bader Ginsburg Says Her 'Impossible Dream' Is for Citizens United to be Overturned," *Vox*, July 11, 2016, accessed November 30, 2016, http://www.vox.com/2016/7/11/12148066/ruth-bader-ginsburg-citizens-united.

6. *See*, for example, *Masterpiece Cakeshop, Ltd. v. Colorado Civil Rights Commission*, 584 U.S. ___ (2018). (The sole owner of a for-profit limited liability company sought First Amendment protection from state antidiscrimination laws. The U.S. Supreme Court did not decide this case on substantive grounds but found unacceptable bias against the owner by state officials prior to their rendering a state-level decision.) Similar First Amendment cases, some involving legal persons and some involving natural persons, make their way through the state and federal administrative and judicial systems. *See*, for example, *Arlene's Flowers Inc. v. Washington* (Petition granted, judgment vacated and case remanded for further consideration in light of *Masterpiece Cakeshop, Ltd. v. Colorado Civil Rights Commission* on June 25, 2018); and *Klein v. Oregon Bureau of Labor and Industries* (petition granted, judgment vacated and case remanded for further

consideration in light of *Masterpiece Cakeshop, Ltd. v. Colorado Civil Rights Commission* on June 17, 2019).

7. Hobby Lobby homepage, "Our Story." Hobbylobby.com, accessed November 30, 2019, http://www.hobbylobby.com/about-us/our-story.

8. Catholic Concern for Animals home page, "The Catechism of the Catholic Church," Catholic Concern for Animals (CCA), accessed September 23, 2019, https://catholic-animals.com/about/.

9. In some cases, managers and controlling shareholders might be motivated by greed. In other cases, they might act from a sincere belief that they know better than their non-controlling shareholders what is good for them. This is a form of pride. Neither case evidences virtuous behavior.

10. Robert C. Clark, *Corporate Law* (New York: Aspen Publishers, 1986), chapter 16. This section of chapter 5 relies extensively on Clark's treatise.

11. Milton Friedman, "The Social Responsibility of Business Is to Increase Its Profits," *The New York Times Magazine*, September 13, 1970, accessed December 5, 2016, http://www.colorado.edu/studentgroups/libertarians/issues/friedman-soc-resp-business.html.

12. *Sinclair Oil Corp. v. Levien*, 280 A.2d 717, 720 (Del. 1971).

13. Russell L. Ackoff, *The Democratic Corporation* (New York & Oxford: Oxford University Press, 1994), 36–45.

14. R. Edward Freeman, "Managing for Stakeholders," in *Ethical Theory in Business*, 8th ed., ed. Tom L. Beauchamp, Norman R. Bowie, and Denis G. Arnold (Upper Saddle River, NJ: Pearson Prentice Hall, 2007).

15. Business Roundtable, "Business Roundtable Redefines the Purpose of a Corporation to Promote 'An Economy That Serves All Americans'," Business Roundtable (BR), accessed October 22, 2019, https://www.businessroundtable.org/business-roundtable-redefines-the-purpose-of-a-corporation-to-promote-an-economy-that-serves-all-americans.

6

The Market for Reputation: A Fresh Take on the Ford Pinto Scandal

■ ■ ■

"What is History but a fable agreed upon?"

—attributed to Napoleon Bonaparte, among others

The Ford Pinto fiasco has long been the poster child of business-ethics scandals. In fact, the phrase "Ford Pinto" has itself become a byword for its own type of scandal, like Watergate (political cover-up), Enron (financial and accounting shell game), and Bernie Madoff (rip-off of wealthy-but-naïve clients).

When a story becomes legend, sifting truth from myth becomes hard. In the telling and re-telling, people embellish those facts which fit their preferred moral and airbrush out the ones that don't.

So it has become with the Ford Pinto. Ask most people about the Pinto scandal, and they will tell you that rather than spend $11 more per car, Ford went forward with a knowingly faulty gas-tank design. As a result, hundreds of people burned to death when rear-end collisions ruptured the Pinto's gas tank and ignited the fuel.

But that's not how things happened. The $11 fix did not relate to a gas-tank defect on the Pinto. The $11 involved a valve that would slow gas leakage in the event of a rollover. And the rollover-leakage issue concerned not just the Pinto, but Ford's entire fleet.

Misinformation also surrounds the fire risk from the Pinto's allegedly faulty fuel-tank placement. This risk needs to be placed in context. An estimated 27 to 180 people died as a result of rear-impact-related fuel-tank fires in the Pinto. Moreover, given the number of Pintos on the road, the car may not have been substantially less safe than comparably sized cars of the competition.[1]

This chapter does not argue that Ford was blameless. The truth of the Pinto case depends on the intentions of, and care shown by, dozens, if not hundreds, of people. As a result, the truth remains unknown and perhaps unknowable. So, this chapter will not offer one version of the story but several versions. That's because the real-world lesson of the Ford Pinto is not about what actually happened. The lesson is about how to avoid being caught naked and defenseless in a world in which, "A lie gets halfway around the world before the truth has a chance to get its pants on."[2]

THE UNDISPUTED FACTS

Let's start with what all sides appear to agree upon.

Between 1971 and 1980, Ford Motor Company sold approximately 3.2 million units of its Pinto subcompact car.[3]

Inexpensive and fuel efficient, the Pinto was a top seller. Its popularity helped keep Ford afloat during the Energy Crisis and recession of the mid-1970s. During that period, gas prices spiked fourfold and overall U.S. automobile sales fell 25 percent. In the middle of this turmoil, Pinto sales peaked at 544,000 cars in 1974.

The Pinto's Origins

The Pinto was the brainchild of Ford Motor Company President Lee Iacocca.[4] Lido (Lee) Iacocca was the Allentown, Pennsylvania-born son of Nicola and Antonietta Iacocca, immigrants from the Campania Region of Italy.

Iacocca joined Ford Motor Company in 1946. Trained as an engineer, Iacocca actually made his mark in sales and marketing. His successful "56 for '56" campaign fast-tracked him for senior management. This campaign offered car buyers loans on 1956 model–year cars with a 20 percent down payment and $56 in monthly payments for three years.

Iacocca also shepherded design and release of Ford's blockbuster 1964/65 Mustang sports car, as well as a number of other successful models.

In the mid-1960s, Iacocca and other senior Ford executives saw the looming threat that cheap imports posed to Ford's strong position in the U.S. small-car market. Within Ford, a power struggle broke out over how to respond. Iacocca won. He became Ford's President and ramped up the Pinto's development and launch.

Design Constraints and Trade-Offs

Iacocca intended the Pinto to compete head-to-head against low-priced, imported subcompacts. Consequently, he imposed the "limits of 2000" on design and sales and marketing teams. The finished car absolutely, positively, could not weigh more than 2,000 pounds nor cost more than $2,000.[5]

These constraints forced a number of engineering trade-offs. Moreover, designers also had to take into account not just the first-to-be-released, two-door sedan, but follow-on station-wagon and hatchback models. All three models would have to share a common frame and placement of certain systems like the gas tank and fuel filler pipe.

Ford weighed two main options for gas-tank placement: either above the rear axle, or else behind it. Siting the gas tank above the rear axle better protected the tank from a rear-end collision. But this location lay directly underneath the rear-passenger compartment. These passengers would face a greater risk of harm should the tank rupture and the gas ignite.

Above-the-axle placement also required a longer, oddly shaped fuel filler pipe. A longer pipe with multiple bends held more fuel and was more prone to damage and leaks. Finally, there was the issue of handling. When full, the gas tank would weigh just under seventy pounds. The Pinto's curb weight was only 2,000 pounds. Placing the fuel tank above the axle raised the car's center of gravity, which in turn degraded handling and overall safety.

There were, of course, several practical considerations also arguing against above-the-axle placement. It reduced storage space, complicated servicing, and failed to accommodate station-wagon or hatchback models.

The second main option, placing the fuel tank behind the rear axle, reduced filler pipe risks and solved the practical problems described previously. Such placement increased fire risks in the event of a rear-end collision but was farther from the passenger compartment. Such placement also matched that of nearly every American-made car at the time.

How Safe Is "Safe Enough"?

Ford's design and safety deliberations did not take place in a vacuum. A number of federal bodies claimed at-times-overlapping authority to regulate automobile design, operation, and marketing.

The federal National Traffic and Vehicle Safety Act of 1966 established the National Highway Traffic Safety Administration (NHTSA). Located within the Department of Transportation, the NHTSA has primary authority to regulate vehicle design and safety. In addition, the Environmental Protection Agency (EPA) regulates automobile emissions. Established in late 1970, the EPA reports directly to the President. The Federal Trade Commission (FTC) focuses on consumer protection, with particular emphasis on adequate disclosure and truthful advertising. Established in 1914, the FTC received significant additional powers in 1975, just as the Pinto scandal was heating up.

In addition to recently established or strengthened regulators, the period in which the Pinto was designed and sold saw the rise to prominence of non-profit advocacy organizations. These organizations viewed themselves as watchdogs tasked with protecting consumers from unfair or unethical practices by businesses.

Chief among these organizations in the automobile industry was the Center for Auto Safety, founded by Ralph Nader. Like Iacocca, Nader was the U.S.-born child of immigrants. He graduated from Harvard Law School in 1958. He first came to prominence in 1965, with his book *Unsafe at Any Speed: The Designed-In Dangers of the American Automobile*. A best seller, Nader's book criticized the safety record of American automobile manufacturers and played a key role in the creation of the NHTSA a year later.[6]

Nader and automobile industry executives hated each other. In fact, General Motors so resented *Unsafe at Any Speed* that the car maker unjustifiably hired private detectives to dig up dirt on Nader. Nader sued

General Motors for invasion of privacy. The parties settled for $425,000; Nader used the money to found the Center for the Study of Responsive Law.[7]

In January 1969, while the Pinto was under development, the NHTSA preliminarily proposed its first fuel-leakage standard governing rear-end collisions. Under the standard, called Standard 301, a stationary vehicle struck by a 4,000-pound barrier moving at twenty miles per hour should leak fuel at a rate of less than one ounce per minute.

Ford crash-tested Pinto prototypes in light of Standard 301. Several failures resulted. The company adjusted the fuel-tank design and rolled these changes out with the first production run in summer 1970.

Unfortunately for Ford (and other automakers), the NHTSA moved the goalposts. Shortly after the Pinto starting rolling off the assembly line, the NHTSA announced that instead of a twenty-miles per hour (mph) *moving*-barrier standard, the regulator would propose a twenty-miles per hour *fixed*-barrier standard, with an eye to ultimate adoption of a thirty-miles per hour *fixed*-barrier standard.

In a moving-barrier test, the barrier hits a stationary car. The movement of the car after impact dissipates over half of the collision's force. In a fixed-barrier test, on the other hand, the car is pushed or towed at speed into an immovable barrier. Since the barrier does not move, the entire force of the collision concentrates on the point of impact. By analogy, imagine the difference between a quarterback being sacked by a linebacker moving at twenty miles per hour and a receiver moving at the same speed who runs into an unpadded goal post.

Many engineers believed that the twenty-miles per hour moving barrier better simulated real-world crashes. Rear-end collisions almost always involve a car being struck from behind by another car. Drivers almost never back into a wall at speed. In addition, in the days before smart-phone-distracted drivers, 85 percent of rear-end collisions took place at speeds at or under twenty miles per hour.

Not surprisingly, the automakers fought adoption of fixed-barrier standards. At the same time, they anticipated eventual adoption of a *thirty-miles per hour moving*-barrier standard. To this end, in early 1971, a junior Ford engineer considered various ways to improve fuel-tank safety. His ideas included (1) placing the tank over the axle; (2) repositioning the spare tire; (3) installing body rails; (4) redesigning the filler pipe; and (5) installing a rubber bladder inside the tank itself.

Ford rejected all of the previous options for the Pinto as they involved design changes too late in the process. The bladder substantially improved tank crash-worthiness in ideal conditions. But, in cold weather, the bladder made the tank difficult to fill. In tests simulating very hot weather, the bladder simply failed.

Unrelated to the gas-tank issue, in February 1973, the EPA fined Ford $7 million for falsifying emissions data on its 1973 model–year cars.[8]

In August 1973, the NHTSA proposed the thirty-miles per hour moving-barrier standard, to apply effective September 1976 for 1977-and-later model years. Regulators wanted to test compliance with car-to-car crash-testing, which mimicked real-world accidents. Auto-industry engineers argued for *moving*-barriers tests. These engineers stated that barrier tests were more consistent and therefore yielded more reliable data.

At the same time, the NHTSA announced a proposed fuel-leakage standard with regard to rollovers. Ford's $11 fix and Cost/Benefit analysis estimating personal injuries took place with regard to this standard, rather than the one governing fuel leakage from rear-end collisions.

Ironically, Ford's Cost/Benefit analysis applied the U.S. government's own figures. The government uses these figures, for example, when deciding whether to place a guard rail on the side of a road, or a concrete barrier in the median between lanes of oppositely moving traffic.

The Scandal Unfolds
The opening shot in the Pinto scandal was fired in late 1973 at a Department of Transportation conference by an independent consultant who claimed that the Pinto fuel-system design was "very vulnerable . . . to even minor damage."[9]

A few months later, Nader's Center for Auto Safety picked up the issue and asked the NHTSA to investigate the Pinto, as well as the Chevrolet Vega, for defects. The NHTSA reviewed the Center's request, along with the Center's supporting information. The NHTSA concluded there was no demonstrable safety issue.

In early 1975, an Insurance Institute for Highway Safety study found that Pintos were disproportionately involved in accidents involving fuel-tank ruptures. But the study stated that it could not draw definitive conclusions about causal relationships or meaningfully distinguish among car models with regard to fuel-tank ruptures.

The mortal blow to the Pinto's reputation came with the publication of "Pinto Madness," in the September/October 1977 issue of *Mother Jones*, a recently founded investigative magazine devoted (in its own words) to "a new brand of socially conscious journalism [that takes] on corporate as well as political power."[10] Citing what it claimed were secret Ford internal documents, the *Mother Jones* article painted a picture of Ford deliberately foisting a defective and dangerous car onto consumers, while fighting to delay adoption of a governmental safety standard which would expose the defect and force change.

In September 1977, Ford attempted to publicly refute the *Mother Jones* article. That same month, the NHTSA opened an investigation into the Pinto's fuel-tank system. Since Ford had modified the system with the 1977 model year, the investigation focused on 1971–1976 model–year Pintos.

A few months later, the Center for Auto Safety started a recall campaign. At the same time, a California jury hit Ford with $125 million in punitive damages for a burn-related death and injuries involving a 1972 Pinto. (Damages were later reduced to $3.5 million.) In addition, the NHTSA conducted eleven car-to-car crash tests involving 1971–1976 Pintos at *thirty to thirty-five miles per hour*. The results included two fires and one other case of significant leakage.

As class-action lawsuits against Ford began sprouting, the NHTSA announced that the 1976 Pinto had failed a thirty-miles per hour *front-end* barrier test. Ford recalled 300,000 Pintos.

In May 1978, the NHTSA made an "initial determination" of a safety defect for Pinto models 1971–1976. In June 1978, Ford recalled all cars without admitting any defects. As part of the recall, Ford replaced the filler pipe and installed a polyethylene shield in front of the gas tank. Ford estimated that such upgrades would cost it a total of $20 million.

In light of Ford's recall and upgrades, the NHTSA closed its defect investigation without a final determination.

In July 1978, Board Chairman Henry Ford II fired Iacocca, despite the fact that Ford's annual earnings were in the range of $2 billion.

FOUR VERSIONS OF WHAT HAPPENED

At the time and in even hindsight, views diverge widely on what happened and why.

Here are four versions. Readers should feel free to take their pick.

Ford Was Evil

This was *Mother Jones*'s version. It's also the version that most likely comes to mind when people hear the phrase "Ford Pinto."

In this version, Ford deliberately or recklessly brought to market a defective and dangerous vehicle. The "limits of 2000" overrode proper engineering controls and sacrificed American lives to a catchy marketing slogan. The senior engineers, in particular, chickened out. As professionals, they had a duty to reject the limits of 2000 or resign, rather than sign off on an unsafe car.

Design engineers knew the fuel-tank risks. They either hid the bad news from senior management, or allowed senior managers to press on anyway.

Senior executives rushed the car to market because their greed overrode their concern for passenger safety. In fact, Ford bean counters had callously run the numbers and decided that the benefits of a defective car outweighed the damages from lawsuits should Ford get caught. Then, Ford spent money fighting government standards that could have gone toward upgrading Pintos on the road.

Uncorrected defects and financial misbehavior sprang from a corrupt and slipshod culture. Witness Ford's falsifying of emissions-test results, as well as the recall of 300,000 1976 Pintos for a front-end fuel-system defect.

Ford Was Negligent

In this version, Ford did wrong, but through lack of due care rather than deliberate choice or recklessness.

To start with, Ford engineers made design trade-offs that no reasonably well-trained, experienced, and careful engineers would have made. Iacocca, as an engineer with over twenty years in the car business, should have known better than to impose such rigid weight and cost limits on the car; a reasonable senior executive would have understood that something had to give. A major tip-off that something was wrong was falsification of emissions-test results. The recall of 1976 Pintos for front-end fuel-systems defects further evidenced sloppy design and quality assurance.

In addition, Ford's cost-benefit calculation was faulty. Ford may have been right to weigh costs and benefits. And any such analysis must place some dollar value on human lives and injuries. As finance professionals, the number crunchers should have realized that the government figures for death and injury failed to place any dollar cost on pain and suffering. A well-trained and careful financial analyst would have realized this omission and adjusted for it. The adjustment would have justified design changes, even if they meant delayed rollout, or breaking the "limits of 2000."

Ford Was Dutiful and Competent, but Mistaken or Unlucky

This version holds that Ford reasonably tried to do the right thing, but simply made decisions that did not turn out well. In this regard, Iacocca's "limits of 2000" was a stretch target reasonably designed to get the best work out of engineering teams. Also, the finance people used the right numbers, but could not reasonably foresee how changing judicial and social standards and sentiments would inflate jury awards in product-liability cases.

Ford Was a Victim

Under this scenario, Ford built a popular car that met then-applicable safety standards. Yes, the "limits of 2000" imposed trade-offs, but all engineering projects involve trade-offs. There was no point in building a car that people did not want or could not afford. The Pinto's safety record compares with other subcompacts; this fact vindicates Iacocca's approach.

Similarly, the financial analysts used accepted Cost/Benefit methods. These applied the same values for loss of life and injuries as the government used in its own calculations.

What happened was that three determined and unscrupulous groups hoodwinked the public and blindsided Ford. The first comprised self-appointed, supposedly non-profit watchdogs like the Center for Auto Safety, as well as anti-business media like *Mother Jones*. These organizations had a vested interest in finding and/or exaggerating problems or wrongdoing by Ford. Without such problems or wrongdoing, these organizations could not attract the funding—or sell the subscriptions or advertising—to keep their staffers employed.

The second group comprised eager and opportunistic regulators. The NHTSA and EPA lacked experience and perspective. They also had the same self-interest as the watchdogs and media in finding and/or exaggerating problems or wrongdoing. Without such problems or wrongdoing, the bureaucrats could justify neither their existence, their funding, nor their ongoing expansion.

When the watchdogs and *Mother Jones* stirred up public hysteria against Ford, the NHTSA refused to take the heat by sticking to its 1974 conclusion exonerating the Pinto design. Rather than follow the law and its own procedures, the NHTSA either caved in to the rabble-rousers, or else saw an opportunity to "cash in" on the hysteria themselves. Smashing cars into each other at thirty to thirty-five miles per hour was dishonest. It showed that the NHTSA intended to carry out more-and-more extreme crash tests until it got the outcome it wanted.

The third group came with the inauguration of Jimmy Carter in January 1977. Carter, a liberal Democrat, staffed the NHTSA, EPA, and FTC at the political-appointee level with anti-business Nader supporters. As a result, Ford faced a stacked deck. In 1974, the NHTSA found no demonstrable evidence of defects in the fuel system. In 1977–1978, the anti-auto-industry activists now in charge of the NHTSA used car-on-car crash tests outside of normal speed parameters to gin up bogus failures.

The NHTSA used the crash-test results to make a preliminary finding of defect. This finding strong-armed Ford into a recall and led to the firing of its President. Nader and the NHTSA got their scalps. Ford lost a visionary leader. That leader would go on to make billions of dollars for Chrysler, one of Ford's prime competitors.

LESSONS LEARNED: THE MARKET FOR REPUTATION

Whichever version readers prefer, certain common lessons from the Pinto scandal apply.

It's Not What You Intended or Did; It's What You Can Prove You Intended or Did

Getting to the right answer isn't enough. In cases like the Pinto, the "right" answer can only be seen in hindsight.

Consequently, businesses should design decision-making processes so that they—and the decisions they produce—are defensible to the outside world. At a minimum, this means enough formal process definition and documentation that the business can demonstrate what the issue was, what the decision was, how it was arrived at, what supported it, and who made it.

A particular lesson from Ford is the need to appoint a Devil's Advocate. The Devil's Advocate should be tasked with challenging the thinking of the decision-making team. He or she should question basic assumptions, processes, and sources and uses of data. The Devil's Advocate should provoke debate and force the team to test the strength of various arguments and courses of action. For example, a Devil's Advocate should have questioned Ford's use of governmental valuations placed on lives lost and injuries sustained. Such questioning should have surfaced the failure to account for the cost of pain and suffering.

For complex or high-value decisions, a business should consider bringing in a knowledgeable reputational adversary under a confidentiality agreement to act as Devil's Advocate. Bringing in someone who is not only independent but adverse will force decision makers to deal with weak points, objections, and counterarguments early on. It will force decision makers to confront how they and their actions might be viewed (or distorted) by third parties. Finally, the adversary's involvement should also help immunize the process and decision from criticism made in hindsight.

Small Ethical and Operational Lapses Create Potential for Large Reputational Damage

Some versions of the Pinto story portray Ford as well intentioned and/or correct in its actions with regard to the fuel-tank system.

There was no defense, however, for falsifying emissions tests. Nor did Ford dispute a design defect in the front end of the fuel system of 1976 model–year Pintos. This recall, as noted previously, made headline news and involved at least 300,000 owners. These real stories fed the Ford was Evil narrative pushed by the Center for Auto Safety and *Mother Jones*.

Mixing truth with exaggeration or lies makes for a potent cocktail. The public at large was ready to swallow the Ford was Evil narrative because it matched the emissions-fraud and front-end-system-recall stories members of the public had already consumed.

This chapter does not argue that Ford was evil. Or that Ford was a victim. The chapter does not maintain that either the Center for Auto Safety or *Mother Jones* lied or exaggerated. The point is that, whatever version readers prefer, businesses simply cannot afford to underestimate the potential for harm created by even small ethical lapses or mistakes in execution.

Be Ready for Reputational Adversaries

The Pinto scandal found Ford unready to deal with its reputational adversaries at the Center for Auto Safety and *Mother Jones*, among others.

Reputational adversaries can come from the Left, Right, or center of the political spectrum. They make their living by making you and your business look bad. These days, such adversaries also include hordes of bloggers and part-time activists for whom trashing your reputation is a hobby or passion. For these adversaries, reputation is a zero-sum game. A business's loss is their gain, and vice versa.

Reputational adversaries may have completely noble or completely selfish motives, or some mixture of the two. But no codes of business or professional ethics guide or constrain their actions. Many of these adversaries will fight dirty. A business must be ready for them.

Here, for example, is what Walmart, the world's largest retailer, did.[11]

Long a piñata for the blows of its reputational adversaries, Walmart developed and executed a game plan to counter the hits it had been taking.[12] The plan included:

1. *Staffing up.* Walmart hired a Senior Director for Stakeholder Engagement. It also built and staffed a war room that monitored conventional and social media for reputational threats and attacks. War-room personnel included a bi-partisan team of media consultants.
2. *Outreach to critics and influencers.* Walmart set up eight community relations centers. It funded an Investor-Responsibility Research Center and became active in environmental and anti-sweatshop efforts. It took part in Business for Social Responsibility activities and reached out to coalitions in Congress such as the Congressional Black Caucus.
3. *Preemptive communications.* Walmart undertook a campaign in one hundred newspapers outlining its positions on wages, benefits, and employment. The company sponsored public-broadcasting outlets and funded journalism fellowships. It also funded a third-party study on its positive effect on employment and cost of living.

4. *Support for worthy causes.* Walmart contributed to environmental organizations and made commitments relating to sustainability and offsetting its carbon and asphalt footprints.
5. *Workplace justice and support.* Walmart publicized its improved health benefits and diversity programs. It also created a grass-roots organization comprising employees and their families and took some public steps to mitigate its impact on Mom & Pop competitors.

The purpose of these steps was to build Walmart's reputational capital and alliances. The company wanted good buzz in the public domain. Good buzz would make people less likely to believe bad buzz, or at least encourage them to put bad buzz in perspective: "OK, maybe they made a mistake, but they're trying to do the right thing, and they definitely do a lot of good things."

With regard to alliances, Walmart built bridges with some of its reputational adversaries. More importantly, it picked off and/or co-opted groups that might otherwise have allied with these adversaries. Labor unions, for example, might never be won over. But, environmental groups which worked with and received donations from the company might be less inclined to publicly side against the company.

This game plan was comprehensive. It worked. But was it ethical?

The answer from a Cost/Benefit perspective is "yes." Cost/Benefit analysis looks only at results, not motives. Even if Walmart acted from completely selfish and cynical motives, the good it did for worthy causes or workplace justice, for example, would still be good.

From a Golden Rule perspective, which looks solely at motives, the plan may have been unethical. A cynic might say it was designed not only to serve selfish interests but to disguise these interests behind a mask of benevolence. Any effort to deceive violates the Golden Rule. The cynic would argue that Walmart simply followed Machiavelli's maxim that one should not practice virtue, but should definitely appear to.

So much for the cynic. It remains possible that Walmart executives sincerely wished to do good, as well as to counter what they perceived to be unfair or inaccurate buzz about the company. Such motives would satisfy the Golden Rule.

In any event, this chapter does not ask readers to judge Walmart's motives but to note well how one of the world's largest and most operationally tight organizations rose to the challenge of its reputational adversaries. Here, Walmart's game plan may in fact have reflected the Virtue Ethics expressed by retired U.S. Marine Corps General James N. Mattis: "Be polite, be professional, but have a plan to kill everybody you meet."

The market for reputation is real. It is vicious. And businesses wishing to safeguard their reputations and their prospects had better come up with and execute a plan. Mattis's view may be dark but should not be dismissed out of hand.

Had Ford, in 1971, put in place a plan like Walmart's, would we be talking about the Pinto now?

NOTES

1. Ben Wojdyla, "The Top Automotive Engineering Failures: The Ford Pinto Fuel Tanks," *Popular Mechanics*, May 20, 2011, accessed, December 7, 2016, http://www.popularmechanics.com/cars/a6700/top-automotive-engineering-failures-ford-pinto-fuel-tanks/.

2. Variously attributed, including Winston Churchill.

3. Encyclopedia of American Cars, by the Auto Editors of Consumer Guide®, cited in How Stuff Works, accessed December 6, 2016, http://auto.howstuffworks.com/1971-1980-ford-pinto14.htm.

4. This chapter relies extensively on David L. Davidson, "Managing Product Safety: The Ford Pinto," *Harvard Business School*, Case No. 9–383–129, May 1, 1984.

5. Lee Patrick Strobel, *Reckless Homicide?* (South Bend, Indiana: And Books, 1980), 82.

6. Mark Green, "How Ralph Nader Changed America," *The Nation*, December 1, 2015, accessed December 7, 2016, https://www.thenation.com/article/how-ralph-nader-changed-america/.

7. Staff, "GM Settles Out of Court; To Award Nader $425,000'," *The Harvard Crimson*, August 14, 1970, accessed December 7, 2016, http://www.thecrimson.com/article/1970/8/14/gm-settles-out-of-court-to/.

8. Louis Heldman, "U.S. Fines Ford $7 Million for Emission Test Violations," *The Chicago Tribune*, February 14, 1973, Section 1, 2.

9. Strobel, *Reckless Homicide?* 145.

10. Mark Dowie, "Pinto Madness," *Mother Jones*, September/October 1977, accessed September 23, 2019, https://www.motherjones.com/politics/1977/09/pinto-madness/. For a description of the magazine's founding and mission, *see* https://www.motherjones.com/about/history/.

11. Walmart's $482 billion in annual sales would make it the world's twenty-fourth wealthiest country by gross domestic product, just behind Sweden and ahead of Belgium. Sources: Yahoo Finance, "Walmart Inc. (WMT)," accessed

December 12, 2016, https://finance.yahoo.com/quote/WMT, and IMF, "List of Countries by Projected GDP," The International Monetary Fund, accessed December 12, 2016, http://statisticstimes.com/economy/countries-by-projected-gdp.php.

12. David Baron, "Case: Wal-Mart: Nonmarket Pressure and Reputation Risk (B)," *Stanford Business School*, P52B-PDF-ENG (2006).

7

"You Deal, You Die": The Godfather and Warren Buffett on Reputation

■ ■ ■

"It's true that I have a lot of friends in politics, but they wouldn't be friendly very long if they knew my business was drugs instead of gambling."

—Don Corleone, in *The Godfather*

In business, reputation matters. A lot. This chapter and the one that follows will look closely at why, and what this means for business ethics.

As the reader may recall, chapter 5 considered whether a business entity *can* be ethical. The answer is "yes," but only where the entity is owned by a tightly knit group of like-minded people. Such entities make up a small fraction of the economy. For more broadly held business entities, on the other hand, which control the lion's share of commerce, the answer is "no." Here, the *Hobby Lobby* case tells us that such business entities lack the psychic components necessary for moral/ethical deliberation and choice.

In such event, the issue becomes not whether the entity acts ethically, but whether the individuals who direct and manage the entity do. Corporate law and Golden Rule/Cost-Benefit analysis tell us that these individuals must pursue the entity's good, not their own.

This said, disagreement exists over just what entity end goals the directors and managers should work toward. Chapter 5 describes the principal end goal alternatives: Dualism, Monism, Modest Idealism, High Idealism, and Pragmatism.

Chapter 6 picked up this discussion by looking at the case of the Ford Pinto. The chapter introduced the concepts of a market for reputation and reputational adversaries. The chapter noted that, whatever end goals directors and managers choose, there will be other players with vested interests in making these directors and managers—and the business entity they serve—look bad. These other players might be commercial competitors. They might be people in non-profits, media, or government who benefit financially or psychologically from harming the entity's reputation.

In the real world, therefore, businesses must tend and defend their reputations. Concern for reputation may in fact free us from having to definitively choose sides in the Dualism–Idealism debate. Dualistic managers cannot chase profits heedless of reputational blowback. At the same time, idealistic directors and managers must take into account how their support for the greater good opens them up to criticism for self-dealing, waste, or mismanagement.

So, reputation indeed matters. This chapter and the one that follows will argue that the value and vulnerability of reputation make it a unique driver of business ethics.

THE REAL GODFATHER'S EDICT ON DRUGS: "YOU DEAL, YOU DIE"

The four gunmen closed in on their target.

It was Christmastime, 1985, in Manhattan. The sun had set early, but lights and decorations brightened the Midtown East neighborhood. At the intersection of Third Avenue and 46th Street, the sidewalks were crowded for a Monday evening. The wet pavement glistened. From a nearby black Lincoln sedan with tinted windows, the crew boss had just given the shooters the "go" order via walkie-talkie.

As Gambino Family boss Paul Castellano emerged from his own car just outside of Sparks Steak House, two of the gunmen shot him down. Castellano's driver, Thomas Bilotti, tried bolting from the car. The other two gunmen put six bullets into his head and chest.

The crew boss in the Lincoln was John Gotti, himself a member of the Gambino Family. He put his car in gear and rolled slowly past the bodies. His No. 2, Sammy "the Bull" Gravano, looked out the window and confirmed the kills. Gotti swung a right onto Second Avenue, then headed back to Sammy's office in Brooklyn.

So ended a Gambino dispute over business reputation.[1]

Carlo Gambino (1902–1976), the "Real" Godfather

The Gotti-Castellano feud had its roots in an edict of Carlo Gambino, perhaps the most powerful organized crime figure in U.S. history. Gambino served as the inspiration for the Godfather character depicted in Mario Puzo's novel and Francis Ford Coppola's film.

Gambino was born in Palermo, Sicily. He immigrated to the United States in 1921. Still only a teenager, he was already a "made," or fully fledged, member of the Mafia.

His timing was lucky. The 1920s saw a consolidation and modernization of Italian organized crime, funded by Prohibition's huge criminal windfall. At the top of the Mafia sat a Commission comprising the heads of the five leading Italian organized-crime families. The Commission dictated policy. It also settled disputes. This included authorizing the murder of mobsters for reasons of policy or expediency.

Gambino emerged from this first phase of his career in 1931 as a captain (*capo*) within the crime family headed by Vincent Mangano. In 1951, Mangano "disappeared," and underboss Albert Anastasia, suspected of murdering Mangano, took over. Gambino became underboss, turning his crew over to his cousin and brother-in-law, Paul Castellano.

In 1957, Gambino seized the top spot. He sided with a rival family against Anastasia, who was shortly afterward gunned down while sitting in a barber's chair. Gambino succeeded his former boss and re-named the family after himself.

At its high point, the Gambino Family was reputed to have up to 800 "made" men spread across thirty crews.[2] Its annual take has been estimated at $500,000,000.[3]

As baseball fans know, many major league players have a great year or two. What makes a Hall of Famer is sustained output. Carlo Gambino headed the Gambino Family for nearly twenty years, until his death from a heart attack at age seventy-four. He died peacefully, in his bed, and, according to Church authorities, in a state of grace.

The Business-Ethics Case for "You Deal, You Die"

As boss, Gambino laid down a simple rule for underlings tempted to enter the drug trade: "You deal, you die." This rule rested on cast-iron economic and business logic.

As noted previously, Gambino stood at the top of an immensely profitable pyramid. "Business as usual" had made him rich and powerful. Fame he neither wanted nor needed.

Gambino saw that reputational risk from dealing drugs far exceeded that from other criminal activities. The post-Prohibition Mafia made the bulk of its money from gambling and prostitution, as well as from infiltration of organized labor and unionized industries like trucking, dock-working, waste hauling, construction, and entertainment. Much of this crime was non-violent. Even the bulk of violent crime connected with it, such as battery, robbery, or extortion, carried relatively light penalties for first or second offenses. Drug dealing, on the other hand, was viewed across society as a dirty and destructive business. It threatened to shred the Mob's political cover. Politicians under pressure from voters might (as they eventually did) authorize greater involvement by federal law-enforcement bodies in fighting trafficking, as well as provide for decades- or even lifelong sentences for wholesale-level drug offenses.[4] Such sentences would give prosecutors the leverage to squeeze convicted mobsters into ratting on Family leadership.

In light of this risk, Gambino decreed, "You deal, you die." This rule encouraged mobsters, rather than dealing directly, to extort non-Mafia drug dealers for a percentage, as was done with gamblers and pimps. "Taxing" dealers in this manner kept the gangster within bounds while only risking extortion's lesser penalties. And, after all, to whom would the dealers complain?

Gambino's approach addressed a problem common in business ethics. Very often, the executives at the top of an organization become risk-averse. These executives have made it and don't want to upset the apple cart. At the same time, lower-level employees have yet to make their fortunes or careers. Such employees must take risks to stand out and to get ahead.

Differing appetites for risk between senior and junior employees can lead to ethical problems. An ambitious lower-level employee will be tempted to risk the firm's assets—including reputation—with gains from the gamble largely going to the lower-level employee. Such gains can take the form of a bonus, raise, promotion, or cut of drug-deal profits.

As discussed in chapter 4, keeping the benefits from an activity while pushing the costs onto others creates an externality. In the context of an organization, an employee who, without permission, takes a benefit for himself at the expense of the organization imposes an "agency cost" on the organization.[5] Even within the context of the Mob, such an agency cost is unethical, from both a Cost/Benefit and Golden Rule standpoint. In Hollywood Mob-speak, the employee has "skimmed" from the organization, wrongly taking for himself some of the cream of proceeds from Mob activities.

Hence, Gambino's edict. It did not eliminate drug dealing completely, but it imposed the maximum amount of risk possible on the lower-level employee—loss of his own life.

This arrangement worked for nearly twenty years. Three factors forced a change. The first was a ratcheting effort by the federal government to go after organized crime, particularly the Commission. Aided by increased resources and the Racketeer-Influence Corrupt Organization (RICO) statute, in 1985, U.S. Attorney Rudi Giuliani indicted all five members of the Mafia's ruling Commission. Mafia leaders found themselves under unprecedented pressure and scrutiny.

Among these five Commission members was Paul Castellano, who had succeeded Carlo Gambino as Gambino Family boss upon the latter's death. Castellano's weakened position represented the second factor. In addition to the RICO prosecution, Castellano's authority was undermined by claims of nepotism. Many Gambino members felt that Castellano had not earned the top spot, but had simply ridden his late brother-in-law's coat-tails. Mobsters did not fear Paul Castellano as they had Carlo Gambino. For tough, street gangsters like Gotti and his Bergin Hunt and Fish Club crew, Castellano's weakness not only encouraged them to flout the rules but to strike at the boss.

The third factor was the increasing attractiveness of white-collar crimes like fraud and corruption. These were the go-go 1980s of junk bonds and

Wall Street's Gordon Gekko. Money was pouring into New York con-struction and other Mafia-infiltrated trades. At the same time, the U.S. federal government had ramped up both drug-enforcement efforts and penalties. Castellano generally preferred profitable-but-lower-risk scams like bid-rigging, price-fixing, and union corruption to Gotti's blue-collar hijacking, strong-arming, and dope dealing. Now a CEO under indict-ment, Castellano needed to lower his organization's risk profile, to get a better risk-adjusted return. This meant that those who were dealing but as yet uncaught had to stop. Gotti & Crew, however, lacked the savvy for high-end, white-collar scams. Giving up drugs meant giving up their most lucrative line of business.

It was too late, anyway. A number of Gotti's men—including Gotti's own brother—had been arrested for large-scale trafficking. Discovery rules required prosecutors to turn over copies of the government's evidence to the defendants. This evidence included surveillance tape recordings of the crew planning drug deals. The tapes also recorded Gotti's men talking over how to keep Family leadership in the dark about their activities.

After Castellano made the defendants' lawyer play him the tapes, war became inevitable. Not only had Gotti's men gotten caught selling drugs, but the scale of Gotti's disloyalty, recklessness, and double-dealing came into view.

As Sammy Gravano later testified, he and Gotti knew that Castellano would order them killed.

So, as we saw at the beginning of this chapter, Gotti and Gravano struck first.

WARREN BUFFETT CUTS OFF HIS RIGHT-HAND MAN

Warren Buffett is the world's greatest investor.

He has served as Berkshire Hathaway's CEO since 1964. A $1,000 investment in his company at that time would now be worth about $20 million. By comparison, a $1,000 investment in the Standard & Poor's Index of the Top 500 U.S. Companies (S&P 500) would be worth $175,000.[6]

Berkshire Hathaway's current market capitalization (i.e., how much all of its shares are worth put together) tops $550 billion. This number makes

Berkshire the sixth largest company in the world by market capitalization. Buffett is currently the world's third richest man, with wealth exceeding $80 billion, having given away over $25 billion to charity.[7]

Like his teacher and mentor, Benjamin Graham, Buffett is a "value investor." This means he looks to buy stocks that are trading well below their intrinsic value.

In Berkshire Hathaway's first decades, Warren Buffett used to buy shares in public companies like Coca-Cola. Over the last ten to fifteen years, however, Berkshire Hathaway has grown so large that Buffett has shifted focus from investing in companies to buying them outright. Nothing else will allow him to deploy the amount of money he has available while achieving his desired level of growth.

Like Carlo Gambino, Warren Buffett is surprisingly low key. The billionaire lives in the same house in Omaha, Nebraska, he bought in 1958 for $31,500. He carries no cell phone. No computer sits on his desk. For over twenty-five years, he has drawn the same $100,000 annual salary from Berkshire. His passions appear limited to playing bridge, drinking Cherry Coke, and making his shareholders rich(er).

The David Sokol Affair—Berkshire Hathaway's Acquisition of Lubrizol

While Buffett may be personally frugal, he does not shy from paying his key subordinates well when they perform. For example, Gregory Abel, chairman and chief executive of Berkshire Hathaway Energy, received $41 million in compensation in 2015. This pay included $1 million in salary, an $11.5 million bonus, and $28 million under an incentive plan tied to the company's performance.[8]

Back in 2010–2011, one of Buffett's key lieutenants was David Sokol. Like, Buffett, Sokol is an Omaha native. He joined the Berkshire family in 2000, when Buffett acquired MidAmerican Energy Holdings Co., which Sokol led.

Once at Berkshire Hathaway, Sokol sourced deals. He was also known as Buffett's Mr. Fix-It, turning around underperforming Berkshire companies.[9] Sokol served as Chairman of the Board of several Berkshire-owned companies. He was also said to be a possible successor to Buffett as CEO of parent company Berkshire Hathaway.

This success notwithstanding, Sokol had a very fast—and very public—fall from grace. The events that ended his career with Berkshire and destroyed his relationship with Buffett took place as follows:[10]

- In the fall of 2010, Sokol met with investment bankers from Citigroup to review a list of eighteen potential target companies for Berkshire to acquire. In a December 13, 2010, follow-up meeting, Sokol told Citigroup that of the companies on the list, only Lubrizol attracted him. Lubrizol was a publicly traded manufacturer of specialty chemicals. Sokol instructed Citigroup to request a meeting for him with Lubrizol's CEO.
- The next day, December 15, 2010, Sokol bought 2,300 shares of Lubrizol at approximately $108 per share. This investment totaled about $250,000. For someone with Sokol's net worth and prospects, this was like dipping his toe in the water.
- On December 17, 2010, Citigroup told Lubrizol of Berkshire's potential interest in investing in, or acquiring, Lubrizol. Citigroup also informed Sokol that it had contacted Lubrizol's CEO, who would alert his Board of Directors.
- On December 21, 2010, Sokol sold his stake in Lubrizol for nominal profit. Then, on January 5–7, 2011, Sokol bought 96,060 shares as part of an order to his broker to buy up to 100,000 shares at no more than $104 per share. This stake cost Sokol just under $10,000,000.
- On January 6, 2011, Lubrizol's CEO met with his Board. He put the wheels in motion to discuss a potential sale of Lubrizol to Berkshire Hathaway. On January 14, 2011, Sokol and the CEO spoke by phone and agreed to meet face-to-face on January 25, 2011.
- On January 14 or 15, 2011, Sokol brought the Lubrizol opportunity to Buffett, who was cool on the deal. Buffett would later state that in this meeting, Sokol mentioned in "a passing remark" that he (Sokol) owned stock in Lubrizol, but that the date-of-purchase and amount of the holdings were not discussed.
- On January 25, 2011, Sokol and the Lubrizol CEO met. They discussed Lubrizol's current business and prospects. After Sokol's report of the meeting, Buffett began warming to the deal.
- On March 13, 2011, Berkshire's Board of Directors voted to approve purchase of Lubrizol.
- On March 14, 2011, the deal was announced: a $9 billion acquisition at $135 per share. With the news, Lubrizol's market price soared 28 percent. Sokol profits on paper were $3 million.
- On March 19, 2011, Buffett learned the specifics of Sokol's ownership of Lubrizol's shares.
- On March 28, Buffett received and accepted Sokol's letter of resignation.

Much of this timeline comes from a press release written in the form of an open letter from Buffett himself.[11] In that letter, Buffett threads a needle. He knows that his letter will be read by class-action lawyers eager to file suit against Berkshire. The challenge was to admit enough to explain Sokol's departure, but not so much as to trigger a lawsuit against Berkshire Hathaway for Sokol's actions.

What is most interesting about Buffett's letter is what it does not say. For example, Buffett does not explain how Sokol's ownership in Lubrizol came to his attention, only when. Buffett says that twice before Sokol had tried to resign to pursue other interests, but that he (Buffett) had talked Sokol out of leaving. The unspoken message is that Buffett made no such effort this time around.

Buffett's letter emphasizes that Sokol purchased his shares before knowing how Buffett would react to the deal, whether terms could be reached with Lubrizol, or whether the Berkshire's Board would sign off on the deal.

In fact, Sokol's activities might easily be construed as illegal insider trading. Sokol was an officer of Berkshire Hathaway. He bought shares in Lubrizol knowing that he would recommend the deal to Buffett. Had Sokol's secretary, knowing Sokol's schedule and correspondence, bought the shares in the same manner he did, she would likely have been prosecuted.

Hence, in threading a needle, Buffett did not claim that he fired Sokol for cause. But neither did he claim that Sokol did nothing wrong. Such a comment might be a material misstatement, which might itself open up Buffett and Berkshire to lawsuits. Instead, Buffett wrote that "neither Dave nor I feel his Lubrizol purchases were in any way unlawful."

While the letter was carefully worded, the bitterness between the two men would eventually burst forth in a less-controlled manner.[12] In the weeks after Sokol's departure, Buffett called Sokol's actions "inexcusable" and "inexplicable," as well as a violation of the company's code of ethics. Moreover, Buffett, likely in an effort to divert trouble away from himself and his company, turned over to the U.S. Securities and Exchange Commission (SEC) information on Sokol's trades that Buffett characterized as "very damning."

Sokol would endure a two-year investigation by the U.S. Securities and Exchange Commission. The SEC ultimately decided not to take action. Sokol at last felt free to vent against his former boss and mentor. Sokol wrote of the hurt done to his family by Buffett. The former Mr. Fix-It summed up his feelings by noting that as the eighty-three-year-old Buffett was "rapidly approaching his judgement [*sic*] day, I [Sokol] will leave his verdict to a higher power."[13]

"We Cannot Afford to Lose . . . Even a Shred of Reputation"

The philosophy driving Buffett's actions in the Sokol Affair appears in a memorandum Buffett sent to all his managers and Board Directors on July 26, 2010. In that memorandum, Buffett wrote:

> The priority is that all of us continue . . . to zealously guard Berkshire's reputation. We can afford to lose money—event a lot of money. But we can't afford to lose reputation—even a shred of reputation. . . . We *must* continue to measure every act against not only what is legal but also what we would be happy to have written about on the front page of a national newspaper in an article written by an unfriendly but intelligent reporter. . . .
>
> There's plenty of money to be made in the center of the court. If it's questionable whether some action is close to the line, just assume it is outside and forget it.[14]

In short, reputation is so valuable that neither the business nor its employees should take any steps that risk it.

In the Lubrizol acquisition, David Sokol played too close to the line. Berkshire's and Buffett's reputation took a hit. At that point, it did not matter what Sokol had done for Berkshire earlier, or what he had sacrificed as a loyal but erring lieutenant. He had to go. In the end, Sokol simply showed enough foresight to resign before Buffett fired him.

LESSONS LEARNED: REPUTATION, REPUTATION, REPUTATION

The philosophy behind Buffett's actions in the David Sokol Affair does not differ that much from Carlo Gambino's or Paul Castellano's.

CEOs need to preserve and grow the business's principal asset—its reputation. This asset must of course be defended from reputational adversaries. Such adversaries include the ones which assailed Ford in chapter 6, as well as the "unfriendly but intelligent reporter" mentioned previously in Buffett's memorandum.

The raw material from which these adversaries work, however, is typically some wrongdoing committed by employees of the business itself. An employee gambling with the business's reputation risks the chips of the employer while hoping to scoop up for himself a disproportionate share of the winnings. This behavior is unethical. Multiplied across an organization, it is also ruinous: numerous employees all gambling with the same set of reputational chips will eventually bankrupt the company.

In some cases, like Gotti & Crew, the wrongdoing is intentional. In other cases, like David Sokol, the wrongdoing may be rationalized: "It's not unlawful." "It's a negligible amount." "Everybody does it." In still other cases, the employee might even think he acts in the employer's best interests.

Buffett's memorandum offers some useful tests for employees to double-check the motives and wisdom of any course of action. First, would the employee be happy for the action to be publicized by a reputational adversary? Second, does the action lie in the center of the court, or close to a line? These are useful rules, and easier to implement than, "You deal, you die."

On a final note, this chapter has paired Carlo Gambino with Warren Buffett for more than shock value or amusement. Many people dismiss business ethics as a crunchy-toasty topic with no real-world application. The real world, these people say, is pure Machiavelli. It is dog-eat-dog. You have to recognize and accept that fact if you want to get ahead and stay there.

To that argument, this chapter answers that no world has been more dog-eat-dog than Carlo Gambino's. And no investor has ever done a better job of getting and staying ahead than Warren Buffett. When polar opposites like the world's greatest mobster and the world's greatest investor come to the same conclusion about ethics and reputation, people ignore that fact at their own peril.

Our next chapter will look at what happened when the world's premier accounting firm did just that.

NOTES

1. Arnold H. Lubasch, "Shot by Shot, an Ex-Aide to Gotti Describes the Killing of Castellano," *The New York Times*, March 4, 1992, accessed December 12, 2016, http://www.nytimes.com/1992/03/04/nyregion/shot-by-shot-an-ex-aide-to-gotti-describes-the-killing-of-castellano.html.

2. Jerry Capeci, "Frank Perdue Meets the Godfather," *New York Magazine*, July 5, 1983, 28–9.

3. Selwyn Raab, "John Gotti Running the Mob," *New York Times Magazine*, April 2, 1989, accessed December 13, 2016, http://www.nytimes.com/1989/04/02/magazine/john-gotti-running-the-mob.html.

4. Lisa N. Sacco, "Drug Enforcement in the United States: History, Policy, and Trends," *Congressional Research Service*, October 2, 2014, 4–10, accessed October 23, 2019, https://fas.org/sgp/crs/misc/R43749.pdf.

5. Agency costs include: (1) the monitoring expenditures of the organization spent to deter or catch skimming; (2) the bonding expenditures by the agent to show that he will not skim; and (3) the residual loss suffered by the organization from an agent who has skimmed. Michael C. Jensen and William H. Meckling, "Theory of the Firm: Managerial Behavior, Agency Costs and Ownership Structure," *Journal of Financial Economics* 3 (1976): 305–60, http://ssrn.com/abstract=94043. It should come as no surprise that there is a vast legal and economic literature on this topic.

6. Andrew Bary, "Berkshire after Buffett," *Barron's*, February 17, 2020, 19.

7. Tanza Loudenback, "24 Mind-Blowing Facts about Warren Buffett and His $84.7 Billion Fortune," *Business Insider*, April 30, 2018, accessed August 7, 2018, https://www.businessinsider.com/facts-about-warren-buffett-2016-12.

8. Stephen Gandel, "Warren Buffett Is Paying This Executive $41 million," *Fortune*, February 29, 2016, accessed December 13, 2016, http://fortune.com/2016/02/29/warren-buffett-berkshire-energy-greg-abel/.

9. Brian Dumaine, "Warren Buffett's Mr. Fix-It (Full Version)," *Fortune*, August 2, 2010, accessed December 13, 2016, http://archive.fortune.com/2010/07/29/news/companies/buffets_mr_fixit_full.fortune/index.htm.

10. Shira Ovide, "Warren Buffett Lieutenant Resigns amid Stock Purchases," *The Wall Street Journal*, March 30, 2011, accessed December 13, 2016, http://blogs.wsj.com/deals/2011/03/30/warren-buffett-lieutenant-resigns-amid-stock-purchases-read-the-letter/.

11. Berkshire Hathaway Press Release, "Warren E. Buffett, CEO of Berkshire Hathaway, Announces the Resignation of David L. Sokol," Berkshire Hathaway Inc., March 31, 2011, accessed December 13, 2016, http://www.berkshirehathaway.com/news/mar3011.pdf.

12. Serena Ng and Jean Eaglesham, "Ex-Protégé Criticizes Buffett over Exit," *The Wall Street Journal*, January 4, 2013, accessed December 13, 2016, http://www.wsj.com/articles/SB10001424127887323689604578222051534145538.

13. Ibid.

14. Warren Buffett, "Memorandum to Berkshire Hathaway Managers," July 26, 2010, accessed December 13, 2016, http://prosperosworld.com/warren-buffetts-memo-to-managers/2011/.

8

The Hazards of Lumpy Risk: How Arthur Andersen Met Its End

■ ■ ■

"We place absolute confidence in the Titanic. We believe the boat is unsinkable."

—White Star [Cruise] Line Vice President P. A. S. Franklin

Arthur Andersen & Co is the *Titanic* of business-ethics cases. The world's largest, wealthiest, and most prestigious accounting firm sank overnight in a sea of scandal, taking down more than 4,700 partners and 85,000 employees.

Of course, disasters on the scale of the *Titanic* rarely spring from a single cause. They typically happen from an accumulation of missteps and misdeeds. Yes, the *Titanic* hit an iceberg, but the great loss of life which made the sinking tragic arose, among other things, from a combination of flaws in ship design and construction, a shortage of lifeboats, lax operations, safety oversights, and misjudgments and miscommunications onboard and among sister ships.

So what sank Arthur Andersen?

Many people see the Enron scandal as the iceberg that sent Arthur Andersen to the bottom. Enron was one of Arthur Andersen's largest audit clients. Widespread fraud by Enron's leadership led to the company's

103

bankruptcy, as well as twenty-four criminal convictions of Enron executives, including the Chairman, the President & CEO, the CFO, and the Chief Accounting Officer.[1] These crimes inevitably implicated Arthur Andersen as the auditor.

Enron represented the largest commercial bankruptcy of its time.[2] But Enron no more fully explains Arthur Andersen's tragedy than the iceberg does the *Titanic's*. Coming to grips with Arthur Andersen—and drawing ethics lessons from it—requires us to explore the caliber and backgrounds of persons who ran the firm, the culture in which they worked, and the larger business context in which Arthur Andersen ultimately met its end.

A DOOMED GATHERING OF THE BEST AND BRIGHTEST

It was March 2002. The fifteen or so senior partners at the meeting took their places around a conference table in a five-star Madrid hotel. A few people had tried some initial gallows humor, but the jokes fell flat. The mood was grim.

The group was small but highly accomplished. Its members led the major European practices of Arthur Andersen & Co. As such, they enjoyed status. They commanded respect. Each of them made upward of $750,000 a year (or nearly $1.1 million in 2020 dollars).

The people around the table knew each other well. They respected and trusted each other. As partners, they were not just senior managers of Arthur Andersen, but its owners, too.

Earning a place at that table came only the hard way. Each person there had spent fifteen years or more working his or her way up through the firm. This meant putting in sixty- to seventy-hour weeks in the "off season," while ratcheting up to eighty, ninety, or more hours per week during peak audit-and-tax season, as well as for major deals.

Beyond working the hours, the men and women at the table had each managed territories, offices, or practice groups comprising hundreds if not thousands of employees. These partners had built and overseen relationships with the Boards and top managers of the world's largest and wealthiest companies. They handled the world's most sophisticated and challenging accounting issues and deals. Mistakes might cost the client billions of dollars, with Arthur Andersen potentially on the hook for the entire amount.

A few months before the meeting, these partners could have looked forward to retiring in their mid-fifties as multimillionaires. But the discovery of massive fraud at a North American audit client had put Arthur Andersen on life support. The partners now found themselves at risk of losing everything they had worked for.

The partners around the table met not so much to save Arthur Andersen as to harvest its organs. Hopefully, the financial damage from the scandal might be limited to Andersen's North American activities, where the fraud had occurred. If so, partners in other geographies might salvage Andersen's extensive and extremely valuable global operations outside of North America.

That was the plan. In the middle of the meeting, though, word came that the firm had been indicted in U.S. federal court for obstruction of justice. A felony charge.

Nobody spoke. The partners knew the indictment itself was a death sentence. No accounting firm under felony indictment could audit a publicly traded client. No client of consequence could work with them. Beating the rap at trial or on appeal would take years and come too late.

Neither salvation nor harvest was possible. Nothing remained to say or do. In silence, the partners packed up their computers and papers, grabbed their roller bags, and left.

For all practical purposes, a firm with nearly 90,000 professionals, and $9.3 billion in annual revenues, had ceased to function.[3]

How could this have happened?

THE RISE AND FALL OF THE WORLD'S PREMIER ACCOUNTING FIRM

In 1913, Arthur E. Andersen and a partner acquired The Audit Company of Illinois in Chicago for $4,000. The two partners split in 1918, leaving Arthur Andersen at the head of his own shop.

Arthur had always stood out. At the age of twenty-three, he became the youngest certified public accountant in Illinois. At twenty-seven, he simultaneously ran his firm, taught accounting at Northwestern University, and served as Controller of Schlitz Brewing Company.[4]

Arthur intended that his firm also stand out. It was to be a cut above, intellectually and ethically. "Think straight and talk straight" was its motto from the beginning. Firm lore has it that Arthur once told a major client that there was "not enough money in the city of Chicago" to persuade Andersen to change an accounting determination in line with the client's wishes but against Arthur's professional judgment.[5] Another time, an Andersen audit had failed to spot a $190,000 cash shortfall in a client's accounts. When Arthur found out, he traveled immediately to the client's headquarters in Ohio. Arthur personally apologized to the president of the client and, to make amends, wrote the client a check for $190,000.[6]

These stories jibed with the "four cornerstones" of Andersen's business, taught to every incoming recruit: (1) provide good service to the client; (2) produce quality audits; (3) manage staff well; and (4) produce profits for the firm.[7]

One Firm, One Voice

What drove Arthur was his vision of accounting as a true profession.

His obsession fueled a despotic management style. As his firm grew, he continued to hold half the partnership units and to take half the profits. He drove out anyone who threatened his supremacy or crossed his will. This included his own brother, whom Arthur fired in 1916 and refused to speak to for the rest of his life.

Arthur's single-mindedness had a purpose. He wanted to transform accountants from lowly ledger keepers to valued financial and business advisors. He developed college-level accounting courses and then hired the best and the brightest graduates. Arthur established uniform, centralized in-house training. Far in advance of his competitors, he developed industry-specific expertise and reference libraries. He started and led professional associations.

The firm grew immensely under Arthur's leadership, but the winds were also at his back. The 1913 introduction of federal income tax mandated accurate accounting and reporting. While the Great Depression bit into mergers & acquisitions work, New Deal securities laws meant boom times for accountants. These laws required publicly traded companies to publish audited financial statements.

Arthur died in 1947, with the firm ready to take his vision global. U.S. companies after World War II expanded rapidly overseas. Arthur's firm expanded, too. An elite, highly trained, and culturally tight partnership, Andersen found itself uniquely positioned to capture global opportunities serving multinational corporations. Of the fifty-one new locations Andersen opened in the 1960s, thirty-one were outside the United States.

Harvest of Success, Seeds of Destruction

By 1988, Andersen had 19,000 personnel, including 2,000 partners, over 600 of whom came from outside the United States.

True to Arthur's vision, accounting had become a highly respected profession, with his firm at its forefront. A number of Andersen's competitors merged to compete with Andersen's scale and global coverage. Alone among the "Big 6" firms, however, Andersen remained a unified global partnership. It had grown organically, with strong emphasis on recruiting, training, culture building, and promotion of "the Andersen way."

Several factors made the 1990s both the best of times and the worst of times. Economies across the developed world boomed. With the collapse of the Soviet Union and China's economic liberalization, vast new markets opened up for global corporations. Andersen and its competitors rushed to supply enormous demand for high-quality accounting and financial services in whole new industries (dot com) and whole regions of the earth.

The firm grew more than fourfold. By 2001, Andersen had nearly 90,000 personnel, including 4,700 partners spread across approximately 382 offices in 81 countries.[8,9] Such growth strained firm culture, as Andersen hired tens of thousands of new employees and promoted thousands of new partners. The firm committed vast resources—nearly 6 percent of annual revenues—to training and culture building. But taking in and advancing so many people broke down cohesion. This was particularly true in emerging markets, where societal, governmental, and business ethics varied widely from values in the United States.

The 1990s also saw a step change in information technology. Andersen had led and guided clients through the introduction of main-frame computers starting in the 1950s. With the launch of personal computers and the Internet, IT cut across all areas of clients' activities, as well as commerce with other firms. For clients, adopting and mastering new information technologies became a matter of survival. As a result, Andersen's IT-consulting arm rivaled audit and advisory services in importance and profitability.

There was also a shift in the United States toward rules-based accounting. Professions must balance rules and standards. Rules tend to be bright-line, objective tests. An example would be: "If a company owns 20 percent or more of a subsidiary, the company must reflect on its financial statements the activities of the subsidiary." A standard, on the other hand, involves subjective or qualitative determinations. For example, auditors' opinions typically include language that "the financial statements . . . present *fairly*, in all *material* respects, the financial position of X Company." Words like "fairly" and "material" require subjective determinations to which the auditor must apply his or her professional knowledge, experience, and judgment.

Like other professionals, accountants must deal with issues which are not black or white. As a result, aggressive American class-action lawyers created a dilemma for publicly traded companies and their auditors. If the company and its auditor made a grey-area decision and the stock price went down, they might be sued for materially misleading financial statements.

Leashing (or muzzling) politically connected class-action lawyers proved impractical. So, the accounting profession—and financial regulators— increasingly adopted bright-line, safe-harbor rules. So long as the company and its auditor stayed within the safe harbor, they could not be sued for material misstatements.

In other jurisdictions, like England, lawyers could not file class-action lawsuits as profitably as in the United States, and so accounting in these jurisdictions remained predominantly standards-based.

There was an upshot to all of these trends. Accounting firm partners who once had done well now became wealthy. In the 1960s, mid-level Andersen partners made $230,000 per year in 2020 dollars. By the end of the 1990s, average profits per partner had nearly quadrupled, to $860,000, in 2020 dollars.[10]

Appetite grows with eating. Partners got used to making over $800,000 per year. As a result, business became cut-throat internally and externally.

Andersen's accounting and consulting units vied for wealth and power within the firm. In addition, while growth had boosted profits, it also saddled Andersen with high fixed costs in the form of expensive personnel. Junior and mid-level staff had to be kept busy with client-chargeable work. Partners therefore came under greater and greater pressure to develop new business. This meant taking some other firm's client, or cross-selling new services to existing clients.

Internal competitiveness paralleled increasingly fierce competition with other major firms across the entire range of services: audit, tax-advisory, financial-advisory, and IT. The emphasis across accounting, as well as law and consulting, shifted from simply doing first-rate work to generating new clients, new types of engagements for existing clients, and, above all, billing, billing, billing.

One Andersen alumnus would comment that the firm's four cornerstones had become "three pebbles and a boulder," with "produce profits for the firm" vastly outweighing all other concerns.[11]

Andersen's Fall from Grace

Enron was the latest and last in a series of accounting scandals involving Andersen. The major ones included:

- *Waste Management.* In 1998, Andersen audit client Waste Management took a $3.5 billion charge against earnings. The company admitted to overstating its earnings by $1.4 billion in 1992–1996. For its part in this overstatement, Arthur Andersen, without admitting fault, contributed $220 million toward settlements with aggrieved shareholders. In 2001, the SEC fined Andersen $7 million for fraud. The SEC also fined four Andersen partners a total of $120,000 and barred them from participating in accounting work for public companies for one to five years. The lead partner left the firm. The others remained, including Robert Kutsenda, who was promoted to managing partner of global risk management.[12]

  The SEC alleged that Andersen had known of its client improper accounting from 1991 to 1996. Andersen had even given the client a plan for bringing its books into compliance with accounting rules. But, when Waste Management rejected this advice, Andersen continued to give the client's financial reports clean bills of health.

  In levying the fine, the SEC cited lack of independence as a root cause. For the entire period in question, a former Andersen partner served as Chief Financial Officer of the client. In addition, over and above audit fees of $7.5 million from 1991 to 1996, Waste Management paid Andersen $11.8 million for other services. In the SEC's view, the relationship and fees bent the Andersen partners too readily to the client's will.

Andersen put a brave face on a bad outcome. A spokesman said, "The SEC has not questioned the underlying quality or effectiveness of our overall audit process, nor has the SEC limited our ability to conduct audits for other public companies."[13]

- *Baptist Foundation of America*. In 1999, investors lost $570 million as a result of fraud by Andersen audit client Baptist Foundation of America (BFA). Without admitting fault, Andersen agreed to a $217 million settlement (which would break down in the aftermath of Enron).

  The bankruptcy trustee for BFA alleged that an Andersen auditor had received a credible tip of criminal fraud by BFA but failed to follow up earnestly. Andersen disputed the credibility of the tip but acknowledged that it had tried to obtain verifying documents from BFA. The client rebuffed Andersen's request. At this point, Andersen could have withdrawn from the representation, or refused to go forward until it received the documents. Instead, Andersen, so it claimed, used an alternative verification method. When this alternative method checked out, Andersen signed off on financial statements. In fact, the method was faulty. Widespread fraud had occurred, and Andersen's audit report had missed it.[14]
- *Sunbeam*. In 2001, Andersen LLP agreed to pay $110 million to settle an accounting-fraud lawsuit over work it did for Sunbeam Corp. The audit had failed to detect fraud by Sunbeam's CEO.[15]

The Big One: Enron

Enron was one of the biggest corporate scandals of its generation.

Enron was the darling of the New Economy. But, within just over a year, its market capitalization plunged from approximately $70 billion to zero. Several of its senior officers went to jail. And a federal jury convicted Enron's auditor, Andersen, of felony obstruction of justice.

Enron started out as an energy-trading firm. In the late 1990s, under an ambitious young president, Enron branched out into making markets across a range of commodities, services, and financial instruments. Enron's stock price soared from $28 at the beginning of 1998 to over $90 in 2000.

Enron and Andersen staff enjoyed deep professional and personal connections. During the 1990s, Enron became one of Arthur Andersen's marquee clients. By 2000, Enron was Anderson's second largest account, generating $52 million in fees, of which $25 million were for audit services and $27 million for consulting services.[16]

As often happened with fast-growing clients, numerous personnel had left Andersen to join the client. Many people at Andersen and Enron had thus worked together as colleagues for years. They continued to socialize outside of work. Andersen's lead partner for Enron, for example, was a personal friend of Enron's Chief Accounting Officer, himself an Andersen alumnus.

As a result, an Andersen auditor might readily find himself working with a former peer, subordinate or superior. The former Andersen staffer at Enron might in fact have trained or supervised the Andersen auditor—and have deeper relationships with partners at Andersen than did the Andersen auditor himself.

Work for Enron involved cutting-edge issues at the height of the New Economy and emerging-markets booms. Within this environment, Andersen (and other advisors) had to advise and audit clients at a time when conventional approaches for valuing companies and assets appeared to be breaking down. Chaos reigned. Investors were paying hundreds of millions of dollars for start-ups that lacked profits, revenues, and sometimes even a clear business model. Stock and real-estate bubbles formed and popped in emerging markets.

In this environment, Andersen grappled with advising and auditing Enron. A group of senior Andersen accountants might take a half-day to walk through the issues of a single Enron transaction. At the same time, Enron pushed Andersen to sign off of on accounting treatment for deals or structures that did not fit traditional accounting models. In the frothy markets of the times, untraditional treatment made at least some sense, based on analogies to other industries, particularly telecommunications and securities.

In many cases, Andersen signed off because the treatment met a bright-line test, even if it might not otherwise have met a "fairly, in all materials respects" standard. In some cases, before signing off, Andersen successfully lobbied the U.S. government, on Enron's behalf, to change accounting rules.

Enron did not uniquely pressure Andersen. Andersen had numerous, large, high-profile audit clients. More to the point, as a global partnership, Andersen's partners had a keen personal financial stake in stopping clients from pushing individual partners around. In light of this, Andersen had set up a Professional Standards Group (PSG). Local Andersen partners serving individual clients had to get PSG sign off on major, novel, or potentially controversial decisions.

The PSG comprised senior, technically expert, and highly respected Andersen partners. These partners also had direct ties to the U.S. Securities and Exchange Commission, as well as national accounting bodies.

The PSG had a mandate to ensure the integrity and consistency of significant accounting decisions. Andersen wanted to thwart a powerful client from overwhelming or corrupting local partners. The PSG also maintained uniformity of approach on new or complex issues. Professionalism required that multiple Andersen clients with the same accounting issue receive consistent advice.

Did the PSG fail? Some commenters on Andersen and Enron say "Yes." These people believe that Enron put sufficient pressure on Andersen to corrupt, ignore, or override the PSG. This pressure, it is said, included sidelining a particular PSG member who stood in the way of Enron getting what it wanted.[17] Other commentators, including at least one former Andersen partner with direct knowledge but no obvious axe to grind, say "No." They hold that the PSG did its job.

So what did happen, and why?

First and foremost, Enron's business strategy failed. Enron initially did well making markets. But, as new competitors joined in, Enron's trading margins fell sharply. Moreover, compared to major banks which traded, Enron had a weak balance sheet. The company could not sustain trading losses which playing against the big boys required.

Rather than pull out of the game, Enron's senior managers cheated. They set up special purpose entities (SPEs). Taking advantage of bright-line rules, Enron engaged in sham transactions which inflated reported profits while hiding significant losses.

To pull this off, several levels of Enron management lied to Andersen. While the bright-line rules allowed for SPEs, the SPEs also had to have some outside, independent ownership. Instead, Enron had some of its senior officers take an ownership interest in and run the SPEs. Outside, independent ownership in the SPEs did not exist. But Enron certified to Andersen in writing that it did.

In 2001, things quickly began unraveling. The truth of Enron's failed trading model, accounting tricks, and outright fraud came out. Enron's share price rapidly slid. Regulators and investigators swung into action. By year's end, Enron declared bankruptcy, at the time the biggest corporate bankruptcy in U.S. history.

Amid the turmoil, Andersen and Enron fell out with each other. Andersen anticipated investigations. In September/October 2001, two senior Andersen people—the partner for the Enron account and an in-house lawyer specializing in auditor liability—told Andersen's audit team for Enron to comply with Andersen's document retention policy.

Under this policy, draft working papers and other draft supporting documents must be retained until a final audit decision letter, as well as final drafts of the documents supporting the letter, have been produced. At that point, the draft working papers and other draft supporting documents should be deleted/shredded while the final letter and supporting documents must be retained.

The U.S.-based team did not follow this procedure. The team instead responded to instructions from the Enron account partner and in-house lawyer by shredding working papers and deleting emails in advance of issuance of the final audit letter and supporting documents. Over a ton of paper and 30,000 emails disappeared. This behavior ran completely against Andersen's policy.

Had the U.S.-based team completely misunderstood instructions? Or had it astutely "read between the lines" and done what the partner and in-house counsel had really been telling them to do? The U.S. Department of Justice strongly suspected the latter. It notified Andersen that it was under investigation for obstruction of justice.

Arthur Andersen LLP v. United States

In the past, some firms in a position similar to Andersen's had cried *mea culpa* and put themselves under a respected outsider's control to drain the swamp.

One example would be Salomon Brothers.[18] Salomon was a major New York investment bank. In 1991, it discovered that two of its government-securities traders, including the Managing Director in charge of the trading group, had broken the U.S. Treasury Department's bidding rules on more than one occasion in 1990 and 1991. Federal authorities decided to ban

Salomon from further trading in U.S. government securities. Such a ban would bankrupt Salomon.

Salomon responded by having its two senior-most executives resign. Salomon also elevated Warren Buffett (*see* chapter 7) from independent director to interim chairman. Buffett vowed to clean up the mess, and the government partially rescinded its ban so he could try. Buffett succeeded. Salomon was saved, to the benefit of its shareholders, employees, and clients.

Andersen chose a different path—and got a different result.

Andersen's CEO, Joseph Berardino, was an expert negotiator. His partners had elected him to head the firm, in part, for skillfully handling the split between Andersen's accounting and consulting units.

Unlike Salomon's CEO, Andersen's CEO did not resign. And rather than admit fault and task an outsider of unimpeachable reputation with cleaning house, Andersen tried to cut a deal. Andersen suggested that, if the U.S. government agreed not to seek an indictment, Andersen would pay a $750 million fine. Payments would comprise $250 million up-front and $100 million per year for the next five years.

The government countered by indicting Andersen. This happened in March 2002 and ended Andersen's prospects as a going concern.

Once indicted, Andersen refused to plea bargain. The case went to trial in mid-2002. The jury convicted.

Andersen then appealed the conviction. Three years later, the U.S. Supreme Court, by a 9–0 vote, overturned the conviction. The government saw no point in retrying an effectively defunct company.

Andersen had won the battle. But its 85,000 employees and 4,700 partners had lost the war.

LESSONS LEARNED: THERE BUT FOR THE GRACE OF GOD. . .

The easy answer for what killed Arthur Andersen is, of course, "Greed." The big money had corrupted the organization from the top down. On top of this, growth had eroded culture and cohesion.

According to this answer, Enron represented the final and most extreme outgrowth of an institutional rot that had previously led to Waste

Management, Baptist Foundation of America, and Sunbeam, among other scandals. In the case of Enron, the Andersen partner in charge of the Enron account was an ambitious career climber. Too eager to please an important client, he cut corners, then simply ignored the PSG's quality and integrity controls. By that point, Andersen lacked the institutional chops to push back and to reassert its early values. In the context of the culture and climate, the "preserve document" instruction was intended to have the opposite effect. The local partner and in-house counsel had corruptly persuaded the team to obstruct justice. Andersen's win at the Supreme Court hinged on a technicality. The firm got what it deserved.

The Greed answer makes for a good story. But it is too neat; and, as a result, shallow and unconvincing.

As a partnership, Andersen was run by its owners. These owners had huge sweat equity in the firm. They had made it. They were on top. Like Warren Buffett, they had no rational incentive to chase money outside the center of the court.

Moreover, Andersen's partners represented the smartest, most experienced accounting-and-audit minds in the world. They understood the importance of risk management, process controls, and transparency. If any organization had the wherewithal to counteract greed, it was Andersen.

To this end, Andersen structured partner income so individual partners would not make wild short-term bets with house chips. For example, the partner in charge of the Enron account made about $1.1 million in annual income, or "draw" (in 2020 dollars). His bonus for a great year might be an additional $140,000–210,000, in 2020 dollars. This arrangement discouraged high risk-taking; it rewarded careful stewardship. An Andersen partner made his money by sticking with the firm until retirement, not by having one or two great years.

Likewise, Andersen's partners charged the PSG with managing risk. Yes, Enron was Andersen's second largest client, but the $52 million in fees Enron paid represented less than 0.6 percent of Andersen's $9.3 billion in annual revenues. The PSG gained next to nothing by cutting Enron, or any other client, slack. Letting a local partner ignore or override PSG rulings endangered the partnership as a whole. It made no sense for very sensible and sophisticated partner-managers to allow it. And even if the firm as a whole had lost cultural cohesion, the key decision makers with regard to

Enron and the PSG came from Andersen's old guard. They each had fifteen or more years at the firm. They had come up together and knew each other well. They had every reason to uphold long-standing firm values.

Greed there certainly was. But this chapter argues that the reasons—and lessons—behind Andersen's fall lie deeper.

What Does Not Kill You Makes You Stupid

Pride goeth before a fall. The immediate cause of Andersen's demise was the arrogance of its top leadership.

In hindsight, the series of scandals leading up to Enron could only end in disaster.

Viewed at the time, however, Andersen's leadership might well have drawn the opposite conclusion. In the years leading up to Enron, Andersen had weathered a series of high-profile scandals. The firm had gotten away with relatively modest fines and no admission of wrongdoing. In other words, the Andersen ship had hit several icebergs, yet steamed on more profitably than ever. To Andersen's top leadership, the firm might have seemed unsinkable.

Andersen's top leadership failed to see the damage earlier scandals, as well as other scandals not involving Andersen clients, had done to Andersen's reputation and to that of the accounting profession generally. In the aftermath of the Dot Com Bust, the public mood was not just sour, but seething.

Had Andersen's leadership understood this situation, it would—like Salomon—have admitted mistakes, fired the partners involved, accepted the resignation of top leaders, and brought in a respected outsider to clean house.

In this context, Andersen's offer of $750 million to avoid indictment looked like an insult borne of arrogance. The first-year's payment amounted to less than 3 percent of Andersen revenues, then about 1 percent of revenues for each of the next five years. This was loose change from Andersen's couch. After all the other scandals, did Andersen think that Enron was business as usual?

Andersen's CEO failed to appreciate that reputational harms, like icebergs, come in unpredictably sized lumps. A big enough lump will sink the business. Carlo Gambino knew this. So did Warren Buffett. That's why they forbad their employees from running reputational risk: it was impossible to know in advance how big the harm might be. It was consequently foolhardy to expect that otherwise-lethal damage could always be survived by spreading it out over time. With his $750 million offer, Andersen's CEO tried to spread the damage out—and failed.

When Andersen proved itself unwilling to make an example of its leadership and Enron-related partners, the U.S. government decided to make an example of Andersen.

Trust, but Verify

The broad and deep personal connections between Andersen and Enron made for a strong client relationship. These connections also undermined the independence Andersen auditors needed to bring to their work.

On a personal level, post-collapse Andersen partners still wonder how they could have been lied to so brazenly by ex-Andersen people working at Enron. After all, these were people the partners had known and worked with for years. They had come up through the same culture. In many cases, they were even personal friends. They hung out together, took trips together.

Professionally, younger Andersen auditors found themselves at a disadvantage. They might be required to conduct an audit interview of a close friend or former boss. They might have to defend their own accounting determination against the views of a client representative who had trained them at Andersen. Most importantly, the younger auditors had to worry that ex-Andersen personnel at Enron might use their personal connections to go over the auditors' heads to a partner. Displeasing a client representative having such connections could threaten an auditor's career.

In such a situation, Andersen auditors at all levels might have trusted too much and verified too little. In Andersen's defense, a concerted conspiracy among client personnel can defeat a standard audit. But, how likely is it, given the extent of personal relationships between Andersen and Enron, that such a conspiracy could have taken place without someone from Enron confiding to someone from Andersen in a corner of an office, over dinner, or at a party or a bar after a few-too-many drinks?

The U.S.-based audit team's response to the document-preservation order says much. **Even if some or all of the partners had been fooled, the shredding and deletions suggest that many audit-team members**

had not. They understood that wrongdoing had occurred, that the team had had a hand in it, and that the course of dealings between the two firms meant getting rid of the evidence.

The fact that the truth could not make its way up Andersen's organization—and the document-preservation policy could not make its way down—points to a failure of culture and leadership.[19]

Ethics Demands More Than Compliance

Readers will recall from chapters 2 and 3 that Golden Rule ethics looks at motivations, not outcomes.

As a result, if someone thinks he has been trying to do the right thing, he will be slow to recognize or to own up to ethical lapses. Witness that throughout numerous scandals, including Enron, Andersen agreed to pay fines but refused to admit wrongdoing.

On the technical side, auditing standards obliged Andersen to follow certain procedures. If these procedures were followed, and no problem or inconsistency presented itself, the auditor could issue an opinion that "the financial statements present fairly, in all material respects, the financial condition" of the client. This was not the same as guaranteeing, or representing and warranting, that no problem or inconsistency existed. The opinion merely stated that Andersen had applied generally accepted standard audit procedures and accounting rules and had found nothing materially out of place.

On the business side, accounting and auditing had become intensely competitive. So, Andersen accountants worked hard and hustled for business. If they didn't, the firm couldn't make payroll and keep itself going. Yes, Andersen accountants made great money. This meant they were keeping clients happy. It also meant they had earned the respect of Andersen's partners, who decided their compensation and advancement.

Stepping back, however, readers should bear in mind that competition can take various forms. Coke and Pepsi, for example, compete viciously in marketing, but not on price. The airlines compete on price, but fly the same or similar planes.

Through the 1990s, the accounting profession changed profoundly. Blue-chip accounting firms like Andersen battled each other for business more fiercely than ever.

But, on what things did they, and didn't they, compete? The blue-chip firms certainly competed on client satisfaction. This included breadth of services, depth of expertise, timeliness, geographic reach, and, to some extent, price.

Where competition faltered was in professional independence and concern for the public interest. Yet, these were the very foundations on which Arthur had carved his reputation and built his firm.

Chapter 7 quoted Warren Buffett's call to his manager's to make money for Berkshire Hathaway "in the center of the court." He also told them that "if it's questionable whether some action is close to the line, just assume it is outside and forget it."

What happened to Andersen—and the accounting profession as a whole—is that they forgot where the line was, and consequently, where the center of the court lay.

Shifting from standards- to rules-based accounting played a major part. Bright-line rules did more than entice accountants and their clients to play "close to the line." They focused attention on the wrong line!

By the wrong line, I mean that what is legal is not always what is right or ethical. Accountants lost sight of that fact. Enron's SPEs might have met the bright-line rule, but they would not, without the rule, have met the "fairly and in all materials respects" standard. Note that Enron's scandals took place in jurisdictions where rules-based accounting applied, but not where standards-based accounting held sway.

Time and time again, Andersen's defense to a client scandal was that Andersen had followed applicable procedures and rules in good faith. Andersen indeed may have done so. In such case, the problem lay with the procedures and rules themselves. But then Andersen and other accounting firms should have done something about them.

Chartered (or certified public) accountants have a duty not just to their clients but to the public interest. **Many partners across the accounting profession mistook their desire to please the client executives who hired them for the accountants' professional duty to serve the client entity, as well as the public interest.**

This duty means that sometimes an accountant needs to say "no" to a client executive, or to resign, rather than to go along with a move which may be legal but is not right. If we credit the stories about Arthur as more than legend, he clearly understood what line to look for and where the center of the court lay.

More than saying, "no," this duty means that accountants should have pushed for changes in procedures and rules in order to serve both clients and the public interest. The rise in class-action lawsuits, for example, placed accountants and their clients in a true bind. The solution they found—bright-line rules—worked well for client executives and the accountants, but not necessarily for the clients themselves, or the public.

Finding a better answer than bright-line rules might well have required enormous effort by the accounting profession—in the teeth of opposition from the trial lawyers. This is a challenge Arthur would likely have taken on; it was one his successors should have.

EPILOGUE: ON EMPATHY AND LEARNING

Some readers might think that this chapter treats Andersen and its people too gently.

Perhaps so.

But, the story of Arthur Andersen & Co is a tragedy. Tragedy does not spring from bad people doing bad things. Nor is tragedy about innocent people who have evil things done to them. Rather, tragedy arises from the collision of character *and* circumstance. It's about basically good people who make bad choices because of who they are and the situations in which they find themselves—and who, as a result, suffer ruin.

Tragedy should evoke both pity and fear. If we don't see something of ourselves in the people who worked at Arthur Andersen, we will learn very little from their example. In such case, we set ourselves up as the tragic characters in some scandal for future readers.

Running an ethical business is hard. Arthur Andersen comprised the best and brightest, and it failed.

What, then, must we do to do better?

The next section will look at the key rules and tools you need to succeed.

NOTES

1. Associated Press, "10 YEARS LATER: What Happened to the Former Employees of Enron?" *Business Insider*, December 1, 2011, accessed September 20,

2017, http://www.businessinsider.com/10-years-later-what-happened-to-the-former-employees-of-enron-2011-12.

2. George J. Benston, "The Quality of Corporate Financial Statements and Their Auditors before and after Enron" (PDF), *Policy Analysis*. Washington, DC: Cato Institute (497): 12, November 6, 2003, archived from the original (PDF) on 2010–10–18, accessed September 20, 2017, https://www.cato.org/publications/policy-analysis/quality-corporate-financial-statements-their-auditors-after-enron.

3. Ianthe Jeanne Dugan, Devon Spurgeon, et al., "Andersen Partners Are in Peril as Enron Debacle Roils the Firm," *The Wall Street Journal*, March 21, 2002 (updated), accessed August 7, 2018, https://www.wsj.com/articles/SB101666095271132040.

4. Mary Moore and John Crampton, "Arthur Andersen: Challenging the Status Quo," *Journal of Business Leadership* 11, no. 3 (2000): 72, accessed September 23, 2019, http://citeseerx.ist.psu.edu/viewdoc/download.

5. Ken Brown and Ianthe Jeanne Dugan, "Arthur Andersen's Fall from Grace Is a Sad Tale of Greed and Miscues," *The Wall Street Journal*, June 7, 2002, accessed December 15, 2016, http://www.wsj.com/articles/SB1023409436545200.

6. Moore and Crampton, "Arthur Andersen," 79.

7. Brown and Dugan, "Arthur Andersen's Fall."

8. Kirstin Downey Grimsley, "Up in the Air with Andersen," *The Washington Post*, March 23, 2002, accessed December 30, 2018, https://www.washingtonpost.com/archive/business/2002/03/23/up-in-the-air-with-andersen/0518d1f1-99db-4e2d-85a9-4eb06f4bde18/.

9. Funding Universe, "Andersen History," citing *International Directory of Company Histories*, Vol. 68 (Detroit, MI: St. James Press, 2005), accessed December 30, 2018, http://www.fundinguniverse.com/company-histories/andersen-history/.

10. Brown and Dugan, "Arthur Andersen's Fall."

11. Brown and Dugan, "Arthur Andersen's Fall."

12. Daniel Diermeier, "Arthur Andersen (B): From Waste Management to Enron," *Kellogg School of Management*, Case No. KEL559 (2011), 1.

13. Michael Schroeder, "SEC Fines Arthur Andersen $7 Million in Relation to Waste Management Audits," *The Wall Street Journal*, June 20, 2001, accessed December 19, 2016, http://www.wsj.com/articles/SB992971291203974783.

14. Jonathan Weil, "Arthur Andersen Faces Court Trial Over Baptist Investment Foundation," *The Wall Street Journal*, February 19, 2002, accessed December 19, 2016, http://www.wsj.com/articles/SB1014067925637124880.

15. Nicole Harris, "Andersen to Pay $110 Million to Settle Sunbeam Accounting-Fraud Lawsuit," *The Wall Street Journal*, May 2, 2001, accessed December 19, 2016, http://www.wsj.com/articles/SB98875363447314931.

16. Jonathan Weil, "Audits of Arthur Anderson Become Further Focus of Investigation by SEC," *The Wall Street Journal*, November 30, 2001, accessed September 23, 2019, https://www.wsj.com/articles/SB1007059096430725120.

17. Diermeier, "Arthur Andersen (B)," 4.

18. Carol Loomis, "Warren Buffett's Wild Ride at Salomon," *Fortune*, October 27, 1997, December 21, 2016, http://fortune.com/1997/10/27/warren-buffett-salomon/.

19. For a detailed discussion of how issues and concerns might have been raised both up and down the organization, *see* Mary C. Gentile, *Giving Voice to Values: How to Speak Your Mind When You Know What's Right* (New Haven, CT; and London: Yale University Press, 2010).

Part III

RUNNING AN ETHICAL ORGANIZATION IN THE REAL WORLD

9

Organizational Design: The Who and What of Accountability

■ ■ ■

"Unless the individual truly responsible can be identified when something goes wrong, no one has really been responsible."

—Admiral Hyman G. Rickover, USN

"The best way to rob a bank is to own it" goes the old saw. In fact, robbers don't even need to own the bank, just to work there. So it was with Wells Fargo. So it was with Enron, which was not a bank but traded like one. The individual world record for bank robbery may belong to Nick Leeson, a twenty-something trading-desk manager for Barings plc. In 1995, Leeson's unauthorized trades cost his employer over $1.3 billion, leaving it insolvent.[1]

TAKING THE BENEFITS, OFF-LOADING THE COSTS

The crux of unethical behavior lies in someone taking the benefits from an activity for himself/herself while pushing the activity's costs onto others (including employers) without their free and informed consent.

Previous chapters have explored three different forms of such behavior:

1. *Externalities.* Externalities occur when someone unilaterally takes the benefit of an activity while pushing some or all of the activity's costs onto unrelated third persons or society as a whole. As noted in chapter 4, an externality includes a dog owner whose pooch leaves behind a present on the neighbor's lawn or public sidewalk. The term also includes a chemical plant discharging pollutants into a river in excess of legal levels.

2. *Counterparty Defection/Breach.* As between parties to a contract, defection occurs when one party doesn't perform its obligations under a contract. Where this failure is sufficiently clear cut, we say that the party has "breached" the contract. In such case, the wronged party may seek remedies under contract law, or a commercial or consumer-protection statute, if one applies. An example would be Ford, or a Ford dealer, selling the Pinto, assuming the car had indeed been defective. In many real-world cases, however, a party may have been wronged by the other party's defection but cannot prove a breach occurred. Another problem may be that the remedy, under either contract law or statute, fails to make the wronged party whole for the harm done him or her by the other party's breach.

3. *Skimming.* As noted in chapter 7, "skimming," is a type of agency cost which arises when an employee, without proper authorization, takes a benefit for him/herself at the expense of his or her employer. Of course, skimming might also breach an employee's contractual or other legal duties to the employer. But these breaches would have to be found out and proven. And, as in other cases of defection, finding and proving breach can be difficult; and, getting an adequate remedy, impractical. Examples of skimming include a Gambino member or associate who profits from dealing drugs while pushing reputational risk onto the entire Family, as well as a bank or corporate manager/employee who, without proper authorization, risks his or her employer's assets—including reputation—in the hope of winning for himself/herself a bigger bonus, a larger salary, or a faster promotion. Also bear in mind that skimming does not require active wrongdoing. Loafing on the job counts as skimming, too.

These behaviors constitute both wrongdoing and waste. Under the Golden Rule, it is wrong to treat other people (and/or their property) as means to one's own ends. Cost/Benefit analysis would find wrongdoing and waste since splitting cost from benefit in this manner leads to inefficient allocation and use of resources. Think of a teenager set loose with a parent's credit card.

On a societal, business, and family level, then, such behaviors lead to misery and strife.

If these behaviors are so bad, how should we attack them?

Part III will lay out three inter-connected approaches, all leading toward the same end: creating and enforcing individual accountability. **Individual accountability reduces or eliminates unethical and wasteful behavior by making a specific person shoulder responsibility for an activity's related costs and benefits.**

The present chapter will focus on accountability through organizational design. How should laws, deals, and organizations be designed to force specific individuals to bear responsibility for related costs and benefits? Next, chapter 10 will explore accountability through process control: how to maintain accountability (and promote efficiency) when individuals interact within an organization or with outside parties. Chapter 11 will then consider how culture impacts accountability, particularly in aligning the end goals of employees with those of their employers. Finally, chapter 12 will discuss crises and cross-fires and how they upend normal ethical calculus.

Of course, so long as businesses have human beings working in them, wrongdoing and waste will never disappear. Some people will try to off-load costs onto unrelated third parties. Some contracting parties will cut corners or breach outright their obligations to the other parties. Some fiduciaries and agents within an organization—that is, directors, managers, and employees—will put their own interests before the welfare of the business they have a duty to serve loyally and carefully. Life will never be perfect. At the same time, **no society, no party to a contract, and no organization can hope or expect even a basic degree of ethical behavior without a strong and steady focus on individual accountability.**

PROMOTING INDIVIDUAL ACCOUNTABILITY

Unethical behavior mainly affects the parties directly involved. One side wins; the other side loses. Think of BASF versus Hilton Head residents/ businesses, or Ford and its customers.

But, inefficiency hurts a wider circle of people. Such inefficiency skews the allocation and consumption of resources across society. As inefficiencies throughout society add up, everybody pays.

This situation is not new. So, how have people responded?

Background Rules' Allocation of Risks

As shown with BASF/Hilton Head, the background rules matter. These rules establish in the first instance whose rights and interests come first, and to what degree. These rules determine whether and how BASF should get permission to build and operate its plant.

In general, to promote both fairness and efficiency, background rules should mirror the terms the parties would have agreed to if they had negotiated ahead of time.[2,3]

Well-crafted background rules put the risk inherent in an activity on the party that can: (1) avoid, reduce, or eliminate that risk at the lowest cost; and/or (2) best bear the risk. In the case of the Ford Pinto, for example, modern product-liability law puts financial responsibility for product defects on Ford as the manufacturer. Such law allows consumers to sue the manufacturer directly even if they bought the car through a dealer or other middle man.

Why focus on the manufacturer? Product defects can arise from either faulty design or faulty manufacture. The finished-automobile supply chain has three basic links: the manufacturer, the dealer, and the consumer. The manufacturer, compared to a car dealer or consumer, can most easily and efficiently weigh the pros and cons of various design choices, parts suppliers, and manufacturing methods. The manufacturer should therefore bear the costs associated with its choices and methods. If it has been wronged by other parties, such as a supplier who provided defective parts, the manufacturer is better positioned to pursue remedies than parties further down the supply chain.

Forcing the manufacturer to bear direct liability for defects in its products avoids considerable transaction costs. Otherwise, the consumer would have to sue the dealer, who in turn would have to sue the manufacturer. In long supply chains with lots of middlemen, the transaction costs increase, as do the odds of a middleman going bankrupt. High transaction costs and/or a bankrupt middleman means that some injured parties may go without an adequate remedy, while the manufacturer or parts supplier avoids paying for its mistakes.[4]

Business Deals as Voluntary Allocations of Risks

Background rules set the baseline when no agreement exists between the parties. Or, as in the case of product-liability law, when no direct agreement exists among all of the parties in a supply chain.

Let's now consider the ethics of situations in which the parties agree to deal with each other. I say, "deal" rather than "contract" because dealings represent a broader concept than contracting. In approaching a deal, a businessperson typically thinks first about his or her own overall business goals. Then, the businessperson thinks about the current and future relationship with the other side ("counterparty"). Finally, in light of the business goals and business relationship, the businessperson thinks about the contract. In other words, **the contract makes up only part of the business relationship while the relationship serves only as a means to an end, namely, reaching the business goals.**

The interaction of business goals, relationship with counterparty, and contract is illustrated in figure 9.1.

Figure 9.1 A deal in perspective

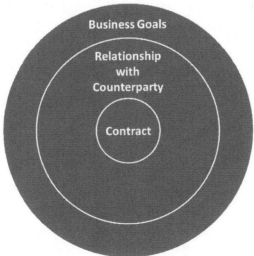

Each side, of course, has its own business goals and may have a very different view of its relationship with the other side. There will, of course, only be one contract. But, how each side interprets and/or performs the contract will depend in part on that side's business goals and view of the relationship.

In this context, a "deal" can be thought of as an allocation of risks. A deal can be good for both sides when each side trades away risks it has for ones it can handle better.[5] At a farmers' market, for example, a baker might trade bread to a dairy farmer in exchange for cheese. Each can now expect a better cheese sandwich at a certain cost than if the baker had to try to make cheese, or the dairy farmer, to bake bread.

Allocations of risk can also involve cash. Suppose a car owner hands over money to an auto mechanic in exchange for repair services. The car owner has off-loaded repair risk at a set price, but will have to chase the mechanic for the money if the repair is not done right. The mechanic, on the other hand, will not have to worry about the customer failing to pay; but, the mechanic has assumed the risk that the repair might take more time, effort, and resources than estimated.

Holding cash also means taking a risk that the value of the cash received may go down. This may ordinarily seem like a small risk. But it is not small if the mechanic lives in a country with high inflation or if the parts are imported, and the mechanic receives payment for services in one currency while paying for the parts in another currency.

There are four basic types of business risk:[6]

1. *Market Risk*. Exposure to adverse market-price movements, such as the value of securities, exchange rates, interest rates or spreads, and commodity prices:
   Example: An electric-motor manufacturer holds a large stock of copper for making wire, and the market price of copper falls.
2. *Credit Risk*. Exposure to the possibility that a borrower or counterparty might fail to honor its contractual obligations:
   Example: A meat-packing plant must write off debts owed by a supermarket-chain customer that has gone bankrupt.
3. *Operational Risk*. Exposure to losses due to inadequate internal processes and systems, or to external events:
   Example: A construction contractor must compensate the property owner when the contractor fails to pour concrete in accordance with agreed specifications.

4. *Business-Volume Risk*. Exposure to revenue volatility stemming from changes in supply or demand, or competition:
   Example: A sporting-goods store is stuck with a large stock of jerseys when the local professional team moves to another city.

When businesses, or businesspeople, do deals, they allocate a combination of these risks. Understanding the risks at play in a particular deal, as well as the capabilities of the parties to assume and manage them, helps the parties structure the deal in a way that is both efficient and ethical. In this regard, *placing* **a particular risk on the party who can best avoid/ mitigate or bear the risk promotes efficiency;** *keeping* **that risk on the party who has accepted it discourages unethical behavior in the form of defection/breach.**

The task of designing contractual methods for placing and keeping a particular risk on a particular party principally falls to the lawyers as "transaction cost engineers."[7] Exploring these methods in detail lies beyond the scope of this book. As Figure 9.1 illustrates, of course, such methods make up only part of the story. Voices other than the lawyers' need to be heard so that contracts serve, rather than dictate, the parties' business relationships and goals.[8]

The nature of business relationships and goals also plays a large role in discouraging one or more of the parties from defecting or breaching, or, in other words, cheating. To varying degrees, one or both of the parties can set the nature of their business relationship or goals. But, also to varying degrees, relationships and goals will be shaped by the subject matter of the deal, the nature of the industry, and the overall business climate. So, for example, will the deal be a one-off, or will the parties repeatedly trade with each other over the long haul? If a party is caught cheating on the deal, will getting caught dissuade other people from doing business with the cheater? Can one or both of the parties plan for the long term, or are general business conditions so uncertain, or one or both of the parties so desperate, that long-term business goals or relationships don't make sense?

As discussed in chapter 7, the need to build and safeguard reputation plays a large role in furthering ethical business relationships and business goals. Another large role is played by firm, industry, and societal culture, which is the topic of chapter 11. All other things being equal, **a wise businessperson will seek out—or try to structure—contracts, relationships,**

and goals that: (1) promote long-term, repeated dealings with specific counterparties; (2) make dealings with counterparties transparent; and (3) raise the reputational cost of cheating (defecting or breaching). Such conditions make defection or breach less likely because the penalties for cheating will be higher and the odds of getting caught, more likely. Put more simply, such conditions build trust, which is the currency of ethics.

Business Deals within Firms: Agents and Agency Costs

Thus far, this chapter has considered externalities between strangers. This is the sphere of background rules. This chapter has also explored defection and breach by parties to a deal. Here, the discussion touched upon the interaction among and structure of business goals, business relationships, and the contract.[9]

But deals don't just happen between businesses. In a very real sense, day in a day out, fiduciaries and agents within a firm (directors, officers, employees) deal with the firm itself, as well as with other fiduciaries and agents within the firm. The same framework of business goals, business relationship, and contract therefore applies, not only to a fiduciary's or an agent's deal with the company, but with the fiduciary's or agent's colleagues as well.

To work on the company's behalf, fiduciaries and agents must have discretion to act. But this discretion also gives them room to skim. As noted at the beginning of this chapter, just because a person works for a company does not mean that that person has shed his or her self-interest. Often the first and greatest victim of a company's unethical fiduciary or agent is the company itself.

If so, how does a business balance discretion with deterring or catching skimming?

Part of the answer lies in organizational design and key performance indicators. Just as the structure of background laws and deals address externalities and defection or breach, respectively, so the organizational design of the business and the KPIs help fix individual accountability and thereby discourage skimming.

To see how organizational structure and KPIs work together, let's look at a simplified example involving WidgetCo.

Imagine that WidgetCo sells widgets and widget-maintenance services. There is a Chief Executive Officer (CEO) and Chief Operating Officer

Figure 9.2 Accountability through structure: Sales

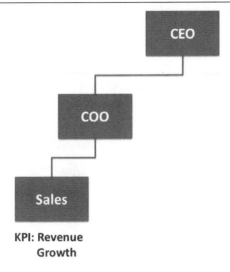

KPI: Revenue
Growth

(COO). They tell WidgetCo's VP of Sales to sell as many widgets and widget-maintenance services as he can (*see* figure 9.2).

So, the VP of Sales tells his sales force to go out there and sell. He succeeds. But there's a catch. In order to close deals, sales-team members make promises WidgetCo can't deliver. Customers start getting upset. Some cancel their contracts. They threaten to sue.

The CEO barks at the COO, who calls up the VP of Fulfillment. The VP of Fulfillment says she will take responsibility for customer satisfaction but wants the right to review the sales team's proposals before they go to a prospect. The Fulfillment Group wants to make sure that Sales does not overcommit the company. The COO says, "OK," telling the VP Fulfillment that her performance will be measured based on customer satisfaction. The CEO tells the COO that he must balance revenue growth against customer satisfaction (*see* figure 9.3).

All seems well. Sales grow. Customers are delighted. But a new problem arises. Namely, WidgetCo loses money hand over fist. First of all, to close deals, the VP of Sales lowballs on price. Also, to make customers happy, the VP of Fulfillment employs a huge team of people. Some cater to customers' every whim, and many have nothing to do when business isn't booming.

The CEO barks at the Chief Financial Officer (CFO), who calls up the VP of Finance. The CFO tells the VP of Finance that WidgetCo has to run profitably. The VP of Finance says he will take responsibility for profitability, but wants the right to review the sales team's proposals for pricing and productivity. The VP of Finance also wants a say in the VP of Fulfillment's staffing numbers and costs. The CFO and COO call a meeting with the CEO, who agrees to a new set of KPIs (*see* figure 9.4).

Figure 9.3 Accountability through structure: Sales versus Fulfillment

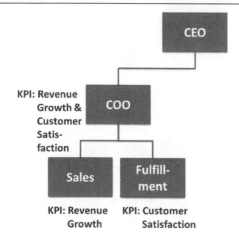

Figure 9.4 Accountability through structure: Sales versus Fulfillment versus Finance

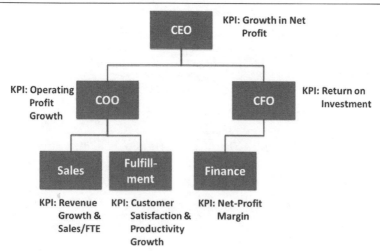

The VP of Sales was previously measured on growth in revenues. Now, the VP of Sales must also answer for his team's efficiency in terms of sales per full-time equivalent (FTE) salesperson. Similarly, the VP of Fulfillment will be assessed not only on customer satisfaction but her ability to increase productivity. No more gold-plating or featherbedding. Further up the organization, the COO will be measured by growing operating income while the CFO focuses on WidgetCo's return on investment.[10] The CEO will be measured on growth in overall net profit.

The problems seem solved. WidgetCo is now making money hand over fist. The Board of Directors gets ready to congratulate the CEO and to award her more stock options. Then, a new issue surfaces. One reason the company is doing so well is that numerous employees have been breaking the law. Salespeople have bribed customers' procurement officers. Fulfillment has cut corners by violating safety standards. Finance has pumped up earnings by improperly booking maintenance expenses as capital investments.

In response, the Audit Committee of the Board insists that a Compliance Department be formed. The VP of Compliance will report to the CFO, but also have a direct line to the Audit Committee. The Compliance Department will have the right, company-wide, to mandate compliance training, to set up reporting procedures, and to conduct investigations and audits. The Board builds an adherence/risk-adjustment factor into KPIs across the company (*see* figure 9.5).

If this situation seems to be getting complicated, it is. Life is complicated. And yet, these same tensions and trade-offs would exist if a lone craftsman, such as Geppetto, started making widgets instead of puppets. Geppetto would have to balance Sales, Fulfillment, Finance, and Compliance. He would have to ensure that he was both operating profitably and getting a high enough return on his investment in his workshop. Finally, he would measure his financial success by growth in his risk-adjusted net profit.

When these concerns reside in a single person, he or she is solely accountable, and there is no skimming. However, as an organization's staff grows and people specialize, these concerns disperse among employees responsible for various functions. With dispersion comes the opportunity for employees to skim.

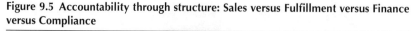

Figure 9.5 Accountability through structure: Sales versus Fulfillment versus Finance versus Compliance

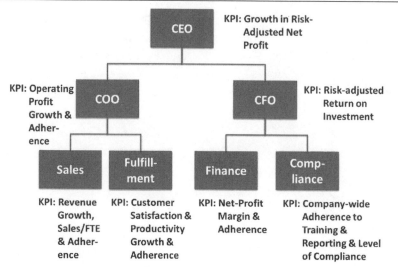

Defining and fixing individual accountability within an organizational structure help directors and managers bring the organization's parts—and people—back together in a way that encourages efficiency while discouraging skimming. Organizational structure and KPIs work like the design and mainspring of a mechanical watch. The parts must interlock to form a whole; they must also remain under tension. Otherwise, they won't move properly.

Tensions among the various functions of an organization are therefore not only normal but essential to ethical behavior. People within a firm will and should fight their corners. As in any deal, they are negotiating allocations of risk. Distribution of functional responsibilities largely defines their business relationship, while KPIs represent the "contract" among the various members of the organization. Where conflicts arise, a senior manager whose competence embraces both lower-level functions may have to mediate or arbitrate.[11] In our WidgetCo case, for example, the COO might have to resolve a dispute between Sales and Fulfillment over what promises to make to prospective clients on delivery times and service levels.

For each employee and manager, KPIs should remain few in number. Once someone has more than two to three KPIs, effort diffuses, and supervisors have difficulty assessing performance. KPIs must therefore be selected with care.

They must also be pursued in good faith. Poorly thought-through KPIs may create perverse incentives; people may also feel tempted to satisfy the letter of a KPI while violating its spirit. In this regard, a famous Russian cartoon from Soviet times shows a nail factory meeting a monthly production quota expressed in tons by producing a single, giant, utterly useless nail.[12]

Similar stories from that era include a shoe factory that met its quota for a specific number of shoes by only producing those for the left foot.[13]

LESSONS LEARNED: ORGANIZATIONAL DESIGN IS NECESSARY BUT INSUFFICIENT

This chapter has touched upon economics, law, and organizational behavior. These are vast and complex topics. A single chapter, or a single book, cannot even scratch the surface.

Hopefully, though, the preceding pages have driven home the message that business ethics involves recognizing and balancing competing legitimate interests. This challenge takes place at a societal level, among parties to a deal, and within organizations. Tensions, negotiations, and periodic re-balancing are inevitable and desirable.

This work cannot be done with slogans. The retired CEO of a publicly traded company once told me that his rule for business ethics was simple: "Put the client first, the company second, and yourself third. End of story."

This statement may sound good, but what does it mean in practice? How do we treat someone who isn't a client? What do we do when the client is an entity, with numerous employees, each of whom has his or her own outlook, agenda, and interests? How do we handle this same situation as it applies to the company itself? Think back to WidgetCo, its customers, and employees.

The retired CEO commands respect. He led his company from a struggling start-up to a public company to a $1.4 billion sale. In the process, he made clients happy, and a lot of shareholders and employees, including himself, rich. But, be sure that in order to do so, he shed blood, toil, tears, and sweat on organizational design and key performance indicators. A similar degree of effort and care went into crafting and keeping business relationships that served his company's overall goals.

The CEO might not have thought of organizational design, KPIs, and business-relationship structuring as fundamental drivers of business ethics, but they are. As businesses expand, the employees within them specialize. When tasks spread throughout an organization, so does accountability. Temptations and opportunities to skim sprout exponentially.

As noted earlier, organizational design tells the individual parts and persons within an organization their function. KPIs represent the means by which managers bring these parts and persons back together into an holistic and useful whole.

As with a mechanical watch, of course, correct design is necessary but insufficient. To tell time accurately, the parts of a watch must not only fit together and cover all essential functions. They must move, harmoniously and to a common purpose. In business, such movement is known as "process." It is to the role of process control in business ethics that we now turn.

NOTES

1. Andy Martin, "A View from the Top: How 'Rogue Trader' Nick Leeson Made a Career out of Killing a Bank," *The Independent*, June 15, 2017, accessed November 13, 2017, http://www.independent.co.uk/news/business/analysis-and-features/a-view-from-the-top-nick-leeson-barings-bank-debt-singapore-prison-sentence-a7791881.html.

2. Ronald Coase, "The Problem of Social Cost," *The Journal of Law and Economics* 3, no. 1 (1960): 1–44. Guido Calabresi, "Some Thoughts on Risk Distribution and the Law of Torts," *Yale Law Journal* 70, no. 4 (1961): 499.

3. In contract law, the general case does not always hold. In certain cases where parties have private information when they bargain with each other prior to entering a contract, background rules may be more efficient if they encourage disclosure of the private information, rather than simply reflect the preferences of a majority of similarly situated parties. Eric A. Posner, "There Are No Penalty Default Rules in Contract Law," *Law Review* 33, no. 3 (2006): 564–87. Ian Ayres and Robert Gertner, "Filling Gaps in Incomplete Contracts: An Economic Theory of Default Rules," *Yale Law Journal* 99, no. 1 (1989): 87–130.

4. Of course, product-liability laws as written or interpreted may swing the pendulum too far in the opposite direction. The result can impose on manufacturers frivolous lawsuits, verdicts based on dubious expert testimony, and excessive awards.

5. Generally speaking, parties to a deal take responsibility for their own assessments of deal risks and benefits. Exceptions typically involve lack of free and informed consent to the deal. In such cases, contract law or statutes may free a party in whole or part from a deal it made. Contract law examples include minors, who are deemed legally incompetent to make contracts. The law also excuses someone who made a deal under duress, or who made a mistake—known to the other party—with respect to the contract. For an example of a unilateral mistake, imagine that a Farmer Brown buys a wagon of grain from Farmer Smith not knowing, as Farmer Smith does, that the grain has already spoiled. To avoid such situations, statutes, among other things, may require specific disclosures be made by one or both parties to a deal.

6. Kevin S. Buehler and Gunnar Pritsch, "Running with Risk," *McKinsey Quarterly*, November 2003, accessed November 2, 2018, https://www.mckinsey.com/business-functions/strategy-and-corporate-finance/our-insights/running-with-risk.

7. Ronald J. Gilson, "Lawyers as Transaction Cost Engineers," in *The New Palgrave Dictionary of Economics and the Law*, ed. Peter Newman (New York: Stockton Press, 1998), 508–14.

8. *See* Lisa Bernstein, "Beyond Relational Contracts: Social Capital and Network Governance in Procurement Contracts," *Journal of Legal Analysis* 7, no. 2 (2015): 561–621.

9. Of course, contract law and commercial statutes provide background rules for cases where the contract itself is silent, or where the law forbids the parties from varying from the background rules.

10. Operating income measures the amount of profit realized from a business's core operations, after deducting expenses such as wages, depreciation and cost of goods sold (COGS). Operating income does not take into account interest payments or taxes. Return on investment (ROI) measures the efficiency of an investment. To calculate ROI, the benefit (or return) of an investment is divided by the cost of the investment. The result is expressed as a percentage or a ratio.

11. Russell L. Ackoff and Patrick Rivett, *A Manager's Guide to Operations Research* (New York: John Wiley & Sons, 1964), 3–4.

12. Cartoon by Viktor Vasil'ev (1906–1954), *Krokodil*.

13. Doug Farrago, "1000 Left Shoes," *Authentic Medicine Blog*, January 23, 2016, accessed November 1, 2018, https://authenticmedicine.com/save-more-with-aetna-and-sams-club-by-aaron-levine-md/.

10

Process Control: The How of Accountability

■ ■ ■

"If you can't describe what you are doing as a process, you don't know what you're doing."

—W. Edwards Deming

Chapter 9 dealt with the Who and the What of an organization's activities. This chapter deals with the How.

Before starting in, I should note that some readers might be feeling cheated. They bought a book on business ethics. Where's the discussion of environmental sustainability? Of corporate social responsibility? Of globalization and labor justice? "The Organizational Design chapter was bad enough," these readers might say. "What on Earth does process control have to do with ethics?"

Here's what. For two main reasons, this book avoids the flavor-of-the-week approach common to many business-ethics books and courses. The first reason is that issues, like fashions, come and go. An ethics topic gets hot and attracts funding. People, conferences, and papers dedicated to it pop up like mushrooms after rain. (After all, academics, experts, and public officials have families to feed, too.) Time passes. A scandal erupts in a different area. Or some ambitious and creative expert, academic, or public servant sparks interest with a new angle or topic. Funding starts to flow in that direction. People, conferences, and papers sprout anew. Funding for previous topics dries up, and interest in them withers.

This book aims at something more lasting and therefore more helpful. How should we think about business ethics? How should businesspeople understand their ethical obligations? How should these people embed ethical sensibilities and habits into the actions of their colleagues and companies? What should we reasonably expect or demand of business entities owned and run by imperfect human beings? Coming to grips with these questions will enable us to grapple with any specific issues we face now, or may face in the future.

A second reason for this book's approach arises from the popular but mistaken practice of viewing of business ethics in isolation. In business schools, this tendency leads to courses, and even departments, solely dedicated to ethics. As a result, other courses can skip the topic and teach the stuff that really matters. In companies, this tendency can lead to appointment of a Chief Ethics Officer, sometimes with his or her own staff. The Office of Chief Ethics Officer issues a company Code of Conduct. All well and good. But who has accountability for integrating the Code into company operations? In other words, is business ethics treated like a devout but odd relative at a family picnic? This person can't be kept out, and probably won't shut up. But, with luck, he'll stay off to one side so everybody who wants to can ignore him.

This book recommends a different approach to business ethics, if not to eccentric relatives. It argues that good ethical practices cannot be separated from good managerial practices. The former flow from the latter, and so stay front and center rather than off to the side.

Consequently, as chapter 9 recounted, sound organizational design and KPIs are necessary to ethical behavior. The same applies to process control. **A business that has not defined and does not monitor its business processes cannot manage them.** Unmanaged processes lead to skimming, which in turn spawns losses, scandal, and ruin.

Now *that* cheats readers, big time.

THE ROLE OF PROCESS CONTROL IN BUSINESS ETHICS

A process is a series of actions or steps taken in order to achieve a particular end.

Figure 10.1 Flow diagram for "shampoo your hair"

You can see a process described every time you pick up a shampoo bottle: "Lather. Rinse. Repeat." These actions represent stages in the process called, "Shampoo your hair."

We can illustrate stages in what is variably called a **flow diagram, flow chart, or process map** (*see* figure 10.1).

"Shampoo your hair," of course, may form part of a larger process called "Take a shower," which, in turn, might be part of an even larger process called, "Get ready for work or school."

Since shampoo bottles do not magically appear in shower stalls, the process "Take a shower" depends upon another process called, "Buy toiletries."

In areas like construction, complex manufacturing, and financial services, flow diagrams might easily comprise hundreds of processes and tens of thousands of stages/steps. For present purposes, it is enough to note that in business,

> every activity, every job is part of a process. A flow diagram will divide the work into stages. The stages as a whole form a process. The stages are not individual entities. . . . Work comes into any stage, changes state, and moves on into the next stage. Any stage has a customer, [which is] the next stage. The final stage will send product or service to the ultimate customer, [which is] he that buys the product or the service.[1]

Flow diagrams can specify not only what steps make up a process but who is responsible for particular actions, decisions, and deliverables. The following example illustrates the process of trying out for a club soccer team. We start by identifying the parties involved in a chart like figure 10.2.

In figure 10.2, "swim lanes" identify the parties who will be responsible for various stages/steps: the Player, the League Office, the Club Office, and the Club Coach (or Trainer).

Figure 10.3 shows the initial steps in the process. In our example, the Player initiates the process by submitting an application packet to the League Office. Next, the League Office determines whether the application is complete.

Figure 10.2 Flow diagram with swim lanes

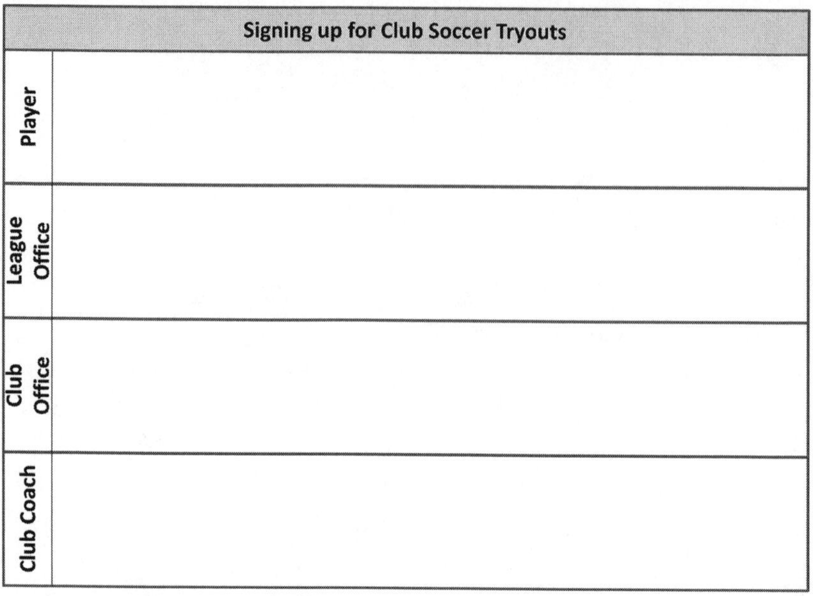

Signing up for Club Soccer Tryouts
Player
League Office
Club Office
Club Coach

Source: Adapted from a template by creately.com. Used by permission.

Figure 10.3 Flow diagram with swim lanes: first steps

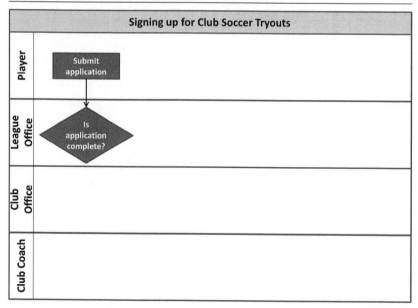

Signing up for Club Soccer Tryouts
Player
Submit application
League Office
Is application complete?
Club Office
Club Coach

Source: Adapted from a template by creately.com. Used by permission.

By convention, a rectangle denotes performance of an action. A diamond denotes the making of a decision (in this case, determining whether the submitted application is complete).

Our flow diagram next defines the further steps that result from a "yes" or a "no" answer (*see* figure 10.4).

As in figure 10.4, an answer of "no" results in the League Office sending the Player an email requesting re-submission. A "yes" answer results in the League Office passing the completed registration form to the Club Office for another decision: Does the Club's team have an opening?

As before, the flow diagram will illustrate what results from the determination, as well as succeeding decisions and steps (*see* figure 10.5).

As shown, the complete flow diagram ends with issuance of a Decision Email, illustrated by the four-sided icon in the upper right, the shape of which customarily denotes a document.

In addition to steps and decisions, process definition can also specify service levels. In the previous example, service levels might include the deadline for submitting an application, the amount of time by which submission review should take place, and so on.

Figure 10.4 Flow diagram with swim lanes: further steps

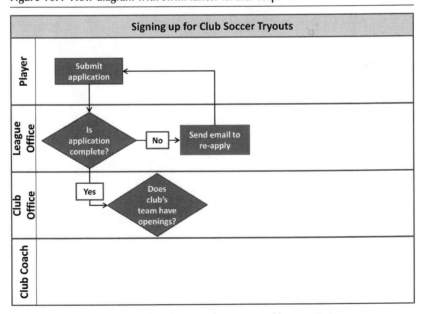

Source: Adapted from a template by creately.com. Used by permission.

Figure 10.5 Flow diagram with swim lanes: complete process

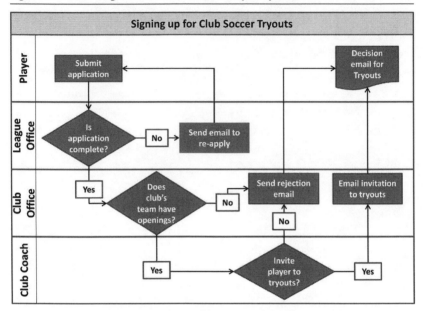

Source: Adapted from a template by creately.com. Used by permission.

Obviously, real-world processes involve much greater complexity. Even the action of sending an email, for example, can be represented as a process broken down into sub-steps/stages. The larger point, though, is that by identifying the Who's and describing the precise order of the What's, flow diagrams make us work through the How.

What Is Process Control?

The reader can see how flow diagrams depict the Who, What, and How of processes. Fixing accountability, though, requires a deeper understanding. As noted previously, some steps in a process depend upon preceding steps. Some processes in a system depend upon other processes. A teenager with greasy hair on yearbook-photo day may blame his or her parents for failing to buy shampoo. A club office may be unable to send an email to a player on time because the league office passed through as complete an application that was in fact lacking the player's email address.

Fixing individual accountability requires management to establish control over an organization's processes. Control means: (1) defining each process (addressed previously); (2) understanding the natural variability of the process; (3) distinguishing between common and special causes of variability; and (4) working to eliminate special causes while whittling away common causes through continuous improvement.

We have already looked at (1). Now, let's consider (2) through (4) in turn.

(2) Natural Variability in a Process

No process produces exactly the same result every time. For example, as hard as McDonald's works to make each meat patty of every Quarter Pounder exactly 0.25 pounds, some patties will come out less than 0.25 pounds, and some more.[2] If we weighed each meat patty and charted the results, we would expect a "normal," or bell-shaped, curve centered on an average of 0.25 pounds per patty (*see* figure 10.6).

As the process for making patties improves, variability in weight (whether lighter than 0.25 pounds, or heavier) will go down. Consistency

Figure 10.6 A normal, or bell-curve, distribution

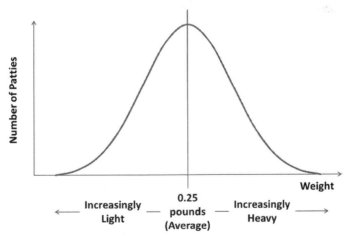

PRE-COOKED QUARTER POUNDER® PATTIES BY WEIGHT
(SINGLE HYPOTHETICAL PRODUCTION LINE)

QUARTER POUNDER trademark by MCDONALD'S CORPORATION

Figure 10.7 Production line variability/consistency

PRE-COOKED QUARTER POUNDER® PATTIES BY WEIGHT (THREE HYPOTHETICAL PRODUCTION LINES)

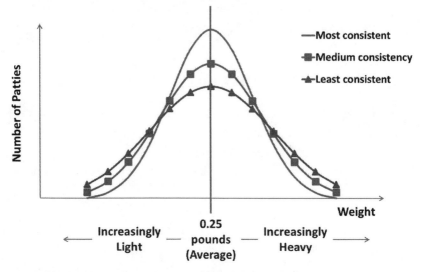

QUARTER POUNDER trademark by MCDONALD'S CORPORATION

Source: Adapted from an example created by Prof. Dana Lee Ling. Used by permission.

will go up. The distribution of patties by weight will cluster more and more closely around the figure of 0.25 pounds. We can illustrate the variability/ consistency of three hypothetical Quarter Pounder production lines as follows (*see* figure 10.7).

Note that the average weight of Quarter Pounder patties produced by each line is the same: 0.25 pounds. But the production line illustrated with the smooth curve operates with lower variability/higher consistency than the production lines illustrated with curves that are accented with squares or triangles.

The reader should recall as well that the term "customer" means not only the ultimate customer, but also each stage in the process that receives output from a previous stage. To the extent that Quarter Pounder processes for packaging, shipping, cooking, sandwich-assembly, and consumption depend upon Quarter Pounder patties weighing as near as possible to 0.25 pounds, the production line illustrated with the smooth curve produces the highest-quality output.

The term "tolerance" means the degree to which a good or service can vary from a specified characteristic and still meet internal- or external-customer expectations or needs. Goods or devices outside of this range are "defective." The Quarter Pounder process has a relatively large tolerance. A Quarter Pounder meat patty much heavier or lighter than 0.25 pounds won't jam the packing equipment or cause a grill to break down or to catch fire. It's quite possible that a Quarter Pounder meat patty could weigh 5 percent more, or 5 percent less, than 0.25 pounds without the customer even noticing.

Other processes, however, must operate with less tolerance. In machine parts or medical services, deviation by a fraction of a percent might trigger not just failure but catastrophe. Examples include jet-engine components and surgical implants. The fact is, the more consistent and precise the outputs of a process, the more confidently and safely internal and external customers can rely on them. This situation applies both to processes that produce goods as well as those that deliver services.

A critical but counterintuitive aspect of process control is that as the quality of a process goes up, so does productivity. The reason is less re-work. Defective goods, if caught before shipping, must be repaired or scrapped. Defective goods spotted by the customer upon delivery damage the business relationship. In addition, the customer might cancel the order, insist on urgent replacement of defective goods, or demand a sizable price discount. Defective goods incorporated into the customer's products/services before failing can cause widespread reputational and physical harm. In the case of now-bankrupt airbag manufacturer Takata, for example, defective Takata products passed through to auto-manufacturer customers led to a reported eighteen deaths, 180 injuries, and the recall of tens of millions of cars. Damage claims exceed $30 billion.[3] *Ouch.*

(3) Common versus Special Causes of Variability

As noted previously, no process produces exactly the same output every time. The reasons for variability, however, fall into one of two categories: common and special.[4]

Common causes arise from features of the process itself, unrelated to specific or assignable person(s) or conditions. Imagine a garment factory that produces shirts. Workers might on average produce a certain number of defective shirts (torn fabric, split seams, misaligned pockets, missing buttons, etc.). For these workers, common causes of defects might include general use of inferior fabric or thread, poor overall lighting, or unclear specifications. Although these workers produce defective goods, eliminating such defects from future production requires changing the process itself.

Special causes arise from features specific to some group of workers, or to a particular worker, or to a specific machine or local condition. Special causes include workers sitting in a poorly lit part of the factory or being given a shipment of defective buttons, or a worker who needs eyeglasses, has never been properly trained, has been assigned a malfunctioning sewing machine, or lacks the manual dexterity for the work.

Confusing common with special causes not only represents slack management but erodes morale and creates ethical problems. Assume, for example, that shirt-factory lighting is generally poor. Everything else being equal, those workers sitting closest to the windows will perform the best while those sitting farthest from the windows will perform the worst. In such case, relative performance does not arise from the special cause of individual abilities but the general cause of poor lighting. Rewarding the group nearest the windows while disciplining the group farthest away treats workers unfairly, kills morale, and leads to resentment. Resentful employees may consciously or subconsciously sabotage the company.

At the same time, treating a special cause as a common cause stops managers from addressing and eliminating defects. Think of a manager who, instead of checking workers' eyesight, simply assumes that a certain level of defects will always result from low-wage, low-skilled workers.

Competent and dutiful managers must therefore distinguish between common and special causes.

(4) Statistical Control and Continuous Improvement

Distinguishing between common and special causes requires managers to find out whether a particular process is in "statistical control." Statistical control means that all special causes of defects have been identified and addressed. Once only common causes remain, reducing variability and eliminating defects must come from changes to the process itself.

Responsibility for this task ultimately rests with management since only management has authority to implement such changes.

How does this work in practice?

The world can thank two statisticians, Walter Shewhart of Bell Labs,[5] and W. Edwards Deming of the U.S. Census Bureau, for seeing and evangelizing the connection among process control, continuous improvement, and productivity. Efforts to implement and refine their work include Total Quality Management, Six Sigma, and Lean Manufacturing.

Among the tools and methods Shewhart and Deming popularized is a control chart. A control chart plots how often over a given period of time a process has produced outputs with a particular, measured characteristic of quality. For example, out of 1,000 Quarter Pounder patties sampled from a production line over the course of an hour, how many patties weighed between 0.25 and 0.26 pounds? How many weighed between 0.24 and 0.25 pounds, and so forth?

To produce a control chart, we start by calculating average output, whether the average weight of a sample set of Quarter Pounder patties, or the number of defective shirts found by sampling a factory shift's production over eight hours. This average becomes the centerline of the control chart (*see* figure 10.8).

Figure 10.8 Sample control-chart center line

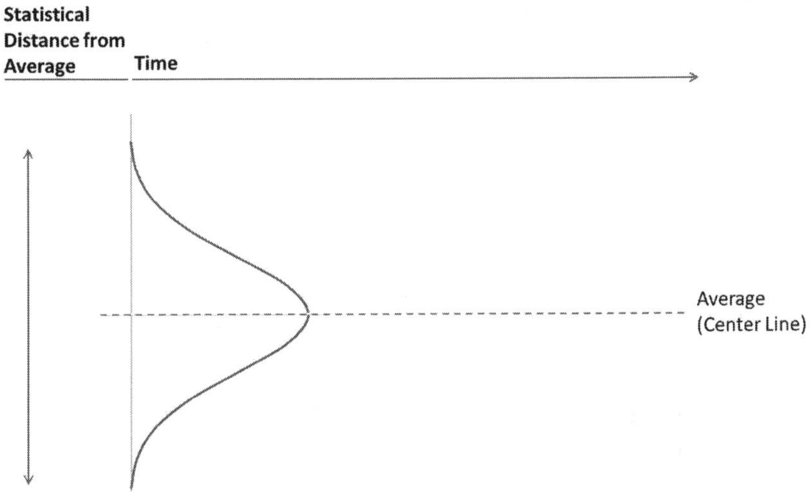

Figure 10.9 Sample control charter with upper and lower control limits

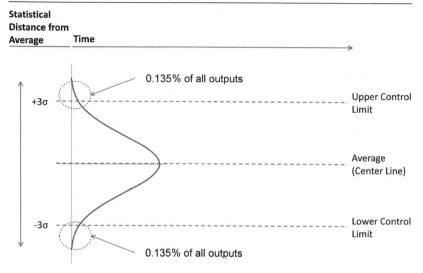

Charts typically assume that a measured output which has a 0.135 percent or less chance of occurrence (1.35 cases or fewer out of 1,000) might result from a special cause. As illustrated in the following control chart, this output falls outside of what are labeled upper or lower control limits (*see* figure 10.9).

In our Quarter Pounder example, suppose that the control chart recorded that a half-pound hamburger patty comes down the conveyor belt one time in a thousand patties. This patty's weight would exceed the upper control limit. A half-ounce tidbit coming down the belt one time in a thousand patties would, by contrast, exceed the lower control limit. In either case, we would assume that a special cause might have produced the grossly mis-sized patty. We would therefore go hunt for that special cause.

Measured outputs that fall outside of upper or lower control limit give us immediate grounds to investigate for special causes. For outputs between the upper and lower control limits, on the other hand, we typically assume that variability arises from common causes of the process. In the Quarter Pounder plant, for example, failure to regulate plant-wide humidity and temperature might affect the moisture content of the meat and lead to variations in weight occurring more often than 1.35 times in 1,000.

Figure 10.10 Sample control chart showing standard deviations from average (center line)

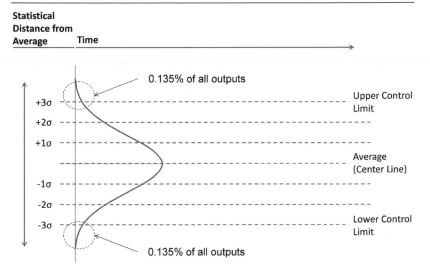

But there is more to a control chart than upper and lower control limits. We also care about measured outputs which happen more frequently than 1.35 times in 1,000. Why is this so? Because certain output patterns that emerge within the upper and lower control limits also give us reason to look for special causes, even though no single output measurement has fallen outside of the upper or lower control limit.

To plot these patterns, we sub-divide the control chart into zones that measure statistical distance from the average. The unit for measuring statistical distance from the average is called a "standard deviation." It is represented by the lower-case Greek letter "sigma," or "σ." In the following control chart, each "zone" marks out one standard deviation (*see* figure 10.10).

Readers who like math will see that "3σ" is another way of saying "Fewer than 1.35 times in 1,000."

For our purposes, though, the terminology does not matter so much. What matters is that statistics enable us to sample and chart outputs in ways that help distinguish common causes from special causes.

The following is a sample control chart showing not only a single measured output outside a control limit, but three other patterns that suggest

Figure 10.11 Four patterns evidencing lack of statistical control

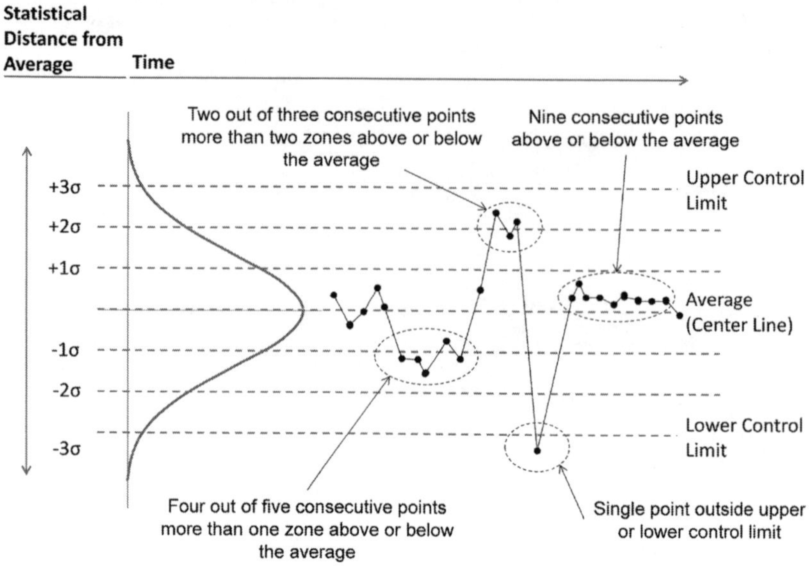

the presence of special causes and, hence, lack of statistical control (*see* figure 10.11).

There are of course other patterns beyond the four mentioned earlier that indicate a lack of statistical control. One or more of these patterns means that special causes probably lurk within processes. Tracing and eliminating these special causes will achieve statistical control. There will still be variability and may be defects. But they will arise solely from common causes. This means that further reduction in variability and defects must come from changing the process itself, or the system in which the process makes up only a part.

Maintenance of statistical control, and the constant search for, and reduction in, common causes, lead to continuous improvement. Shewhart and Deming represented this process as shown in figure 10.12.

Other theorists and practitioners have since refined or modified Shewhart's and Deming's approach.

Why Process Control Matters for Business Ethics

The previous discussion has very briefly summarized a complex topic. Here, as elsewhere, a little knowledge is a dangerous thing. No one reading

Figure 10.12 The Shewhart cycle for continuous improvement

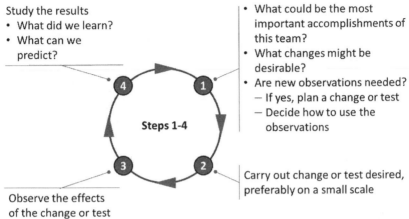

Study the results
- What did we learn?
- What can we predict?

Observe the effects of the change or test

- What could be the most important accomplishments of this team?
- What changes might be desirable?
- Are new observations needed?
  - If yes, plan a change or test
  - Decide how to use the observations

Carry out change or test desired, preferably on a small scale

Step 5 – Repeat Step 1, with knowledge accumulated

Step 6 – Repeat Step 2, and onward

Source: Adapted from Deming, W. Edwards, Out of the Crisis, PDSA Cycle, page 88, © 2000 Massachusetts Institute of Technology, by permission of The MIT Press.

this chapter should go out and start creating control charts. Deming himself stated that teaching the theory and use of control charts requires knowledge of statistical theory at least at the master's level, plus training under a master.[6] Such a background I do not have, though the manuscript of this chapter has been reviewed by someone who does.

This said, you don't have to have a medical degree to know you should see a doctor when it's time for an annual checkup or when you're feeling really sick. Few people will ever develop the technical expertise to lead process-control efforts. But everyone serious about business ethics needs an awareness of and appreciation for process control.

Process control matters to business ethics because it attacks skimming and other agency costs. Defining processes through things like flow diagrams specifies how the various parts of an organization, and people within it, should interact. Such definition assigns nominal responsibility.

Responsibility is nominal because of interdependence. People and groups don't always do what they are supposed to. Where people and processes are interdependent, how do we judge whom to hold accountable?

This is where process control helps. And where business ethics also come into play. Managers who fail to distinguish special from common causes ether skim themselves or enable skimming. Such managers take the pay, perks, and prestige of management but not the accountability. In the shirt-factory example, a manager who treats common causes of defects as special causes pushes the cost of defects onto workers by blaming them for conditions that only management controls. Where managers treat special causes as common causes, such managers cheat the company by allowing problems to fester.

Process control and continuous improvement as preached by Deming favor redemption over damnation. Some special causes will arise from individual workers. For causes such as poor eyesight or inadequate training, helping the worker makes more sense than punishing him or her. In areas where a worker simply lacks capability to do the job, Deming recommends transfer to another position rather than termination. In this way, Deming encourages organizations to drive out fear so that managers and workers will focus on spotting and eliminating causes of variability, both special and common, rather than fight over whom to blame. Deming would likely scorn modern-day zero-tolerance policies, which ignore natural variability and devolve into counterproductive management by slogan.[7]

USING STATISTICAL ANALYSIS TO CATCH CHEATERS

As noted previously, Deming argued for driving fear out of organizations. But even he saw that, statistically, every barrel will probably hold a certain number of bad apples. Process control further contributes to business ethics by red-flagging statistical anomalies which, when investigated, may reveal fraud or other forms of unethical conduct. This section considers real-world examples from the fields of financial services and professional sports.

Stumpf & Wells Fargo, Revisited: Learning the Right Lessons

Readers will remember chapter 1's recounting of CEO John Stumpf's trip to the Senatorial woodshed. The bank he ran, Wells Fargo, had fired over 5,300 employees who had opened over two million phony accounts in the names of hundreds of thousands of customers.

Stumpf blamed the head of the division where these employees worked, but allowed this executive to retire with her financial package largely intact.

Stumpf's white-heart, empty-head defense of his actions and those of his senior executives did not sit well with the Senate Committee on Banking, Housing, and Urban Affairs. Nor with Warren Buffett, CEO of Wells's largest shareholder, Berkshire Hathaway. A few days after Stumpf's public debacle, he was out.

What role should statistical analysis have played in Wells Fargo's operations?

Many business sectors in the world economy rely on computers and computerization. Financial services are among the world's most digitalized sectors.[8] When, for example, Wells Fargo employees opened accounts, real or fake, these employees did so by creating electronic accounts showing things such as the name of the account holder, type of account, date of account opening, and so on. Once accounts opened, the bank's computer systems would have tracked every aspect of account activity.

In addition to increasing productivity, digitalization makes available vast quantities of data for automated analysis. The era of Big Data is here. This includes statistical analysis of processes to spot and red-flag anomalies. It would have been relatively easy for Wells Fargo's head of division to have the bank's IT or Compliance Department write programs tracking and reporting information such as:

- The number of accounts opened by specific employees.
- The dates on which such accounts were opened.
- Post-opening activity on accounts opened by specific employees.

Control charts based on this information would have spotted anomalies such as: (1) employees consistently opening a high or low number of accounts; (2) employees opening a high number of accounts just before the end of a sales period; or (3) dearth of activity in accounts opened by a specific employee generally or near the end of a sales period.

Faking natural variability takes great knowledge, skill, and nerve. So, employees opening fake accounts to meet sales targets would have shown unnatural consistency period to period in the number of accounts opened. In addition, employees opening fake accounts to meet month-end sales goals would likely have shown an unusually high number of accounts opened in the last few days of the month. Finally, since fake accounts don't show activity after opening, an unusually high number of inactive accounts would have evidenced fraud.

If almost everyone were cheating, then a high number of inactive accounts might not have seemed unusual. But then, those few *honest* employees would have evidenced an unusually high number of *active* accounts. Investigating special causes of active accounts would have unearthed widespread cheating by dishonest colleagues.

If statistical analysis were so simple, why didn't Wells Fargo's head of division put it in place? The bank's systems were digitalized. The Bank already employed or could readily have hired skilled IT people and statisticians.

The only plausible answer for the head of division's failure to set up statistical controls is that she did not *want* to know the results. The next question is why Stumpf, the Compliance Department, and the Board of Directors did not insist on knowing what anomaly spotting, statistical analysis, and investigative follow-up the division was carrying out to catch cheaters.

Lambasting Stumpf for greed made good political theater. It was fun to watch. But it failed to expose and drive home the right lessons. The Board, the CEO, and the Compliance Department failed to put in place and to monitor process controls, which would have quickly spotted—and thereby largely deterred—the kind of cheating that occurred. Bear in mind that if only 1 percent of the 5,300 employees had cheated, that would still be fifty-three people committing fraud. That is still a significant number and one that process controls could have rooted out.

Bernie Madoff: Checking from the Outside In
Bernie Madoff is a thief.

From 1960 to 2008, Madoff ran an investment-advisory firm that actually operated as a pyramid scam. Madoff attracted clients. Instead of investing their money, he spent much of it on himself, his family, and his friends. To cover up this fraud, Madoff took in money from new clients and used it to pay "profits" to earlier investors.

Madoff could keep the scam going as long as enough new money came in to distribute fake profits to existing investors, as well as to cover the accounts of those investors who pulled out their money.

For much of Madoff's career, few investors withdrew their funds. After all, who would pull out their money when Madoff, on paper, generated handsome returns year after year while paying out real cash as profit?

Madoff's house of cards collapsed in 2008. The Great Recession hit numerous Madoff clients with losses in other investments. To cover these losses, Madoff's clients needed to pull their money out of their accounts with Madoff. Only Bernie's cupboard was bare.

Madoff himself estimated that he lost $65 billion in paper wealth and $17.5 billion in cash. His victims include tens of thousands of individuals, pension plans, and charitable organizations, among others.[9]

Madoff will spend the rest of his life in federal prison. The bank J. P. Morgan Chase, which was accused of ignoring red flags while it handled Madoff's business, kicked in $2 billion toward a fund to compensate Madoff's victims.

The circle of wrongdoers widens, however. Many investment advisors counseled their clients to invest with Madoff. These advisors failed to perform adequate due diligence. Madoff was so well known, so well connected, and so popular with other sophisticated advisors and clients that everybody relied on someone else to have double-checked. Madoff's word-of-mouth marketing, rather than setting off alarm bells, added to his mystique.[10]

Why could no one see that the emperor had no clothes?

Actually, years before the scandal broke, a few financial analysts could and did. They tried, to no avail, to alert the market and the Security and Exchange Commission.[11,12]

What tipped these analysts off was a lack variability (or "volatility" in financial terms) in Madoff's reported returns. After only a few hours of statistical analysis of publicly available information, these analysts saw that Madoff's reported returns couldn't be kosher. They showed not only unnatural consistency period to period, but they improbably diverged from the markets and investing strategies with which they were supposedly linked. As one analyst informed the SEC back in 2000, Madoff had to be committing fraud by either: (1) employing an investment strategy different from the one he told investors he was using; or (2) running a pyramid scam.[13]

Many books have been written about Madoff, as well as the failure of regulators and investment advisors to do their jobs. For the purposes of this chapter, however, what the Madoff case demonstrates is the power of statistical analysis to spot anomalies by looking from the outside in, often with limited data.

Roger Clemens: Too Good to Be True

If Roger Clemens hadn't been so good, he would already be in the Major League Baseball Hall of Fame.

Clemens may fairly be considered the greatest pitcher of all time.[14] Over twenty-four seasons, he won his league's pitching Triple Crown sixteen times (wins, strikeouts, and earned-run average). He won more Cy Young awards (seven) than anyone else, while placing ninth in career wins (354) and third in strikeouts (4,672).[15]

Clemens's problem is that he did the improbable: he got better from his mid-30s through his mid-40s. The most logical explanation is that he took banned performance-enhancing drugs (PEDs).

Baseball lends itself to statistical analysis. Various eyewitnesses testified that Clemens took PEDs, which Clemens denied. What was inarguable was Clemens's abnormal late-career performance compared to other durable pitchers, that is, those pitching at least ten games in each of fifteen seasons, as well as a total of at least 3,000 career innings.[16]

The following graphic charts durable pitchers' Age against their Walks+Hits per Inning Pitched. As a measure of performance, Walks+Hits per Inning Pitched is like a golf handicap: the lower the score, the better the player (*see* figure 10.13).

The graphic shows that the average durable pitcher improved over the first ten years of his career, peaked in his early 30s, and then worsened. Clemens, on the other hand, actually worsened over the first part of his career, then began *improving* at 35, an age when other durable pitchers have typically already begun their decline.

Looking at another metric, a second analyst reviewing Clemens's later career noted that

> Clemens . . . posted five qualified seasons from age 35 or older with an adjusted ERA [earned run average] of at least 120 [i.e., 20 percent better than the league average]. Since 2006, when amphetamines joined steroids and other PEDs on baseball's list of banned substances, all the 35+ pitchers in baseball combined have done it only 12 times.[17]

Figure 10.13 Career trajectories: Roger Clemens versus the average durable pitcher

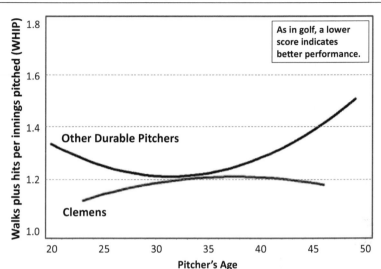

Source: Chart by Justin Wolfers, Freakonomics Blog. Used by permission.

Statistical analysis requires skill and care. Confirmation bias may lead one to focus only on the data that fits the story one wants to tell. Clemens, in fact, provided his own statistical analysis, focusing on his career ERA, to show no performance anomalies. Moreover, adjusting raw data may be appropriate, even necessary, to permit apples-to-apples comparisons. In the case of pitching, for example, should "raw" ERA data be adjusted for other variables, such as the quality of team defense, or the offensive capabilities of opponents? In a similar vein, the number of thirty-five-year-olds still pitching in the major leagues is not large; more information might be needed to confirm whether Clemens's adjusted-ERA performance falls outside the established upper control limit of a normal distribution. Hence, we appreciate Deming's demand for professionalism and expertise in data gathering and assessment. My paternal grandfather, a small-business owner who was short on formal education but long on real-world experience, put things more bluntly: "Figures don't lie, but liars can figure."

Statistical analysis like that above, coupled with eyewitness testimony from individuals, proved insufficient to convict Clemens in a court of law.[18] But, in the court of public opinion, Clemens's performance-enhancing-drug use seems well established. His achievements have an ethical asterisk next to them, and he has thus far been shunned by the Hall of Fame.

That may be justice enough.

LESSONS LEARNED: RUNNING LIKE CLOCKWORK

Process control should play a large role in sound management and ethical business behavior, including fixing and enforcing accountability.

Managers need to define processes so the various parts and people within an organization know how to interact. Defining processes means documenting them. The scope and level of detail will depend upon the risk connected with a particular process as well as the maturity of the organization.

As noted previously, interdependencies among the stages of a process, or among various processes, make accountability difficult to determine from process documentation alone. Surrendering to these difficulties means unethical behavior, waste, and poor performance. Tackling these difficulties requires management to put in place and to maintain statistically driven process control and continuous improvement.

This effort should never end. Management must involve statistics professionals, as well as the organization's rank and file. Commitment and determination for this effort, though, must come from the top without pause or slackening. The resulting mindset and actions will cut through superficial pieties concerning "greed" and focus everyone's attention and energies on continuous improvement in process design and performance.

Good management practices undergird ethical conduct. For decades, Deming demonstrated statistically not just the inefficiencies but the unfairness arising from managers' refusal or inability to distinguish between common and special causes. He also encouraged managers to foster cooperation throughout the organization by driving out fear.

Deming passed away in 1993, at the age of ninety-three. Since his time, increasing computerization and digitalization of business processes have made Big Data analysis of processes cheaper and easier. This analysis includes automated oversight and red-flagging of statistical anomalies for audit and investigation. Such anomalies don't equal incontrovertible proof, but they provide persuasive evidence of special causes. This alone deters wrongdoing while also helping catch cheaters.

For those who think statistically based process control too abstract and esoteric, this chapter closes with a down-to-earth example. It comes from a scene in the movie *Casino,* in which a casino boss (played by Robert De Niro) schools his dimwitted slot-machines manager:

CASINO BOSS

[You paid out] three . . . jackpots in 20 minutes? Why didn't you pull the machines? Why didn't you call me?

SLOT-MACHINES MANAGER

Well, it happened so quick. Three guys won. . .

CASINO BOSS

[interrupts]

You didn't see the scam? You didn't see what was going on?

SLOT-MACHINES MANAGER

Well, there's no way to determine that. . . .

CASINO BOSS

Yes there is. An infallible way! They won!

SLOT-MACHINES MANAGER

Well, it's a casino! People gotta win sometimes.

CASINO BOSS

[grows more irritated]

Now you're insulting my intelligence. . . . You know goddamn well that someone had to get into those machines and set those . . . reels. The probability of one four-reel machine [hitting a jackpot] is a million-and-a-half to one; the probability of three machines in a row [hitting a jackpot]; it's in the billions! It cannot happen!

At the end of this exchange, the casino boss fires the slot-machines manager for the special cause of sheer stupidity. Ironically, by firing the employee, rather than transferring him to a job requiring less smarts, the boss triggers his own downfall.

Deming would have applauded.

NOTES

1. W. Edwards Deming, *Out of the Crisis*, Massachusetts Institute of Technology, Center for Advanced Engineering Study (Cambridge, MA: MIT Press, 1982), 87.

2. Quarter Pounder is a trademark of McDonald's Corporation. To meet changing consumer tastes, McDonald's has reportedly increased the size of Quarter Pounder meat patties from 4 ounces to 4.2 ounces. Katie Little, "McDonald's Quietly Changes Its Quarter Pounder® Size," *CNBC*, August 11, 2015, accessed November 7, 2018, https://www.cnbc.com/2015/08/11/mcdonalds-quietly-changes-its-burger-sizing.html. Our example will continue to assume that the patty size remains 4 ounces, or 0.25 pounds.

3. Maki Shiraki, "Exclusive: Takata Creditors Seek $30 billion, Far More Than It Can Pay—Court Filing," *Reuters*, November 8, 2017, accessed November 8, 2017, https://www.reuters.com/article/us-takata-bankruptcy-exclusive/exclusive-takata-creditors-seek-30-billion-far-more-than-it-can-pay-court-filing-idUSKBN1D822X.

4. Deming, *Out of the Crisis*, 309–10.

5. Walter A. Shewhart, *Statistical Method from the Viewpoint of Quality Control* (Graduate School, Department of Agriculture, Washington, 1939; Dover, 1986).

6. Deming, *Out of the Crisis*, 131.

7. Robert Zafft, "Why Your Company Should Have Zero Tolerance for Zero Tolerance," *Corporate Compliance Insights* (blog), May 13, 2016, https://www.corporatecomplianceinsights.com/company-zero-tolerance-zero-tolerance/.

8. Prashant Gandhi, Somesh Khanna, and Sree Ramaswamy, "Which Industries Are the Most Digital (and Why)?" *Harvard Business Review*, April 01, 2016, accessed November 9, 2018, https://hbr.org/2016/04/a-chart-that-shows-which-industries-are-the-most-digital-and-why.

9. Katie Benner, "Victims of Bernard Madoff's Ponzi Scheme to Receive Millions More," *The New York Times*, April 12, 2018, accessed November 9, 2018, https://www.nytimes.com/2018/04/12/business/madoff-ponzi-scheme-compensation.html.

10. James Bandler and Nicholas Varchaver, "How Bernie Did It," *Fortune*, April 30, 2009, accessed November 9, 2018, http://archive.fortune.com/2009/04/24/news/newsmakers/madoff.fortune/index.htm.

11. Harry Markopolos, *No One Would Listen: A True Financial Thriller* (Hoboken, New Jersey: John Wiley & Sons, 2010).

12. Michael Ocrant, "Madoff Tops Charts; Skeptics Ask How," MAR/Hedge (RIP), No. 89 May 2001, accessed November 9, 2018, https://nakedshorts.typepad.com/files/madoff.pdf.

13. U.S. Securities and Exchange Commission Office of Investigations, "Investigation of Failure of the SEC to Uncover Bernard Madoff's Ponzi Scheme—Public Version," August 31, 2009, Report No. OIG-509, accessed November 9, 2018, https://www.sec.gov/news/studies/2009/oig-509.pdf.

14. Jay Jaffee, "Roger Clemens, Arguably the Greatest Pitcher of All-Time, Is Trending toward Hall of Fame Induction," *Sports Illustrated*, December 13, 2017, accessed November 12, 2018, https://www.si.com/mlb/2017/12/13/roger-clemens-hall-fame-ballot-2018.

15. Baseball Reference, "Roger Clemens," Baseball-Reference.com, accessed November 12, 2018, https://www.baseball-reference.com/players/c/clemero02.shtml.

16. Justin Wolfers, "Analyzing Roger Clemens: A Step-by-Step Guide," *Freakonomics* (blog), February 11, 2008, accessed November 12, 2018, http://freakonomics.com/2008/02/11/analyzing-roger-clemens-a-step-by-step-guide/.

17. Tom Verducci, "Roger Clemens' Recent Statements as Strange as Some Recent Contracts," *Sports Illustrated*, November 18, 2014, accessed November 12, 2018, https://www.si.com/mlb/2014/11/18/roger-clemens-free-agency-james-shields-russell-martin.

18. Del Quentin Wilber and Ann E. Marimow, "Roger Clemens Acquitted of All Charges," *The Washington Post*, June 18, 2012, accessed November 12, 2018, https://www.washingtonpost.com/local/crime/roger-clemens-trial-verdict-reached/2012/06/18/gJQAQxvzlV_story.html.

11

Culture: The Why of Accountability

■ ■ ■

"Culture, more than rule books, determines how an organization behaves."

—Warren Buffett

Chapters 9 and 10 covered the Who, What, and How of individual accountability. Employing the metaphor of a mechanical timepiece, chapter 9
described how organizational design and key performance indicators
define the various parts of an organization and their specific functions.
They establish accountability's Who and What.

Process control (chapter 10), meanwhile, represents the movement of the
timepiece, the How. Such control establishes how the various parts interact
to achieve a common purpose. In this regard, process control comprises
process definition: how products, services, and information flow through
an organization, as well as how they change at each stage. Process control
also embraces statistical analysis of variability to fix accountability among
interdependent people, stages, and processes. Such analysis helps flag and
trace common and special causes of variability and defects. This analysis
also catches cheaters by spotting statistical anomalies that evidence possible wrongdoing.

So far, so good. Now, we come to the "Why." "Why" is different. In
fact, "Why" exists on a different plane than Who, What, and How.

The reason is that "Why" deals with meaning. And meaning is a
uniquely human concern.

Why is this so? To return to our timepiece analogy, modern clocks and watches can tell time with extraordinary precision. The world's most precise clock may be accurate to one second in 30 billion years.[1] This clock can tell what *time* it is. But neither this clock nor any timepiece can tell what time *is*. Comprehending the nature of time is an exclusively human activity. So is comprehending time-related concepts such as punctuality, delay, hurry, and lateness. Along similar lines, no human can defeat top-flight, modern chess programs. But no program or computer understands what chess is, what it means to play a game, or to win or lose.[2] When IBM's Deep Blue became the first computer chess program to defeat the reigning human world champion, at that time Garry Kasparov, it meant nothing to Deep Blue. Kasparov, on the other hand, was devastated.

ALIGNING INDIVIDUAL SELF-ESTEEM WITH THE GROUP'S END GOALS

For better or worse, we have reached an age in which machines have begun designing machines, with results beyond human capabilities. For example, humans uploaded the rules of chess (Who and What) into a self-learning, artificial-intelligence program called AlphaZero. AlphaZero taught itself the How of chess by playing itself over the course of four hours. Afterward, AlphaZero crushed the world's previously best computer program, called Stockfish.[3] In a matter of hours, on its own, AlphaZero pushed the How of chess far past what anyone or anything had ever done before.

Brave new world? Yes and no. While human-designed and self-learning machines and processes may run with extraordinary precision and ever-greater capabilities, human affairs and organizations do not. Humans are, and will be, human. The ability of those in authority to specify, measure, monitor, and enforce will always face limits. So will the ability—and the willingness—of those on the receiving end of authority to listen, comprehend, and execute what those in authority have laid down.

Human limitations and flaws mean that the lessons and techniques of organizational design and process control will be necessary but not sufficient. Try as we might to create background rules, to design organizations, to assign KPIs, and to control processes, we will never make them completely foolproof or villain-proof. Gray areas and blind spots will exist.

These uncertainties lead to vulnerabilities. Those with the skill and will to game the system will find opportunities to externalize, defect, breach, or skim.

This predicament brings us to the "Why" and the reason it matters so much.

When facing uncertainties and opportunities, the people involved will ask themselves "Why" they are doing what they are doing. Their answer will determine a society's, group's, or organization's ability to further its end goals.

The Role of Culture

The *Merriam-Webster Dictionary* defines "culture," in part, as: "the set of shared attitudes, values, goals, and practices that characterizes an institution or organization."[4]

Cultures don't have to be nice. Nazi Germany had a culture. The Mafia has a culture. Law-firm cultures keep the world awash in lawyer jokes.

Cultures provide a Why both individually and collectively. In some cases, a culture can prove so all-encompassing that individuals within it might not realize the culture exists. In other words, their perspectives and value system have become so bounded by those of the surrounding group's culture that these individuals cannot conceive of alternate ways of being, doing, thinking, or wanting. As one saying puts it, "Fish can't see water."

Of course, other individuals with cross-cultural exposure or strong intuition might openly or secretly reject the dominant culture. They might even work to sabotage it. In some cases, dilemmas arise when people feel allegiance to more than one culture, the values of which are in conflict. The prototypical example might be an immigrant, or the child of an immigrant, torn between the cultures of home and adopted countries.

In giving the "Why," a culture tells people what to do when gray areas or blind spots appear in organizational designs or processes. Or when nobody is watching. Successful cultures align individuals' goals with the end goals of the society, group, or organization. An individual who has internalized the surrounding culture's "Why" will much more likely act in furtherance of that culture's rules and goals.

For businesses, management guru Peter Drucker put things more starkly: when it comes to achieving end goals "Culture eats strategy for breakfast."

Virtue Ethics in Culture

(1) Virtue Ethics, Cost/Benefit, and the Hierarchy of Motivation

Ethics represent part of a culture's "shared attitudes, values, goals, and practices." Ethics and culture go hand in hand. They evolve together and influence each other.

Readers may remember the quick-reference ethical framework chart from the end of chapter 3 (*see* figure 11.1).

The interplay of culture and ethics raises a question. In the context of business ethics, what ethical framework works best for a group or organization?

This book argues that to promote ethical behavior, business leaders should ground their organization's cultures in Virtue Ethics. This happens when individuals' self-esteem (i.e., their sense of self-identification, self-worth, and self-actualization) aligns with the group's or organization's end goals.

Let's think through an example. Imagine a company (and there are many) with a culture built on Cost/Benefit. People working in such a company will constantly ask, "What's in it for me?" Every interaction becomes

Figure 11.1 Basic ethical frameworks

Basic Ethical Frameworks

Framework	Underlying Idea	Challenges/Questions
Cost/Benefit (Teleological)	Do the greatest good for the greatest number	• Who calculates cost/benefit? • How is cost/benefit calculated? • How far out do we measure? • How do we allocate cost/benefit?
Golden Rule (Deontological)	• Act consistently with a rule you would want everyone to follow • Treat people as ends in themselves, not as means to your ends	• How do we prioritize competing rules? • Does lack of concern with outcomes lead to *kitsch*?
Blind Bargaining (Contractarian)	• Rules should benefit least well off • Promote equal outcomes	• How do we assess whether starting positions are adequate? • What is "me" v "mine"? • May we exploit the talented or fortunate without end?
Virtue (Aristotelian)	Pursue happiness through excellence by cultivating good habits (e.g., courage)	How do we translate this general rule into specific action?

a transaction. Such cultures do not breed loyalty or cohesion: mercenaries are not famous for their fidelity or their respect for rules. Rather, they are known for switching their allegiance to the highest bidder and, when the chance arises, making off with the loot.

The material inducements of a Cost/Benefit culture also suffer from diminishing returns. As Steve Wynn, the former CEO of Wynn Resorts, observes,

> In this world, money is important if you're struggling and have no [financial] security. But if you have a job and think you're being paid fairly, money is not the issue anymore.[5]

Wynn's comment matches psychological research on the hierarchy of human motivation.[6] Once basic physical needs are met, motivation shifts to a sense of belonging and love, then to esteem, and finally to self-actualization. As Wynn further states,

> If employees think they're being paid fairly, [w]hat is important is their happiness, their state of mind, and their fundamental identification with the enterprise. . . . That is to say if performance on the job enhances self-esteem, you have plugged into the ultimate energy available on this planet. Money doesn't touch it. . . . [I]f. . . [employees'] self-esteem is at risk in the way. . . [they] do. . . [their] job every day, now you got something.[7]

Wynn seeks to align the hierarchy of employee motivation with service to the company. An employee's basic need for financial security is met through fair compensation. A sense of belonging comes through "fundamental identification with the enterprise." Self-esteem (both the regard of others and realization of one's own potential) comes, or is lost, through "performance on job . . . the way you do your job every day."

This is the language of Virtue Ethics: employees achieve happiness through excellence in their work. But there is more to the matter. On an abstract level, the hierarchy of motivation may apply to everybody. What fulfills that motivation, however, will depend on each person's make up, as well as the culture in which that person lives. For example, a person in a materially obsessed culture will more likely seek self-esteem by accumulating wealth and conspicuously spending it. Recall, for instance, chapter 1's discussion of former McKinsey & Company Managing Director Rajat Gupta. No objective Cost/Benefit analysis would have justified his committing felonies that risked his wealth, reputation, and freedom. But if Gupta had lost himself in a world of billionaires where belonging, esteem, and self-actualization required him to own his own jet, the urge to cheat might have proven overwhelming. At that level of wealth, in that culture, people don't make more money or buy more things for the incremental material benefit. They do it to keep score.

The distinction between the hierarchy of motivation and its fulfillment matters. Beyond basic physical needs and security, the hierarchy of motivation does not tell us what provides a sense of belonging, esteem, or self-actualization. In a similar vein, as figure 11.1 lays out, Virtue Ethics promotes attributes such as courage and diligence, but does not always make clear how to manifest these attributes in specific cases.

A culture will succeed on its own terms by aligning individual self-esteem with the culture's end goals. Such a culture will generate its own ethics. These ethics might be coherent and consistent. But they also might, from a larger perspective, be immoral. Nazi Germany's ethics led to some of the greatest crimes in human history. Mafia ethics mandate the death penalty for ratting on the organization to law enforcement, or laying hands on a "made" man. Wells Fargo's culture signaled to members of the Retail Banking division to "Do whatever it takes to make your sales numbers."

Leaders drive the culture, which in turn, drives the ethics. If the CEO does not value—and reward through the hierarchy of motivation—traits such as honesty, fairness, and respect for others, neither will the company's culture, nor will the ethics that flow from it. As Warren Buffett advises, "In looking for people to hire, you look for three qualities: integrity, intelligence, and energy. And if you don't have the first, the other two will kill you."

Buffett's words ring true, but more must be said. If you hire such people but place them in a culture that doesn't value integrity, one of three things will happen: they will quit, they will be driven out, or they will break bad. In such case, the culture will have killed you. That will be on the CEO.

(2) Virtue Ethics, Golden Rule, and Blind Bargaining Frameworks

This chapter has thus far argued that Virtue Ethics trumps Cost/Benefit as a framework for business culture. This position does not mean that people within a business do not or should not use Cost/Benefit reasoning.

Cost/Benefit reasoning has its place. But a culture emphasizing Virtue Ethics will, from the perspective of the business's end goals, better guide employee behavior and decision-making when structural and process controls are at their weakest, namely, when employees encounter gray areas, blind spots, or lack of enforcement oversight.

Cost/Benefit is, of course, only one framework. Does Virtue Ethics work better than other frameworks, such as Golden Rule (Deontological) ethics or Blind Bargaining (Contractarian) ethics?

Golden Rule ethics, as noted earlier, has two basic formulations. First, act in a way consistent with a rule you would want everyone to follow. Alternatively, always treat other people as ends in themselves rather than as means to your own ends.

So far, so good. A business in which everyone tells the truth, acts honestly, and displays compassion and respect for other people sounds like a great place to work.

But a problem with Golden Rule ethics arises when rules conflict or leave a gap. Which rule should be followed? Bear in mind that culture matters most when standard rules leave gray areas or blind spots, or when oversight is lacking.

A greater issue with Golden Rule ethics as the overriding framework for a business culture is its indifference to outcomes. Remember, what matters in Golden Rule ethics are *intentions*. But a business cannot long turn a blind eye to results and hope to last. Similarly, a business with a Blind Bargaining culture that tries to grow beyond a handful of people will likely wither from lack of individual incentives or blow apart from jealousies and recrimination. By analogy, while people might cheer harder for scrappy Little Leaguers than spoiled professional baseball players, it's the big boys who make the big bucks. In other words, it's fine to *applaud* effort, so long as you also *reward* performance. Golden Rule and Blind Bargaining organizations might be great businesses to work in, but they might not work out so great as businesses.

IRON CHEFS OF ORGANIZATIONAL CULTURE AND ETHICS

Having considered the theory of culture and Virtue Ethics, let's see how they play out through some real-world examples.

Readers may be familiar with television cooking competitions like *Iron Chef* or *Chopped*. On these shows, master chefs or skilled up-and-comers create unique dishes using the same basic ingredients employed by their competitors.

So it is with organizational culture. Successful leaders employ certain common ingredients, but adapt the overall recipe to their particular personalities, circumstances, and goals.

This chapter will consider three Iron Chefs of organizational culture: (1) Steve Wynn, former CEO of Wynn Resorts; (2) the late Admiral Hyman G. Rickover, father of the U.S. Nuclear Navy; and (3) Marissa Mayer, former senior executive at Google and CEO of Yahoo. In all cases, these leaders sought alignment of employee self-esteem with the goals of their respective organizations. In reviewing their stories, please note that the differences among their approaches have as much to tell us as the similarities: great leaders will adapt and improvise in light of their own genius and the needs of the moment and longer term.

Steve Wynn—Storytelling

Steve Wynn has been called the "king of Las Vegas."[8] With an estimated net worth of $3 billion, Wynn ranks 271st on the Forbes list of the 400 richest Americans.[9]

Wynn's life story stands out as a neon-and-bling version of the American dream. In 1963, the twenty-one-year-old Wynn's plans to enter Yale Law School derailed when his father died, leaving behind $350,000 in gambling debts (worth nearly $3 million in 2020 dollars) and a failing family bingo-parlor business. Over the next four years, Wynn righted his family's fortunes. Then, he headed west to make it big.

With money from the bingo business, Wynn bankrolled purchase of a small stake in the Frontier Hotel and Casino. In 1970, finding a mentor in Las Vegas's preeminent banker, Wynn bought a plot of undeveloped land on the Las Vegas Strip from the famously tight-fisted, reclusive billionaire Howard Hughes. Ten months later, Wynn flipped the property to Caesar's Palace, doubling his money and using the proceeds to buy a controlling interest in the Golden Nugget Casino. He was then thirty-one years old.

Over the next forty-five years, Wynn reinvented Las Vegas, transforming his industry and becoming a multibillionaire. Gambling became "gaming."

Operations expanded to Atlantic City. Hotels & casinos transformed into billion-dollar-plus luxury resorts with thousands of rooms, effectively five-star Disneylands for adults.

In 2000, Wynn sold his main company, Mirage Resorts, to MGM Grand Inc. for $6.6 billion. He then started Wynn Resorts Limited, taking it public in 2002. In addition to massive projects in Las Vegas, Wynn Resorts pushed hard into Asia.

Though perhaps not as deadly as in the days of Murder, Inc. mobster Bugsy Siegel, running a casino still calls for steady nerves and sharp elbows. Wynn's record as a CEO includes accusations of waste and self-dealing. In February 2018, Wynn resigned from Wynn Resorts in the aftermath of sexual-misconduct allegations, which he denies.

Wynn does not appear in this chapter as a paragon of personal ethics, but as a CEO who has aligned employee Virtue Ethics with his organizations end goals.[10] Here, he has proven a true Iron Chef.

Wynn's line of work makes this challenge hard. He plays in the deluxe end of the gaming-resorts business. Margins at this level may be high, but only through meeting the equally high expectations of wealthy customers. In Wynn's experience, "It's the non-casino stuff that gets people to come back again and again." The "question of all time" for him lies in infusing his standards and approach into an organization with tens of thousands of often low-wage, low-skill employees. Many of these employees have line responsibility as parking attendants, reception clerks, bellhops, maids, busboys, waiters, and so on. They interact directly and frequently with customers expecting top-notch service.

Delivering this combination of premium pricing, scale, and numerous client touch points is daunting. As Wynn noted in 2001, "I'm frightened . . . in my isolation as a Chairman who doesn't see everything the bigger we get that, basically, I don't really know what's going on."

Wynn's emphatic answer to this dilemma has been "culture," and, as discussed earlier, aligning employee self-esteem with Wynn Resorts' end goal of providing customers with a superb experience. Wynn achieves this alignment through storytelling.

His approach works as follows. At the beginning of every shift, that is, three times per day, every supervisor of at least three people meets with his or her team and asks if anyone has a story of great service to tell.

Employees who come forward receive praise from the group. Exceptional stories result in coverage from an internal public-relations team. The team broadcasts the story on the resort's employee intranet. Posters of the model employee appear in staff areas, along with a recounting of his or her tale.

For Wynn, storytelling critically differs from spotlight programs like Employee of the Month or Employee of the Year in that the storytellers nominate themselves; they don't have to attract a supervisor's notice. Nor is recognition limited each month or year to one or two employees.

Making a hero of the employee may sound corny, but it works. As Napoleon reportedly boasted, "A soldier will fight long and hard for a bit of colored ribbon. Give me enough ribbon to cover the tunics of my soldiers, and I will conquer the world."

The power of Wynn's (and perhaps Napoleon's) approach lies in its effect on the hero's peers. According to Wynn, when other employees see their colleague win acclaim, they say to themselves, "I gotta get me a story!" Wynn sums up storytelling's aggregate impact on his organization's culture:

> Now I got 12,000 employees walking up and down this place looking for . . . guests with a problem. They [the employees] can't wait to interact. . . . That culture of making people responsible in terms of their own self-esteem is the power that makes a guy like me sleep good at night because I'm driving the culture; the employees are driving the [customer] experience.

Skeptical readers will rightly ask for evidence beyond Wynn's own statements. I have analyzed several hundred employee reviews on Glass Door and similar websites, which support Wynn's claim of positive organizational culture and employee engagement. The stock price performance of Wynn Resorts prior to his departure also suggests that he was onto something.

Admiral Hyman G. Rickover—Personal Growth through Professional Attainment

Hyman G. Rickover (1900–1986) may have been the most influential U.S. Navy admiral of his time. He was certainly the most hated, especially by the navy itself.[11]

A Polish Jew, Rickover immigrated with his family to the United States when he was six years old. Winning an appointment to the U.S. Naval Academy, he became a career naval officer.

With advanced training in electrical engineering, Rickover accepted mid-career designation as an Engineering Duty Officer. This designation meant that rather than command ships, he would serve within the navy as a senior technical expert and leader.

The U.S. Navy of Rickover's day did not like Jews or other minorities. Nor did Rickover make efforts to fit in. He did not play golf, bridge, or tennis. He did not go out for drinks after work at the Officers' Club. Rather, he was a workaholic. He drove himself and his people hard and often ignored navy regulations or processes he thought pointless or counterproductive. In a service that emphasized collegiality, he cultivated for tactical reasons a reputation as a fierce and uncompromising son-of-a-bitch. It deterred people from tussling with him.

In the late 1940s, as an obscure captain, Rickover realized that nuclear energy might power a new class of submarines, able to travel long distances under the surface undetected. Through a blend of will, doggedness, and cunning, Rickover winkled authorization and funding from skeptical military and civilian bureaucracies.

The difficulty of Rickover's task challenges description. He built a team from scratch while simultaneously developing both the science and engineering of nuclear propulsion. Dozens, then hundreds, then thousands of people had to be recruited and trained within the navy, civilian agencies, and the hundreds of vendors engaged for the work. Technical commitments for tons of exotic metals (such as hafnium and zirconium) had to be made before the metallurgy was fully understood or a process for refining these metals at scale even worked out. Completely novel processes and standards had to be devised, with vendors taught to perform at unprecedented levels of quality.

Rickover delivered his nuclear-propulsion reactor on time and on budget. He accomplished in a few years what other "experts" thought would take at least twenty-five years, if it could be done at all. With the benefits of nuclear propulsion made real, the navy tasked Rickover with building reactors for surface ships, such as cruisers and aircraft carriers. Based on this track record, President Eisenhower authorized Rickover's team to design and launch a prototype nuclear-power station. Years later, after an accident at the civilian, Three Mile Island nuclear-power plant, President Carter (himself a Naval Academy alumnus and graduate of Rickover's program) called upon Rickover to investigate.

Rickover was a technical and managerial genius. His accomplishments made peers envious. His manner and methods infuriated them. Moreover, as nuclear propulsion spread across the fleet, Rickover developed a stranglehold on naval officers' careers. Only graduates of Rickover's program could command nuclear-powered ships. And only officers personally approved by Rickover could get into his program. Rivals within the navy tried several times to force Rickover into retirement, but his track record and relationship with Congress kept him in the service and saw him promoted, eventually to four-star rank.

Rickover did not run a for-profit business. But he understood and demanded strict adherence to professional ethics. Like a business leader, he operated under tight budgetary, time, and regulatory constraints. His competitors included not only the Soviet Navy, but rivals within the U.S. military, civilian agencies, and industry. Rickover also had to contend with unforgiving Nature: a nuclear accident onboard ship could destroy both vessel and crew. Such an accident might spell the end of Rickover's program and of nuclear power.

Rickover's end goal was producing novel, high-performance technology under budgetary and time pressures and operating it without mishap. Developing this technology required technical expertise, innovation, and professional integrity. Manufacturing the resulting equipment demanded great precision and control. Operating the equipment required an understanding of basic principles, common sense, and discipline.

In light of these constraints, Rickover had to attract people with potential and to develop and retain them over the long term. In this way, his organization built up expertise, institutional memory, and teamwork.

To accomplish this goal, **Rickover promoted a culture of personal growth through professional attainment, or, in other words, Virtue Ethics.** He gave subordinates challenging and intellectually rewarding work so they would develop and stay. As part of this arrangement, they received, early on, considerable authority and responsibility, plus freedom to seek added work and responsibility. He wanted employees to constantly feel stretched.

Generally throughout the organization, Rickover demanded steadily rising levels of adequacy. He emphasized continuing education and self-study. Nuclear-program schools for enlisted sailors taught basic principles in detail, and then related these principles to operating procedures. For enlisted personnel accustomed to rote memorization, this training was often the first time they had ever been taught—or even expected—to think. For many, it came as a revelation. As one chief petty officer explained,

> I was in the Navy for nearly fifteen years before this program came along. . . . If the average human being uses 10 percent of his brain, I was using 1 percent. Everybody figured sailors were supposed to be stupid, and who were we to argue? Now I'm working my tail off, but I'm alive . . . I'm actually a thinking human being. And I think about how I just threw away fifteen years of my life because nobody kicked my ass. You know what really woke me up? On my old ship, we didn't have toasters, 'cause sailors are too dumb to work toasters, right? So we had cold, hard, dry toast from the galley. Then one day we had toasters on the tables. And I asked around, "How come?" And you know what I found out? They said Captain Rickover had told the top Navy brass that if sailors were smart enough to run a nuclear power plant, they could damn well run a toaster. And I said, "There's a guy I want to work for."[12]

The chief's comments give an enlisted-man's view of what made the culture of Rickover's program different. What set it apart at the executive level? One of Rickover's principal lieutenants described it this way:

> With a few exceptions, we all knew we were not as smart as. . . [Rickover], but we did know more than he did about certain things—each of us in his own area—and he was not threatened by that situation. In fact, as he said, he was counting on it, and that was empowering. We found it exciting to be surrounded by exceptionally bright and creative people who could always get an open-minded hearing for their ideas. In that sense, Naval Reactors was almost like an idealized university setting.[13]

Rickover's approach did a couple of things. It quickly identified those with the aptitude and appetite for personal and professional growth. It also provided subordinates with a feeling of ownership and pride in work. Within headquarters, the Naval Reactors Group had a flat, loosely designed organizational structure. Job titles were vague. Self-motivated employees could identify an area requiring further research or development. Rickover would approve a project, obtaining in return the employee's commitment for deliverables by a date certain. Then, Rickover would hold the employee's feet to the fire.

With delegation came supervision. Rickover used various methods to keep tabs on his people. He had over forty people reporting to him directly. This gave direct oversight, quick feedback, and fast decisions. Rickover required frequent oral and written reports to clarify thinking and to memorialize issues, discussions, and reasons. Finally, in the days of manual typewriters, every evening, Rickover received a pink carbon copy of every document typed in his Group that day. These carbon copies, known as "pinks," served as Rickover's "directed telescope."[14] Anybody writing anything in the Naval Reactors Group during the day had to consider that Rickover might, that evening, read what had been written and, the next day, comment on it at high volume. Every supervisor had to worry that Rickover might learn something about, or find some problem in, the supervisor's team or project before the supervisor did. Woe to that supervisor.

Rickover also set a personal example. He worked relentlessly and sweated details. He set priorities and deadlines. He got directly involved in finding and fixing problems, with tenacious follow-up. At the same time, he insisted on facing facts. He encouraged robust debate and demanded that work be checked independently and impartially since even the most talented and dedicated employee makes mistakes.

Was there a contradiction between Rickover's delegation and his personal involvement in finding and fixing problems? No. Rickover wanted subordinates who sought greater work and responsibility. He also had enough real-world experience to expect problems. He wanted supervisors to constantly seek, surface, and solve problems. So, that is how he managed. Furthermore, as an engineer, he knew that Nature could not be fooled. He therefore insisted that his people alert him to problems right away so they could be discussed and dealt with.

Assessing Rickover's methods of management, including culture building, comes with a caveat. He distrusted management as a distinct discipline. He despised cookie-cutter approaches to running things. Instead, he stressed deep technical expertise, professionalism, and hard work.

Still, Rickover himself laid out the elements of his managerial philosophy.[15] Despite his reputation as an SOB, he recognized the soft side of motivation. There was at least as much carrot as stick. More importantly, one can see in his approach the alignment of organizational end goals with Virtue Ethics. In Rickover's case, instead of storytelling, he built a culture of personal growth through professional attainment.

Admiral Rickover ran the Naval Reactors group for thirty-three years, ending in 1982. His example and influence, dubbed "The Rickover Effect," continue to the present day. As of this writing, the U.S. Navy claims over 162,000,000 miles safely steamed on nuclear power.[16]

Marissa Mayer—Finding Your Rhythm

Readers will remember Marissa Mayer from chapter 1. That chapter focused on her travails as CEO of Yahoo. This chapter will look at her earlier successes at Google, as well as her ultimately unsuccessful efforts to kick-start Yahoo's culture.

At the time of her appointment as Yahoo's CEO in 2012, Marissa Mayer seemed to be the woman who had it all and could do it all.

Among the first twenty employees of Google when she joined in 1999, Mayer was the company's first female engineer.[17] Mayer, had, of course, already made a habit of standing out. In K-12 in Wisconsin, she was accelerated two grades.[18] Against stereotype for a math-and-science whiz, she was a state-champion debater and captain of the state-champion dance team.[19] Her eclectic ways continued at Stanford University, where she earned a bachelor of science degree in symbolic systems while dancing ballet, competing in parliamentary debate, and doing volunteer work.[20] She earned an MS in computer science from Stanford shortly before joining Google.

Mayer's accomplishments at Google have been discussed in chapter 1. She embraced the company's proudly geeky culture, with its emphasis on meritocracy, teamwork, and data-driven analysis. She also worked immensely hard. One hundred plus hour weeks were the norm during her early years, with Mayer estimating that during her first five years at Google, she pulled at least one all-nighter a week.

As a senior Google executive, Mayer needed to continually design and launch complex, innovative software products. Like Rickover, she had to attract and retain top engineering talent that could take the pressure and pace. More so than Rickover, however, Mayer faced competitive pressures. For those interested in nuclear propulsion, Naval Reactors was the only game in town. Mayer, on the other hand, had to beat established and start-up rivals to market. She also had to contend with her people getting poached by other companies, or breaking away to found their own start-ups.

Mayer's early tenure and success at Google put her in a position to influence the culture. She did this in part by continuing to enjoy and celebrate her "unique blend of passions."[21] As one former Stanford classmate noted, "Marissa has a totally individual sense of what floats her boat. . . . She's not afraid to be a leader and embrace the things she loves . . . like baking cakes and admiring fashions. She likes throwing holiday, Halloween, and cocktail parties for her work colleagues as long as they involve cake."[22] Mayer herself has said, "My hobbies actually make me better at work. . . . One of the trade-offs that often happens for girls is that they think, 'I like art. I like fashion. And I'm going to have to hide that or dial that back in order to get taken seriously' . . . . It's important to send the message that you don't have to give up your femininity in order to be in a male-dominated space like the Internet."[23]

Mayer saw a particular need—and opportunity—to recruit more women into Google and computer science generally. But she did not view her approach as solely benefiting women. As she noted,

> If you see a number of women who are all working and succeeding on their own terms, it hopefully gives women and men alike [the confidence] to pursue what they want to do in the way they want to do it.[24]

Mayer employs what might be called a "whole person" approach. At Google, she knew that getting and keeping the best talent required the company to value and nurture the whole person. Causing or requiring employees to suppress key aspects of their lives or personalities represented a bad long-term bet. For example, with regard to Google's associate-product-manager program, Mayer said, "We need to make sure we're really investing in them and their careers. . . . [T]hese guys are all my kids. I go to all their weddings and send them all presents for their first child's birthday, and we have big reunions."

Mayer also made it a management practice to have each employee identify some non-work activity that mattered to him or her and to support that employee in making time for that activity. It varied by person. For one, it might be a weekly dinner with friends; for another, attending a child's game or recital, and so on. According to Mayer,

> Burnout is about resentment. . . . Find your rhythm. Your rhythm is what matters to you so much that when you miss it you're resentful of your work. . . . So find your rhythm, understand what makes you resentful, and protect [against] it. You

can't have everything you want, but you can have the things that really matter to you. And thinking that way empowers you to work really hard for a really long period of time.[25]

Burnout, as Mayer uses the term, is psychological and emotional rather than physical. Mayer recognized that to stay productive over the long term, Google employees needed to find belonging, esteem, and self-actualization outside of work, too. This challenge differed from that Rickover and Wynn, who focused on motivation at work, with employees who did not necessarily start out as top talent, but had the potential to shine at their given tasks.

Like both Wynn and Rickover, however, Mayer sought to align employees' individual goals with those of the organization using Virtue Ethics. Google remained an intense, results-oriented business. But **Mayer understood that the best results for Google would come from employees pursuing excellence in line with their individual identities and psychological needs.**

Of course, nothing succeeds like success. Google was one of the fastest growing companies in the world. Starting from a $1.5 million investment by four people in 1998, the company would build over $200 billion in market value by 2012.[26] Such performance gives everything about Google's early years a rosy, if not golden, hue.

Over this same period, however, Yahoo's fortunes followed the opposite trajectory. Founded in early 1994 as an Internet portal and search engine, the company recorded its millionth user that same year. Yahoo went public in 1996. The stock peaked in early 2000 at $500 per share. This price amounted to nearly $120 billion in total market capitalization. Then, Yahoo's slide began as the dot.com bubble burst and Google and Microsoft Bling ate up Yahoo's search business meat, hide, gristle, and bone. Starting in 2001, Yahoo gave up Search entirely and instead licensed technology from Google and, later, Microsoft (*see* figure 11.2).

By the time Mayer signed on as Yahoo's CEO in July 2012, she was Yahoo's sixth CEO in as many years. Nearly the total value of Yahoo stock represented its holdings in Chinese e-commerce giant Ali Baba.

Yahoo employees cheered Mayer's appointment. Investors showed similar enthusiasm.

Figure 11.2 Yahoo market capitalization, 1996–2016

April 1996 to July 2012
Dollars

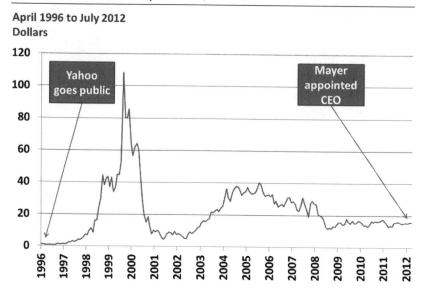

Mayer's effort to turn around Yahoo's culture had five basic parts.[27] The first was to communicate and overcommunicate. Since exiting the Search business over ten years before, Yahoo had failed to define itself. Mayer now faced a strategic decision. Would Yahoo get back into Search? Would the company focus on being a Portal or a Content Provider/Publisher? Would Yahoo make a push into the booming field of Mobile Applications?

Mayer decided on a push into Mobile Applications, which, unlike Search, lacked dominant players. Mobile also played into Mayer's strength as a product developer. Mayer repeatedly communicated Yahoo's new direction in speeches, meetings, and press events. She also switched out and switched over senior personnel and Mergers & Acquisition activity in line with Yahoo's push into Mobile.

The second element of Mayer's cultural re-start involved getting Yahoo employees to recommit. Among her earliest and most publicized moves was to end employees' working remotely. She wanted them back in the office, working with each other face-to-face, sharing ideas, and imbibing a new spirit.

Third, Mayer gave permission and asked for participation. She continued an open-door policy from her Google days and encouraged more risk-taking. A closely connected fourth element involved providing support to nurture innovation. To this end, Yahoo raised $7.6 billion (before taxes) for development and new efforts by selling half of its stake in Ali Baba.

Finally, Mayer celebrated progress. She used her celebrity status in the business and general media to call out Yahoo's successes and broadcast its great promise.

The previous five elements focused on kick-starting an existing culture. An unstated element of this turnaround was to bring in a new set of players. During Mayer's tenure, Yahoo made over one hundred acquisitions. The company bought numerous mobile start-ups, not for the technology but for the people. The quickest way to put together teams of talented developers was to buy their companies, then put them to work producing the technology Yahoo wanted.

As readers know, this story ends unhappily. Yahoo employees' and investors' early excitement and enthusiasm over Mayer faded as she proved unable to turn the company around. Colleagues initially saw competitive advantages in Mayer's star power and glamor. Toward the end, they mocked her for them.

LESSONS LEARNED: CULTURE AS THE ACID TEST OF LEADERSHIP

This chapter does not close with Marissa's Mayer's failure at Yahoo to belittle her. She was and remains a world-class technologist and manager. But two points from her example bear mentioning.

The first is the difficulty of building and keeping a positive culture through hard times. No hero's journey in fact or fiction seems complete without struggle, without a dark night of the soul, when all seems hopeless. Leaders who not only motivate themselves but others through such times have rare and praiseworthy strength. They inspire. Still, no matter how gifted and determined the leader, repeated failure demoralizes.

The second point is the need to ground culture building in the particulars of people, place, and time. What worked for Mayer at Google didn't work at Yahoo. Actual and would-be Iron Chefs of organizational culture have to make the most of what they have, to constantly be on guard for changing circumstances, and to continually experiment, adapt, and adjust in light of these changes. Beware consultants bearing PowerPoint who plug universal recipes for culture building. Just as "Why" is uniquely human, so is culture building. It cannot be reduced to a series of mechanical steps. It must touch the human heart.

It also takes hard work. Lots of it. This chapter has shown how successful organizational cultures rely on Virtue Ethics, which Steve Wynn has described as "the ultimate energy available on this planet." To tap this energy source, the CEO must drive the culture. Some of this work might be fun, inspiring, and gratifying. Wynn's storytelling and Mayer's rhythm fit into this category. But, as Rickover reminds us, much of the leadership that drives culture involves drudgery. This includes the everyday work of supervising, following up, and tackling seemingly trivial problems which take immense effort to resolve.[28] Wynn has no doubt spent much of his life doing the same. Mayer did not spend one hundred plus hour weeks just baking cakes.

In short, in business and ethics, culture matters most. It represents the acid test of leadership. In this, there is no substitute for Virtue Ethics—or the CEO's hard work and good example.

NOTES

1. Amanda Onion, "New Clock Promises to Be World's Most Precise," *ABC News*, July 13, 2018, accessed November 15, 2018, https://abcnews.go.com/Technology/CuttingEdge/story.

2. Russell L. Ackoff, *Ackoff's Best*, 15–9. Business processes, machines, and computer programs represent *systems* (a "system" being "a whole [comprising two or more elements] that cannot be divided into independent parts"). Finding out the purpose of any system (the "Why?" of that system) requires one to look outside the system. That purpose resides in the minds of the designers and programmers who built the system, or of an observer looking at the system in the context of the environment in which the system operates. By contrast, even where self-learning programs can mimic or surpass human behaviors, such programs remain bounded by their algorithms. Programs cannot look beyond their programming. As a consequence, such programs might describe their actions but cannot *explain* them. Nor can human analysis of the code alone provide *understanding*. A similar situation applies to a human being participating in a business process who lacks awareness of the process's purpose. Such person can only explain the purpose by looking outside the process. Analysis of the process itself will yield neither explanation nor understanding.

3. Mike Klein, "Google's AlphaZero Destroys Stockfish in 100-Game Match," Chess.com, December 17, 2017, accessed November 19, 2018, https://www.chess.com/news/view/google-s-alphazero-destroys-stockfish-in-100-game-match.

4. Merriam-Webster Online Dictionary, accessed November 15, 2018, https://www.merriam-webster.com/dictionary/culture.

5. Wall Street Journal Live podcast, "Part II: Steve Wynn Discusses the Future of His Business," at 12:17–12:26, accessed November 27, 2018, https://www.youtube.com/watch.

6. A. H. Maslow, "A Theory of Human Motivation," *Psychological Review* 50, no. 4 (1943): 370–96.

7. Wall Street Journal Live podcast, "Part II: Steve Wynn Discusses the Future of His Business," at 12:26–12:50, accessed November 27, 2018, https://www.youtube.com/watch.

8. Nina Munk, "Steve Wynn's Biggest Gamble," *Vanity Fair*, June 2005, accessed December 6, 2018, https://www.vanityfair.com/news/2005/06/steve-wynn-las-vegas-resort.

9. 2018 Forbes 400 List, "The Forbes 400: The Definitive Ranking of the Wealthiest Americans," Forbes, accessed December 6, 2018, https://www.forbes.com/forbes-400/#729e9be77e2f.

10. Quotes from this section comes from Peter Robinson's interview with Steve Wynn, Uncommon Knowledge, Parts I & II, Hoover Institution, July 25, 2014, accessed December 6, 2018, https://www.youtube.com/watch.

11. For a highly readable biography of Rickover and history of the Naval Reactors Group by one of his key lieutenants, *see* Theodore Rockwell, *The Rickover Effect: How One Man Made a Difference* (Lincoln, Nebraska: iUniverse, 2002).

12. Rockwell, *The Rickover Effect*, 291.

13. Rockwell, *The Rickover Effect*, 323.

14. van Creveld, *Command in War*, 75.

15. Hyman G. Rickover, "Doing a Job," excerpt from a 1982 speech, accessed December 10, 2019, https://govleaders.org/rickover.htm.

16. Team Submarine Public Affairs Press Release, "PCU Hyman G. Rickover Celebrates Construction Milestone," Story Number: NNS180512–02. Release Date: 5/12/2018 10:46:00 AM, accessed December 11, 2018, https://www.navy.mil/submit/display.asp.

17. Meredith Gethin-Jones and Susan Fleming, "Marissa Mayer at Google," *Darden Business Publishing*, UV6474, August 2, 2012, 7.

18. Ben Elgin, "Managing Google's Idea Factory," *Bloomberg Businessweek*, October 2, 2005, accessed September 23, 2019, https://www.bloomberg.com/news/articles/2005-10-02/managing-googles-idea-factory.

19. Wall Street Journal Video, "Marissa Mayer on Being a Google 'Geek'," April 5, 2011, accessed December 10, 2018, https://www.wsj.com/video/marissa-mayer-on-being-a-google-geek/65DF05B0-1A28-41E8-8B0F-43E2F1196A04.html.

20. Sally Singer, "From the Archives: Google's Marissa Mayer in Vogue," *Vogue*, March 28, 2012, accessed December 10, 2018, https://www.vogue.com/article/from-the-archives-marissa-mayer-machine-dreams.

21. Gethin-Jones and Fleming, "Marissa Mayer at Google," 9.

22. Julian Guthrie, "The Adventures of Marissa," *San Francisco Magazine*, February 8, 2018, accessed December 10, 2018, https://www.modernluxury.com/san-francisco/story/the-adventures-of-marissa.

23. Gethin-Jones and Fleming, "Marissa Mayer at Google," 8, quoting, "Tales from the Front Lines," *Wall Street Journal*, April 10, 2012.

24. Wall Street Journal Video, April 5, 2011.

25. Marissa Mayer, "How to Avoid Burnout: Marissa Mayer," *Bloomberg Businessweek*, April 12, 2012, accessed December 11, 2018, https://www.bloomberg.com/news/articles/2012-04-12/how-to-avoid-burnout-marissa-mayer.

26. Gethin-Jones and Fleming, "Marissa Mayer at Google," 2.

27. Kathy Gersch, "5 Ways Mayer's Trying to Kick-Start the Yahoo! Culture," *Forbes*, July 18, 2013, accessed December 11, 2018, https://www.forbes.com/sites/johnkotter/2013/07/18/the-marissa-mayer-method-5-steps-to-kick-starting-the-yahoo-culture/#5d1de6c63dbc.

28. Hyman G. Rickover, "Paper Reactors, Real Reactors" (5 June 1953), Published in AEC Authorizing Legislation: Hearings before the Joint Committee on Atomic Energy (1970), 1702, accessed December 11, 2018, http://ecolo.org/documents/documents_in_english/Rickover.pdf.

12

Crises and Cross-Fires: Weathering the Storm

■ ■ ■

"Gentlemen, you can't fight in here! This is the War Room!"

—Peter Sellers, as President Merkin Muffley, in *Dr. Strangelove*

Recognizing the primacy of culture does not discount the roles that organizational design and process control play in business ethics.[1] Culture, design, and control should work together. Understanding their natures, purposes, and limitations helps us employ them in concert. The whole should be greater than the sum of the parts.

Addressing crises and cross-fires calls for similar breadth of vision and depth of understanding.

The term "crisis" means, in part, "an unstable or crucial time or state of affairs in which a decisive change is impending."[2] As used here, the term covers the alleged happening or discovery of some misdeed or misfortune that requires business leaders to act. Examples of crises from prior chapters include Wells Fargo's fake-account scandal, Yahoo's security breach, Ford Pinto defect claims, and so on.

In an ethical crisis, the business represents one of the principal actors. Typically at issue is whether some norm has been breached and what to do about it. In a cross-fire, by contrast, the business finds itself caught between contending forces. There might be no need to act. In fact, it might be best to do nothing. Examples of cross-fires to be discussed later in this chapter include Target's restroom/changing-room policies, the participation of

Über's CEO in a Presidential advisory council, and enforcement of "community standards" by social-media platforms like Facebook and YouTube.

By definition, crises and cross-fires belie business as usual. This chapter will first explore how the economics of crises and cross-fires bend and twist normal ethical considerations. The chapter will then consider the particular vulnerability of businesses to cross-fires when situations are so new or so fast-changing that various parties battle over what the norms should be.

Notwithstanding such uncertainty, some rules of thumb will emerge. As this chapter will discuss, they include building social capital as a good neighbor, adapting quickly to fickle and fast-changing public moods, and having crisis/cross-fire-management structures and processes primed and ready to go.

THE ECONOMICS OF CRISES AND CROSS-FIRES— WARPING ETHICAL SENSIBILITIES

As readers may recall, part II of this book ("The Ethical Business and Other Fantastic Beasts") dealt with the meaning and drivers of ethical behavior in and by organizations.

In this regard, chapter 5 ("Owners, Managers and Stakeholders: Whose Business Is It, Anyway?") distinguished among the ethical duties—and interests—of a business and the people who own it, direct it, and/or work for it.

Next, chapter 6 ("The Market for Reputation: A Fresh Take on the Ford Pinto Scandal") introduced the concept of reputational adversaries. That chapter also considered the difference between having done the right thing and being able to prove that one has done the right thing.

Chapter 7 ("'You Deal, You Die': The Godfather and Warren Buffett on Reputation") recounted how and why business leaders value reputation. The chapter also described the temptations subordinates feel to play with house chips, as well as the lengths some leaders have gone to stifle such temptation.

Finally, the last chapter of part II, chapter 8 ("The Hazards of Lumpy Risk: How Arthur Andersen Met Its End"), explored why the unpredictable lumpiness of reputational risk makes it so hazardous. The chapter also looked at how a partnership with some of world's most capable business leaders and risk managers lost sight of ethical lines and thereby cratered their own firm.

How Gold Rushes and Sinking Ships Upend Normal Ethical Calculus

An overarching theme of part II was that reputation constitutes a business's and businessperson's most valuable long-term asset. Enlightened self-interest therefore calls for safeguarding and tending this asset. This calculus assumes, of course, that the long-term matters. As figure 12.1 illustrates, such is not always the case.

In situations in which the long term no longer matters, neither does reputation for ethical behavior. The urge to cheat swells. A gold-rush mentality arises when people can get rich quick. Where someone can rake in enough money in the short term to retire in comfort (sometimes called, "'F*ck you' money"), why care about things in the long term?

At the other end of the spectrum, the more uncertain the future looks, the less people will value the rewards that come over the long term. Since reputation for ethical behavior is a long-term asset that produces long-term rewards, the stronger the gold-rush mentality or sinking-ship desperation,

Figure 12.1 What makes a perfect storm for unethical behavior

Degree of Uncertainty over Future

the less reputation for ethical behavior will matter. If someone doesn't care about such reputation, why not cheat?

Combining a gold-rush mentality with sinking-ship desperation produces a perfect storm for unethical behavior. I lived through such a storm in Russia in the 1990s. People simultaneously snapped up the natural-resource riches of the post-Soviet economy while fearing that any wealth left in-country would be stolen or expropriated. This perfect storm led to bankers getting blown up on Main Street during rush hour while tens of billions of dollars flowed out of the country.

By the millennium, however, things settled down. The fat, easy pickings had been taken. The gold rush ended. In addition, for Russia's new ruling class, millions of dollars in offshore accounts, a townhome in London, and a villa in the south of France brightened the face of the future. Those who had made their wealth did not want to have to check under their cars every morning for bombs, or to fear for their children's safety. The violence subsided. Russia's rich, like their counterparts elsewhere, began preferring to fight it out with lawyers in court than with bombs in the street, or guns in the dark corners of residential courtyards. The long term came back into focus, and it looked flush.

Crises and Cross-Fires in Economic and Ethical Context

Crises and cross-fires can produce both gold-rush mentalities and/or sinking-ship desperation. A situation that is dire for some people in an organization might represent a potential windfall for others within it. Or the organization might have competitors, reputational or otherwise, placed to profit handsomely from the organization's misfortunes.

From a coldly rational perspective, then, a crisis or cross-fire upends how people value reputation and so degrades incentives for ethical behavior. Such situations—*by their nature*—invite wrongdoing. They skew analysis and decision-making. They stress cultures, designs, and controls. They tempt even the most upright.

Beyond warping ethical sensibilities, such situations create pressures that can themselves stun and confuse. Imagine a flash-bang grenade going off in front of your face. As a result, coming to grips with crises and cross-fires must focus on prevention and preparation. Waiting until one is in a crisis or cross-fire may be too late.

THE ETHICS OF DETERMINING THE ETHICS

As mentioned earlier, crises typically involve alleged breaches of a norm and the resulting response. Arguments might arise over the fact and degree of misdeed or misfortune, or the rightness of the response. But people usually do not fight over the existence and meaning of the norm itself.

Ethical cross-fires, on the other hand, often arise in areas that are so new, or so fast-changing, that the norms are unclear. Readers will remember from chapter 4 ("The Trashing of Hilton Head: Who Sets the Ethical Baseline?") how decisive the background rules can be. Cross-fires break out, or become particularly fierce, for this reason. Whoever wins the battle over the background norm will likely win the war.

Cross-Fire Examples

When norms are up in the air, previously uncontroversial decisions or actions can spark a media frenzy or popular protest. Consider some examples:

1. Target—Political Contributions and Gender-Fluid Restrooms/Changing Rooms

In 2010, retailer Target contributed to the campaign of a pro-business gubernatorial candidate who tangentially supported traditional marriage. Target's main interest, as a retailer, was the candidate's promise to cut state sales taxes. Word of the contribution, however, led to a boycott of the company by the Left even though fewer than eighteen months earlier, all major presidential candidates—Democrat and Republican—had likewise supported traditional marriage.

A few years later, in 2016, the State of North Carolina passed a law tying use of single-sex restrooms and locker rooms in government-run buildings to the user's sex as set forth in the user's birth certificate.[3] This law triggered scorn across the country. Target, having been burned in 2010, decided to get ahead of the curve by announcing a gender-fluid restroom and changing-room policy. This step triggered a boycott from the Right that cost the Minnesota-based company an estimated $10–15 billion in market capitalization (more on Target later).

2. Über—Working with an Unpopular Official

In December 2016, Über CEO Travis Kalanick joined President-elect Trump's economic advisory council. Previously, service on a Presidential council counted as an honor and an advantage. A place on the council gave a private citizen an opportunity to serve his or her country. Service also enabled the citizen, if a business leader, to speak for his or her particular sector.

Past was not prologue, however. After President Trump's January 27, 2017, Executive Order curtailed immigration from certain countries, Kalanick's participation on the council became controversial. In addition to internal grumbling among Über employees, more than 200,000 Über customers deleted their accounts.

Über's commercial rivals also pounced. The New York Taxi Workers Alliance organized a protest outside of Über's New York offices. Rival ride-hailing service Lyft pledged $1 million to the American Civil Liberties Union and saw downloads of its application surge.

On February 2, 2017, Kalanick resigned from the council.

3. Facebook & YouTube—Enforcing Community Standards versus Censorship

Major social-media platforms like Facebook and YouTube face criticism for either permitting or prohibiting content in light of the platforms' community standards. In many cases, sanctions have been imposed, and then lifted after public outcry. Claims of bias and censorship abound, as do charges that the platforms turn a blind eye to bigotry and hate speech.

In addition to withstanding consumer backlashes, Facebook and YouTube must also thread a regulatory needle. They have broad legal protections as platforms, but much narrower protections as publishers. Policing content to satisfy various groups risks turning the platforms into publishers responsible for content. With such responsibility comes liability, particularly for defamation and copyright violations.

No Safe Haven for Non-combatants

Several factors have shrunk—or perhaps even wiped out—safe havens for businesses hoping to remain non-combatants in today's political and cultural wars. The first is the increasing politicization of civil life. The phrase "The personal is political" gained currency in the 1960s and 1970s. That viewpoint now suffuses much of contemporary culture. For many people, it also means that politics has become intensely personal: you are either with us or against us. And if you are against us, you must be bad.

As discussed in chapter 6 ("The Market for Reputation: A Fresh Take on the Ford Pinto Scandal"), the period from the 1960s onward also saw the rise of reputational adversaries. These are persons whose vocation or avocation depends on making businesses look bad. Adversaries can include business competitors, crusading media, non-profit consumer organizations, and activists of various stripes. Over the last twenty years, digital information, the Internet, and social media have produced an echo chamber for generating and amplifying news, opinion, and propaganda (a/k/a fake news) while blurring distinctions among them.

RULES OF THUMB

In the present environment, a business leader can feel like the saloon keeper in a Western-movie bar fight who tries to keep his head down, only to get shot in the backside.

Ducking for cover is not an option, though. Business leaders must ensure that, through the mayhem, the saloon not only stays open but thrives.

Thriving in this politicized environment requires senior leaders—the Board of Directors and the C-Suite—to apply certain rules of thumb in anticipating and preparing for crises and cross-fires. These rules include: (1) build good neighbor social capital; (2) adapt to social trends without getting too far ahead, or too far behind, the herd; and (3) handle crises/cross-fires through a combination of advanced planning and strategic awareness.

Build "Good Neighbor" Social Capital

A widely disliked company resembles a lame animal in the wild. Predators will try to cull it and kill it.

A company therefore needs to build up goodwill and alliances. People should see the company as a good neighbor. This means that it obeys the law and commercial custom. It cares about its employees, customers, and other stakeholders. It contributes more than the bare minimum to the community, including by supporting worthy causes. People should believe that the company not only seeks to do well but to do good.

Social capital pays off. Bad buzz on the company will more likely be doubted, discounted, or put into context. Credible allies—preferably from the same side of the political spectrum as predators—reinforce messages favorable to the company and signal to predators that they should look elsewhere for slower and more isolated game.

Traditionally, Board responsibilities have comprised selecting senior management and guiding and monitoring the formulation and implementation of corporate strategy, as well as ensuring the Board's own accountability to shareholders. More recently, the Board has also been charged with overseeing the design and performance of certain control systems. Such systems cover areas relevant to crises and cross-fires, such as risk management, finance, and compliance.[4]

Board structures and processes, however, typically function at too high a level and too slow a pace to handle crises/cross-fires in real time. Often, by the time deliberations occupy the Board, the question at hand is whether to fire the CEO. Debate at this level indirectly signals the Board's failure in overseeing strategy formulation/implementation, as well as control systems.

What senior leaders therefore need to do well before crises and cross-fires arise is ensure that the company's mission, values, culture, and brand cohere with each other and inform company social-capital strategy. In addition to guiding, the Board also monitors through selection of KPIs and assessment of senior-management performance against these KPIs (*see* figure 12.2).

Chapter 6 sketched out Walmart's full-bore social-capital strategy.[5] In brief, that strategy included:

1. Staffing up,
2. Outreach to critics and influencers,
3. Preemptive communications,
4. Support for worthy causes, and
5. Workplace "justice" and support.

As discussed in chapter 3 ("Machiavelli: Self-Interest and Self-Regard Posing as Ethics"), over 500 years ago, Machiavelli counseled princes that

Figure 12.2 Coherent social-capital strategy

it was better to be feared than loved, but that in all events they should avoid being hated or despised.

Walmart's social-capital effort has followed this advice to a "T." In fact, Walmart's worthy-cause efforts seemed precisely designed to split the labor-green-urban-progressive coalition which had previously united in criticism of the company. Ironically, Walmart's reputational adversaries cite the very scale and precision of the company's effort as evidence of Walmart's cynicism and failure to change.

We can note the breadth and coordination of Walmart's plan, as well as the determination with which the company followed through, without judging its sincerity. As a template, the plan shows how to link strategy to mission, values, culture, and brand. For each plan element—staffing, internal change, outreach, communications, and worthy-cause support, the Board should work through with the C-Suite the KPIs that will show success or failure, as well as the methods by which return on investment will be measured.[6]

Adapt without Getting Too Far Ahead of or Too Far behind, the Herd

Abraham Lincoln once observed that "a universal feeling, whether well or ill-founded, cannot be safely disregarded." A major challenge businesses and their Boards face in current times is the speed with which such universal feelings can erupt or shift.

Boards and their senior managers, for example, must grapple non-stop with how new technologies and business models should mesh with people's settled expectations and ways of doing things. A case in point is the interplay of consumer-privacy concerns and online behavioral advertising.

At the same time, sea changes in public sentiment can take place remarkably fast. Over the course of *two years*, gay marriage went from being prohibited by federal law to being a constitutional right, with vendors who refuse to supply or service gay weddings in certain states subject to fines and damages.

New or fast-changing areas like those mentioned previously trigger the ethics of determining the ethics. Collectively, we have to ask whether new rules are required, what processes should apply to working them out, and what the substance of the new rules should be. To explore these questions, this chapter will explore two cases: (1) Target and restroom/changing-room policies; and (2) the Federal Trade Commission and online behavioral advertising.

1. Target Shoots Itself in the Foot

At the company level, a threshold issue for business leaders is whether the company must or should get involved. As the reader may recall from chapter 5 ("Owners, Managers, and Stakeholders: Whose Business Is It, Anyway?"), Directors and senior managers need to guard against mistaking their own values and wishes for the good of the company. This temptation will spike in culturally uniform companies. Like-minded people reinforce each other's views. In such an environment, people more easily misconstrue their personal opinions for universally held feelings or morally unassailable stands.

Speaking out when not in the interest of the company can be a form of self-dealing or waste. For example, in 2017, the Head of Global Diversity & Inclusion of a publicly traded technology company tweeted his company's opposition to a change in federal government guidance on transgender students in public high-school restrooms and locker rooms. Whatever the merits of the tweet's substance, it is hard to divine what *corporate* purpose the tweet served. Using company assets—including brand goodwill—to advance a personal agenda or social-media profile is wrong. Directors should ensure that the CEO has a clear communications strategy and that corporate leaders do not muddle or mix their personal goals and interests with those of the company.

This said, there will be situations where a company's mission→ values→culture→brand rubric calls for action. In the case of retailer Target (discussed previously), for example, action was triggered by the State of North Carolina passing a law regarding use of restrooms and locker rooms in government-run buildings.

Since the North Carolina law did not apply to private buildings, there was no immediate effect on Target's stores in that state. But a raft of pending legislation in other states raised the question of what Target's own policy should be and how it should respond to future legislation or ordinances that might apply to public conveniences like Target stores. Moreover, for many years, Target's mission, values, culture, and brand had led the company to embrace progressive viewpoints and causes.

Without prior warning or public consultation, the company announced a gender-fluid restroom and changing-room policy. Target shoppers would be free to use the facility that aligned with their self-perceived gender. Target's stock price plummeted. Boycotts began. Many shoppers resented being forced to share changing rooms and/or restrooms with people whom they perceived to be of the opposite sex. Moreover, any questionable behavior in a restroom or changing room by a single Target customer in a single Target store made national news.

Some months later, Target tried to mollify unhappy customers by announcing plans to build more one-person restrooms. This half-measure angered both sides, and Target's stock price swooned once more (*see* figure 12.3).

As noted earlier, the policy cost Target $10–15 billion in market capitalization. For a significant period, the company's share price underperformed those of its competitors by over 30 percent[7] (*see* figure 12.4).

Please note that this book does not take a position on the *substance* of North Carolina's law, or of the views of those who supported or opposed it. What matters here is that Target management was running a *business* that belonged to a widely diverse group of public-company shareholders. Target also had millions of stakeholders in the form of customers and

Figure 12.3 Target's stock price in a cross-fire

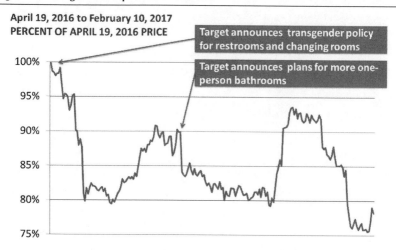

Figure 12.4 Target's stock price versus competitors'

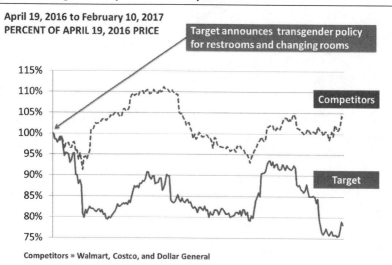

employees. It might have been that Target's progressive corporate ethos compelled action. But needing to act did not justify taking *any* action.

In that case, what should Target, or a similarly situated company, have done? In the area of online privacy, the Federal Trade Commission has given us an example.

2. The Federal Trade Commission Shows the Way

At times, leadership does not mean running ahead of or driving the herd, but urging it forward. In Target's case, the company could have shown leadership consistent with its progressive social-capital strategy by calling for civil dialogue on restroom and changing-room policies among retailers, customers, and other interested groups. This dialogue could have been organized and run by the National Retailers Association, or similar non-profit body.

Calling for civil dialogue is not an empty gesture. **When creating or changing norms people have to live by, persuasion is better than force. This means process is at least as important as logic.** Civil dialogue, even where disagreement is fierce, helps stop the cross-fire by orienting parties toward a common goal. As President Lyndon Johnson once observed in his down-home manner of a political opponent, "Better to have him inside the tent pissing out, than outside pissing in."[8]

Of course, not everybody will want civil dialogue or take part in it. But there are real risks to opting out. It can make one look childish, rather than principled, and call into public question one's good faith and reasonableness. Should the dialogue advance discussion, opt-outs will have marginalized themselves and possibly hamstrung their future sway. Ultimately, the arena is where the action is; players play while non-players sit on the bench, or watch from the stands.

Civil dialogue creates a space and a mechanism whereby a business can serve *all* of its customers, as well as the greater good. The Federal Trade Commission's (FTC) handling of consumer privacy and online behavioral advertising serves as a case in point. This effort brought together the entire spectrum of advocates and positions on consumer privacy.

Online behavioral advertising has been made possible by the Internet and mobile phone technology. The FTC describes behavioral advertising as

the tracking of consumers' online activities in order to deliver tailored advertising. The practice, which is typically invisible to consumers, allows businesses to align their ads more closely to the inferred interests of their audience. . . . An example of how behavioral advertising might work is as follows: a consumer visits a travel website and searches for airline flights to New York City. The consumer does not purchase any tickets, but later visits the website of a local newspaper to read about the Washington Nationals baseball team. While on the newspaper's website, the consumer receives an advertisement from an airline featuring flights from Washington D.C. to New York City.[9]

Some people love this technology. Some hate it. Many don't know or care. In the first ten years of the millennium, online behavioral advertising spread and evolved so rapidly that no one knew what the ethics surrounding use of the technology were, or would be.

To address this situation, in November 2007, the FTC held a two-day Town Hall where all interested parties could meet and express their views. According to the FTC,

> Participants at the Town Hall discussed the potential benefits of the practice [of behavioral advertising] to consumers, including the free online content that online advertising generally supports, the personalized advertising that many consumers may value, and a potential reduction in unwanted advertising. They also discussed the privacy concerns that the practice raises, including the invisibility of the data collection to consumers; the shortcomings of current disclosures about the practice; the potential to develop and store detailed profiles about consumers; and the risk that data collected for behavioral advertising—including sensitive data regarding health, finances, or children—could fall into the wrong hands or be used for unanticipated purposes.[10]

In light of the Town Hall discussion, the FTC published proposed principles for self-regulatory guidelines and invited the posting of public comments on the FTC's website. As a result, FTC staff received sixty-three comments on the Principles from eighty-seven stakeholders, including individual companies, business groups, academics, consumer and privacy advocates, and individual consumers. Finally, in February 2009, the FTC issued its Principles.

This process did not produce a harmonious chorus of "Kumbaya." People across the political/privacy spectrum knocked the Principles. But the process itself paid off in at least one big way: it got warring parties into the same room talking to each other. People had their say. They also had the chance to put written comments in the public record. The process also showed substantive gains. The Principles defined key terms, set forth general principles, described areas of agreement and disagreement, and identified topics for further study. In so doing, the process lessened the cross-fire by finding consensus where it was possible while defining and narrowing matters still in dispute.

Traditionally, democratic societies have had a genius for civil dialogue and compromise. Companies looking to avoid or evade political cross-fires should build upon this tradition. It allows them to demonstrate caring leadership without singling themselves out for attack. It also creates a safe haven and mechanism for working through new or changing issues which have to be addressed.

Since societal and political change never ends, business leaders need to plan and act across three horizons. The first comprises changes the company is implementing. The second covers changes the company is defining, preferably in concert with business associations and other stakeholders. The third describes changes the company is anticipating. In each case, the CEO should identify the relevant stakeholders and describe how the company's social-capital strategy is building bridges with them.

The Board Must Stay above the Fray

Stuff happens. Despite the most artful social-capital strategies and earnest calls for civil dialogue, at some point, a company may find itself in a true crisis/cross-fire or media frenzy.

They are not the same. True crises/cross-fires are rare; media frenzies are not.

As noted previously, the Board represents a poor forum for managing crises or cross-fires. What the Board should do first and foremost is ensure that crisis or cross-fire management and processes have been put in place. Walmart provides a bells-and-whistles example.

Second, the Board must ensure that the company maintains strategic aim. In this regard, the Directors need to provide perspective and guidance from *above* the crisis/cross-fire, not from *within it*. When a crisis or cross-fire hits, directors must stay above the fray and ask—and make sure they get answers to—certain key questions. First, how well is the company operating through the fog of war? Much of the information swirling around a crisis or cross-fire is wrong, incomplete, or out of date. How is top management distinguishing among what it knows, what it suspects, and what it wishes were so? How is top management ensuring that the company is moving fast enough to find out what is actually happening and adjusting as the situation shifts or new facts come to light?

Board oversight should also check whether the company's senior leaders are focusing on the right problem. Throughout much of the Ford Pinto scandal, for example, the carmaker focused on whether the Pinto's fuel system was defective. Management zeroed in on the question, "Did we do something wrong?" By the time the scandal reached the Board for decision, however, the issue had become "How do we want our brand associated with safety and trustworthiness?" Framed this way, the Chairman's decision to recall Pintos and upgrade their fuel systems became clear.

Third, directors need to hear convincingly from the CEO what the company's message is with regard to the crisis or cross-fire, how the company intends to sell that message, and to whom. The company should speak with one voice and stick to—and continually repeat—its core message.

Fourth, the Board must keep the CEO and his or her direct reports focused on the big picture. This picture includes not only the crisis or cross-fire, but the company's operations during it. In this regard, someone has to mind the store and to communicate internally, so that employees can concentrate on their day-to-day tasks. Focusing on the big picture also means the company will cut its losses fast, if need be. Here, the Board must practice what it preaches. Cutting losses can mean firing the CEO and/or forcing resignations among directors.

LESSONS LEARNED: PREVAILING THROUGH
THE NEW NORMAL

Life isn't fair. Businesses face greater competition than ever before. They also face greater scrutiny. Reputational adversaries multiply. Smart-phone cameras and social media turn a single surly employee at the counter, or a single cockroach in the dining area, into global news. In addition, practices that are acceptable one day become scandalous the next, and vice versa.

These pitfalls just involve the things that actually happen. Fake news abounds. It is not just crackpot bloggers or your disfavored cable news network. In December 2018, for example, an award-winning journalist for a leading German publication admitted to fabricating parts of many major stories over a period of years. The publication's Editors-in-Chief assured readers they were "deeply sorry" while stating that the journalist in question "wrote many fantastic features. Unfortunately, most of them included passages that were made up."[11]

Since the editors were also German, they likely didn't intend their comment to be as funny as it was. "Fantastic" features indeed! Of course, as chapter 6 quoted Winston Churchill, "A lie gets halfway around the world before the truth has a chance to get its pants on."[12] Except, of course, that Churchill never said that, probably.[13]

So much for the new normal. What can be done about it?

The first step lies in appreciating the risks the new normal poses. The second lies in understanding how gold-rush mentalities and sinking-ship desperation distort usual perspectives on and incentives for ethical behavior. We will get farther by accepting and accommodating human nature and economic realities than by ignoring or denying them.

The best approach to crises and cross-fires lies in preparation and prudence. Companies need to plan and launch social-capital strategies matching their respective mission, values, culture, and brand. Companies should also put in place crisis and cross-fire-management structures and processes. In larger organizations, structures and processes should be tested through simulations and war-gaming. Former Heavyweight Champion Mike Tyson used to say, "Everyone has a plan until they get punched in the mouth." Crises and cross-fires will stagger people. Practice builds the habits and muscle memory to keep people upright and going until their heads clear.

Companies and managers must also exercise prudence. At root, chapters 9–11 seek to avoid crises by promoting ethical behavior through individual accountability. And, as this chapter has discussed, not every cross-fire calls for action on the part of management. But, where action is required, managers need to move in relation to other interested parties and to leverage the procedural and substantive advantages of collective action.

Lastly, where crises or cross-fires come nonetheless, the Board (or its equivalent in smaller firms) best helps the company by staying above the fray and keeping management on track. Mike Tyson had his Cus D'Amato; and Muhammed Ali, his Angelo Dundee. These trainers coached, advised, encouraged, disciplined, and, if need be, threw in the towel and tried a new fighter.

NOTES

1. This chapter borrows from an article previously published by the author in the May/June 2017 issue of *The Corporate Board* (www.corporateboard.com) © 2017 by Vanguard Publications, Inc., adapted and used here with permission.

2. *See* Merriam-Webster Online Dictionary, accessed December 20, 2018, https://www.merriam-webster.com/dictionary/crisis.

3. Transgender persons born in North Carolina can obtain modified birth certificates on which their sex is different than what was originally identified at the time of their birth, but only if they have undergone sex-reassignment surgery.

4. *See* G20/OECD Principles of Corporate Governance, chapter 6, http://www.keepeek.com/Digital-Asset-Management/oecd/governance/g20-oecd-principles-of-corporate-governance-2015_9789264236882-en#page1.

5. David Baron, "Wal-Mart: Nonmarket Pressure and Reputation Risk (B)—A New Nonmarket Strategy," *Stanford Business School*, Case No. P52B (2006).

6. Measuring Walmart's own success or failure yields no clear answer. The company remains far from loved. Its reputational adversaries continue their attacks. But, Walmart never expected to win over a significant number of these adversaries. Moreover, since launching the plan, Walmart stock has outperformed the discount and department retail industry by approximately 25 percent. The company has successfully expanded into urban areas previously closed to it. It has also fought off unionization during eight years when its adversaries enjoyed the support of, and high positions within, the Obama administration. Overall, the retailer has known progress without peace. Through Walmart's eyes, this may be what winning looks like.

7. CSI Market, "TGT Sales vs. Its Competitors Q3 2019," CSIMarket Company, accessed February 27, 2019, http://csimarket.com/stocks/compet_glance.php.

8. David Halberstam, reviewing, "The Vantage Point Perspectives of the Presidency 1963–1969," by Lyndon Baines Johnson, quoted in *The New York Times*, October 31, 1971, accessed December 31, 2018, https://www.nytimes.com/1971/10/31/archives/the-vantage-point-perspectives-of-the-presidency-19631969-by-lyndon.html.

9. FTC Staff Report, "Self-Regulatory Principles for Online Behavioral Advertising: Tracking, Targeting, & Technology," Federal Trade Commission, February 2009, 2–3, accessed December 24, 2018, https://www.ftc.gov/sites/default/files/documents/reports/federal-trade-commission-staff-report-self-regulatory-principles-online-behavioral-advertising/p085400behavadreport.pdf.

10. FTC Staff Report, "Self-Regulatory Principles," i–ii.

11. Steffen Klusmann and Dirk Kurbjuweit, "Relotius Journalistic Fraud Case: Statement from DER SPIEGEL Editors-in-Chief," *Der Spiegel*, December 20, 2018, accessed December 24, 2018, http://www.spiegel.de/international/zeitgeist/der-spiegel-statement-on-relotius-fraud-case-a-1244896.html.

12. BrainyQuote, "Winston Churchill Quotes," Brainyquote.com, accessed September 23, 2019, https://www.brainyquote.com/quotes/winston_churchill_103564.

13. Quote Investigator, "A Lie Can Travel Halfway around the World While the Truth Is Putting on Its Shoes," Quoteinvestigator.com, accessed September 23, 2019, https://quoteinvestigator.com/2014/07/13/truth/.

We Have Met the Enemy, and He Is Us

■ ■ ■

"Nothing so needs reforming as other people's habits."

—Mark Twain

This book ends where it began. The last chapter, Crises and Cross-Fires, leads back around to the CEO Follies of chapter 1, to the dilemmas faced by John Stumpf, Marissa Mayer, and Rajat Gupta.

After finishing this conclusion, please take a quick look at chapter 1. This time around, do the CEOs and their situations better evoke pity and fear? Do the issues appear both clearer and richer?

Think of the ethical frameworks (Cost/Benefit, Golden Rule, Blind Bargaining, Virtue), as well as the tools and techniques for running an ethical organization (organizational design, process controls, culture, crisis management). Do you feel better prepared to analyze what went wrong and what should have been done differently? Can you state more confidently and precisely how these crises might have been handled better?

If so, this book has served its purpose.

LESSONS LEARNED

Ethical shortcuts and quick fixes work as well—and last about as long—as fad diets. Spend a few minutes on Amazon.com. Books on these topics even have similar titles.

Consequently, in summarizing the key points of this book, I would kindly ask readers not look upon them as "The Seven Simple Steps to Running an Ethical Business."

These points are:

- **To uncover root causes of ethical problems and to find better answers for them, look beyond greed:**
    - One person's greed is another person's ambition.
    - Human beings rationalize their behavior and mistake their wants for their rights.
    - Human nature does not change, so across an organization of any size, replacing one group of employees with another will not markedly improve ethical behavior.

- **Understand and practice using ethical frameworks:**
    - Know the major ethical frameworks (Cost/Benefit, Golden Rule, Virtue, Blind Bargaining) and their underlying ideas.
    - Understand each framework's strengths and weaknesses, as well as the challenges and questions each framework raises.
    - Analyze any ethical issue using multiple frameworks to see which particular framework yields the cleanest or most compelling answer.

- **Recognize that sound ethical arguments can exist for more than one side:**
    - The starting point (background rule) often proves decisive.
    - To find common ground, look for externalities and how to mitigate or re-allocate them.

- **Remember that being ethical isn't enough if you can't prove it:**
    - Cost/Benefit analysis by itself lacks moral content.
    - The fact that you meant well might not be enough.
    - You must contend with reputational adversaries whose job or hobby is making you look bad.

- **Don't do anything that risks your reputation:**
    - Don't use company assets to further your own personal goals or interests.
    - Don't let yourself or others gamble with house chips.
    - Remember that the unpredictable lumpiness of reputational risk makes it truly hazardous.

- **Fix and enforce individual accountability:**
  - In structuring background rules and deals, try to:
    - Place a particular risk on the party who can best avoid/mitigate or bear that risk.
    - Keep that risk (and its consequences) on the party who has accepted it.
    - Promote long-term, transparent, repeated dealings with specific counterparties.
    - Raise the reputational cost of cheating (defecting, breaching, or skimming).
  - Organizational design & KPIs determine structure and function: who and what.
  - Process control defines movement and interdependency: How
    - To manage processes, you must define them: flowchart!
    - Understand variability and its relation to quality control and audit.
    - Bring in an expert to help establish statistical control and to seek continuous improvement.
  - Culture (the uniquely human "Why?") rules:
    - Culture best upholds ethical behavior when it aligns individual self-esteem with the values and goals of the organization.
    - Iron chefs of culture (e.g., Wynn, Rickover, Mayer) employ common ingredients of Virtue Ethics, adapted to their own geniuses and situations.
- **Crises and cross-fires upend normal ethical calculus (Gold-Rush Mentality, Sinking-Ship Desperation, Perfect Storm), so prepare and exercise caution:**
  - Build good neighbor social capital coherently with your organization's mission, values, culture, and brand.
  - Put in place crisis and cross-fire plans and maintain strategic aim.
  - Adapt without getting too far ahead of or too far behind the herd (the ethics of determining the ethics).

Again, please take the previous list with a caveat. Making business ethics work in the real world requires clear thinking, hard work, grit, and humility. One must not only understand general concepts but gauge specific *context*. This includes business context, organizational context, and human context.

Getting things right is hard. Keeping them that way is even harder. People are people. We can either bring humility to the undertaking, or it will surely come to us.

Figure 13.1 The comic strip, "Pogo"

Source: © Okefenokee Glee & Perloo, Inc. Used by permission. Contact permissions@pogocomics.com.

As Walt Kelly's famous Earth Day Pogo comic strip (*see* figure 13.1) reminds us, a sense of humor helps, too. Sometimes, we laugh so we don't cry.

BEYOND THIS BOOK: THE HIERARCHY OF LEARNING

This book represents a small part of a wide-ranging, global conversation about business ethics. The book shares with the reader some stories, concepts, tools, and key lessons learned. To avoid the fairy-tale trap described in chapter 1, I have tried throughout to distinguish what I believe I know from what I only know I believe.

I have also tried to anticipate and answer the reader's questions and objections. That is because the reader, too, takes part in this conversation. Hopefully, this book has not only engaged the reader but also better prepared him or her to contribute further, to draw and pass on his or her own lessons learned.

The learning process should never stop. Moreover, just as there is a hierarchy of motivation (*see* chapter 11), so is there a hierarchy of learning.

This book has emphasized core knowledge and skills.

With regard to knowledge, part I introduced the principal ethical frameworks, along with a Machiavellian gloss on ethical behavior. Part II discussed how the interests and duties of the managers of a business can differ from those of its owners. That part explored various theories on what the "end goal" of business organization should be, as well as why CEOs fight so hard to protect their business's reputation. Part III presented essential tools and techniques to manage for ethical behavior.

This book has also tried to help the reader develop key skills. "Skills" simply mean the ability to apply knowledge to a particular end, which might include gathering more knowledge or acquiring new skills. Skills have to be practiced. In this book, practice has included: (1) playing The Lifeboat Game; (2) analyzing in detail cases like BASF, the Ford Pinto, and Arthur Andersen; and (3) mastering and applying conceptual frameworks, such as WidgetCo's organigram/KPIs, the Shewhart Cycle, and the Perfect Storm for Unethical Behavior.

What remains in the hierarchy of learning are the development of ethical habits and their assimilation into one's character. These tasks are the reader's (*see* figure 13.2).

Habits involve the regular and automatic application of knowledge and skills to specific situations. This includes the pursuit of new knowledge, skills, and habits.

Over time, the exercise of habits, good and bad, defines our character. They become part of who and what we are.

Character plays a central role in the practical realities of business ethics. How central becomes clear from a famous exchange between financier J. P. Morgan and counsel for a Congressional committee.

Figure 13.2 The hierarchy of learning

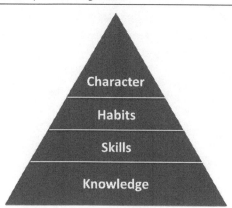

That exchange gives a fitting close to this book.

J. P. Morgan (1837–1913) was America's central banker before it had a central bank. He engineered the starts of industrial titans General Electric, United States Steel Corporation, International Harvester, and AT&T. During the Panic of 1907, he masterminded the rescue of numerous major New York banks, averting a meltdown of the entire financial system.

A few years later, in December 1912, Morgan was called to testify before the House Committee on Banking and Currency. This was the House of Representatives counterpart to the Senate Committee where, over one hundred years later, Senator Warren would deliver her smackdown of Wells Fargo CEO John Stumpf.

Back in 1912, though, it was Samuel Untermyer, Counsel for the House Committee, asking the questions. His exchange with J. P. Morgan included the following:[1]

Committee Counsel:	**"Is not commercial credit based primarily upon [either] money or property?"**
Morgan:	**"No, sir; the first thing is character."**
Committee Counsel:	**"Before money or property?"**
Morgan:	**"Before money or anything else. Money cannot buy it. . . . A man I do not trust could not get money from me on all the bonds [secured guarantees] in Christendom."**

J. P. Morgan was a clear-eyed, tough-minded man of the world. His view is, I think, tested and timeless.

May this book help you put it into practice, for yourself and for others.

Thank you for taking this journey with me.

I wish you Godspeed.

NOTE

1. Untermyer and Morgan, *Testimony of J.P. Morgan Before the Bank and Currency Committee of the House of Representatives, at Washington, D.C., Appointed for the Purpose of Investigating an Alleged Money Trust in 'Wall Street'* (New York: Mail and Express Print. Co., 1912), 5 & 50.

Glossary

■ ■ ■

Agency Costs: Agency costs include: (1) the monitoring expenditures of the organization spent to deter or catch skimming by employees and other agents; (2) the bonding expenditures by an agent to show that he will not skim; and (3) the residual loss suffered by the organization from an agent who has skimmed from the organization.

Blind Bargaining: This book informally refers to Rawlsian Contractarian ethical reasoning as Blind Bargaining, or Equal Outcomes reasoning.

Business-Volume Risk: Exposure to revenue volatility stemming from changes in supply or demand, or competition.

Common Causes: In process control, common causes describe reasons for variability that arise from the process itself and not some special or assignable cause.

Cost/Benefit Analysis: Cost/Benefit analysis requires us to identify and weigh the costs and the benefits connected with various courses of action. Cost/Benefit analysis reflects teleological or utilitarian ethical reasoning by focusing on outcomes that should produce the greatest good for the greatest number of people.

Counterparty Defection/Breach: As used in this book, "counterparty defection/breach" means when one party to a contract fails to perform its obligations reasonably and in a good faith. Where this failure is sufficiently clear cut, we say that the party has "breached" the contract.

Credit Risk: Exposure to the possibility that a borrower or other counterparty might fail to honor its contractual obligations.

Crisis: As used in this book, "crisis" means, in part, "an unstable or crucial time or state of affairs in which a decisive change is impending."

Cross-fire: As used in this book, "cross-fire" describes a situation in which a person or business finds himself/itself caught between contending forces.

215

Culture: The set of shared attitudes, values, goals, and practices that characterizes an institution or organization.

Defective: Description of a good or service which has a specified characteristic falling outside the range that meets internal- or external-customer expectations/needs.

Deontology: A school of ethics focused on acting in accordance with a rule, rather than based upon the expected outcome of the action. Deontology as developed by Immanuel Kant focuses on the motivations of the person acting, rather than the actual consequences of the act. This book informally refers to Kantian deontological reasoning as Golden Rule reasoning.

Devil's Advocate: As used in this book, a Devil's Advocate is a colleague tasked with challenging the thinking and decision-making processes of a team of colleagues.

Dualism: A theory for the end goals of a business entity which holds that a company's directors and managers should seek to maximize the wealth of all of the company's owners.

EPA: The U.S. Environmental Protection Agency.

Ethics: "A code of conduct that allows members of a society to live constructively together and to flourish together."

Externality: The net gain/loss arising when a person unilaterally takes the benefits from an activity while pushing some or all of the activity's costs onto others.

Fiduciaries: Fiduciaries are persons who owe a heightened duty of care and loyalty to another person. The directors and officers of a legal person are typically considered fiduciaries of that legal person.

FTC: The U.S. Federal Trade Commission.

Golden Rule Reasoning: As used in this book, Golden Rule reasoning is the informal term for Kantian deontological reasoning. As developed by Immanuel Kant, deontological ethics can be expressed by categorical imperatives to guide human behavior. The two formulations of the categorical imperative featured in this book are: (1) act so that the principle motivating your action could become a universal law of human action in a world in which you would want to live; or (2) treat other people as ends in themselves rather than as means to your own end. In everyday conversation, the Golden Rule refers to reciprocal conduct based on religious principles, including "Do unto others as you would others do unto you" (Matthew 7:12) and "Whatever is hurtful to you, do not do to any other person" (attributed to Rabbi Hillel, based on Leviticus 19:18 ["Thou shalt love thy neighbor as thyself."]).

Gold-Rush Mentality: A seize-the-day mindset that arises when people can get rich quick, or at least can rake in enough money in the short term to retire in comfort.

Hierarchy of Human Motivation: A theory espoused by A. H. Maslow which posits that once a person's basic physical needs are met, that person's motivation shifts to a sense of belonging and love, then to esteem, and finally to self-actualization.

High Idealism: A theory for the end goals of a business entity which holds that directors and managers must seek not only to generate wealth for company owner(s) but to advance the welfare of stakeholders (e.g., employees, suppliers, customers, and society).

Insider Trading: The unlawful trading of a public company's stock or other securities based on improperly obtained, material nonpublic information about the company.

Kitsch: The self-satisfaction/self-regard felt by people who nominally do something for the sake of others, or who congratulate themselves on the correctness of their feelings.

Legal Person: An entity recognized by the law as having some of the same rights as a natural person. Corporations and limited liability companies are types of legal persons.

Market Risk: Exposure to adverse market-price movements, such as the value of securities, exchange rates, interest rates or spreads, or commodity prices.

Modest Idealism: A theory for the end goals of a business entity which holds that companies should comply with laws and regulations even when non-compliance would be more profitable.

Monism: A theory for the end goals of a business entity which holds that companies do well by doing good. This means that activities and expenditures for the good of stakeholders that reduce shareholder wealth in the short term will maximize such wealth over the long haul.

NHTSA: The U.S. National Highway Transportation Safety Administration.

Officers: The officers of a legal person are managers with actual and apparent authority to run the legal person on a day-to-day basis. Typically, the officers of the company will include vice presidents and executives senior to them.

Operational Risk: Exposure to losses due to inadequate internal processes and systems and to external events.

Pragmatism: A theory which holds that governmental bodies should make greater use of private businesses to implement public policies.

Process: A series of actions or steps taken in order to achieve a particular end.

PSG: The Professional Standards Group of Arthur Andersen, LLP was a body of senior, expert, well-connected partners that had a mandate to ensure the integrity and consistency of significant Andersen accounting determinations.

Rawlsian Contractarianism: A school of ethics derived from the work of John Rawls. This school asks us to imagine that before coming into the world, we find ourselves behind a "veil of ignorance" about our future selves. We don't know our race, ethnicity, or nationality, for example. We don't know our sex or inherent strengths or weaknesses. We don't know our social or economic position. In such a situation, Blind Bargaining posits that people would only agree to rules that will benefit the least well off, since that is the group in which people behind the veil of ignorance may find themselves when the veil is lifted.

Realpolitik: A system of politics based on a country's situation and its needs rather than on ideas about what is morally right and wrong.

Sinking-Ship Desperation: A now-or-never mindset that arises when the near, medium, and long-term futures are so uncertain that people only value actions and gains in the immediate future, with corresponding disregard for harms or losses beyond the immediate future.

Skimming: As used in this booking, "skimming" means a type of agency cost that arises when an employee, without proper authorization, takes a benefit for himself at the expense of his or her employer.

Special/Assignable Causes: In process control, special or assignable causes describe reasons for variability that arise due features specific to some group of workers, or an individual worker, or to a specific machine, input, or local condition, rather than from features common to the process itself.

Standard Deviation: A measure of statistical distance from the average of a group. In mathematical symbols, a standard deviation is denoted by the lower-case Greek letter sigma (σ).

System: A whole of two or more elements that cannot be divided into independent parts. In this regard: (1) the behavior of each element has an effect on the behavior of the whole; (2) the behavior of the elements and their effects on the whole are interdependent; and (3) however subgroups of the elements are formed, each has an effect on the behavior of the whole and none has an independent effect on it (Ackoff, 1999, 15–6).

Teleology: An ethical approach that focuses on the outcome of an action rather than the intent of the person acting.

Tolerance: The degree to which a good or service can vary from a specified characteristic and still meet internal- or external-customer expectations/needs.

Utilitarianism: A school of ethics associated with John Stuart Mill which generally advocates doing the most good for the most number of people. A utilitarian will use Cost/Benefit analysis to weigh competing courses of action in order to maximize utility.

Utility: When costs and benefits are weighed together, the result is called "utility." When the benefits outweigh the costs, we say that utility is "positive." When the costs outweigh the benefits, utility is "negative."

Virtue Ethics: A school of ethics most closely associated with Aristotle. This school argues that happiness represents the highest human goal, since it is the goal to which all other goals (such as wealth, status, power) tend. At the same time, happiness tends toward nothing else. People want to be happy for no other reason than to be happy. Aristotle thought that people best pursued happiness through moral virtue/excellence. They gain moral virtue/excellence by restraining harmful desires (sloth, greed, lust, etc.) and cultivating beneficial ones (courage, wisdom, generosity, self-restraint, etc.)

Bibliography

■ ■ ■

2012 Statistical Abstract of the United States. "Table 744 (2008 Year)." United States Census Bureau, accessed December 1, 2016, http://www.census.gov/library/publications/2011/compendia/statab/131ed/business-enterprise.html.

2018 Forbes 400 List. "The Forbes 400: The Definitive Ranking of the Wealthiest Americans." Forbes, accessed December 6, 2018, https://www.forbes.com/forbes-400/#729e9be77e2f.

Ackoff, Russell L. and Patrick Rivett. *A Manager's Guide to Operations Research*. New York: John Wiley & Sons, 1964.

Ackoff, Russell L. *Ackoff's Best: His Classic Writings on Management*. New York: John Wiley & Sons, Inc., 1999.

Ackoff, Russell L. *The Democratic Corporation*. New York & Oxford: Oxford University Press, 1994.

Ariely, Daniel. *The Honest Truth about Dishonesty: How We Lie to Everyone—Especially Ourselves*. New York: HarperCollins, 2012.

Aristotle. *Nicomachean Ethics*, 2nd ed. Translated by Terence Irwin. Indianapolis, IN: Hackett, 1999.

Associated Press. "10 YEARS LATER: What Happened to the Former Employees of Enron?" *Business Insider*, December 1, 2011, accessed September 20, 2017, http://www.businessinsider.com/10-years-later-what-happened-to-the-former-employees-of-enron-2011-12.

Ayres, Ian and Robert Gertner. "Filling Gaps in Incomplete Contracts: An Economic Theory of Default Rules." *Yale Law Journal* 99, no. 1 (1989): 87–130.

Baker, C. Edwin. "Sandel on Rawls." *University of Pennsylvania Law Review* 133 (1985): 895–928, accessed November 21, 2016, http://scholarship.law.upenn.edu/cgi/viewcontent.cgi.

Bandler, James and Nicholas Varchaver. "How Bernie Did It." *Fortune,* April 30, 2009, accessed November 9, 2018, http://archive.fortune. com/2009/04/24/news/newsmakers/madoff.fortune/index.htm.

Baron, David. "Case: Wal-Mart: Nonmarket Pressure and Reputation Risk (B)." *Stanford Business School,* P52B-PDF-ENG (2006).

Bary, Andrew. "Berkshire after Buffett." *Barron's,* February 17, 2020, 19.

Baseball Reference. "Roger Clemens." Baseball-Reference.com, accessed November 12, 2018, https://www.baseball-reference.com/players/c/clemero02. shtml.

Bazerman, Max and Ann Tenbrunsel. *Blind Spots: Why We Fail to Do What's Right and What to Do about It.* Princeton, NJ: Princeton University Press, 2011.

Benner, Katie. "Victims of Bernard Madoff's Ponzi Scheme to Receive Millions More." *The New York Times,* April 12, 2018, accessed November 9, 2018, https://www.nytimes.com/2018/04/12/business/madoff-ponzi-scheme-compensation.html.

Benston, George J. "The Quality of Corporate Financial Statements and Their Auditors before and after Enron" (PDF). *Policy Analysis.* Washington, DC: Cato Institute (497): 12, November 6, 2003, archived from the original (PDF) on 2010–10–18, accessed September 20, 2017, https://www.cato. org/publications/policy-analysis/quality-corporate-financial-statements-their-auditors-after-enron.

Berkshire Hathaway Press Release. "Warren E. Buffett, CEO of Berkshire Hathaway, Announces the Resignation of David L. Sokol." Berkshire Hathaway Inc., March 31, 2011, accessed December 13, 2016, http://www. berkshirehathaway.com/news/mar3011.pdf.

Bernstein, Lisa. "Beyond Relational Contracts: Social Capital and Network Governance in Procurement Contracts." *Journal of Legal Analysis* 7, no. 2 (2015): 561–621.

BrainyQuote. "Winston Churchill Quotes." Brainyquote.com, accessed September 23, 2019, https://www.brainyquote.com/quotes/winston_churchill_ 103564.

Brown, Ken and Ianthe Jeanne Dugan. "Arthur Andersen's Fall from Grace Is a Sad Tale of Greed and Miscues." *The Wall Street Journal,* June 7, 2002, accessed December 15, 2016, http://www.wsj.com/articles/SB10234 09436545200.

Buehler, Kevin S. and Gunnar Pritsch. "Running with Risk." *McKinsey Quarterly,* November 2003, accessed November 2, 2018, https://www.mckinsey. com/business-functions/strategy-and-corporate-finance/our-insights/ running-with-risk.

Buffett, Warren. "Memorandum to Berkshire Hathaway Managers." July 26, 2010, accessed December 13, 2016, http://prosperosworld.com/ warren-buffetts-memo-to-managers/2011/.

Bureau of the Census. *1970 Census of the Population*, Vol. 1, Part 42 (South Carolina). Washington, DC: U.S. Department of Commerce, 1973.

Business Roundtable. "Business Roundtable Redefines the Purpose of a Corporation to Promote 'An Economy That Serves All Americans'." Business Roundtable (BR), accessed October 22, 2019, https://www.businessroundtable.org/business-roundtable-redefines-the-purpose-of-a-corporation-to-promote-an-economy-that-serves-all-americans.

Calabresi, Guido. "Some Thoughts on Risk Distribution and the Law of Torts." *Yale Law Journal* 70, no. 4 (1961): 499–553.

Capeci, Jerry. "Frank Perdue Meets the Godfather." *New York Magazine*, July 5, 1983, 28–9.

Catholic Concern for Animals homepage. "The Catechism of the Catholic Church." Catholic Concern for Animals (CCA), accessed September 23, 2019, https://catholic-animals.com/about/.

Citizens United v. FEC, 558 U.S. 310 (2010).

Clark, Robert C. *Corporate Law*. New York: Aspen Publishers, 1986.

Coase, Ronald. "The Problem of Social Cost." *The Journal of Law and Economics* 3, no. 1 (1960): 1–44.

Creveld, Martin van. *Command in War*. Cambridge, MA: Harvard University Press, 1987.

CSI Market. "TGT Sales vs. Its Competitors Q3 2019." CSIMarket Company, accessed February 27, 2019, http://csimarket.com/stocks/compet_glance.php.

Danielson, Michael N. *Profits and Politics in Paradise: The Development of Hilton Head Island*. Columbia: University of South Carolina Press, 1995.

Davidson, David L. "Managing Product Safety: The Ford Pinto." *Harvard Business School*, Case No. 9–383–129, May 1, 1984.

Deming, W. Edwards. *Out of the Crisis*, Massachusetts Institute of Technology, Center for Advanced Engineering Study. Cambridge, MA: MIT Press, 1982.

Diermeier, Daniel. "Arthur Andersen (B): From Waste Management to Enron." *Kellogg School of Management*, Case No. KEL559 (2011).

Donaldson, Thomas and Patricia Werhane, eds. "Introduction to Ethical Reasoning." Tuck School of Business, 1–12, accessed November 21, 2016, http://faculty.tuck.dartmouth.edu/images/uploads/faculty/adam-kleinbaum/introduction_to_ethical_reasoning.pdf.

Dowie, Mark. "Pinto Madness." *Mother Jones*, September/October 1977, accessed September 23, 2019, https://www.motherjones.com/politics/1977/09/pinto-madness/.

Dugan, Ianthe Jeanne, Devon Spurgeon, et al. "Andersen Partners Are in Peril as Enron Debacle Roils the Firm." *The Wall Street Journal*, March 21, 2002 (updated), accessed August 7, 2018, https://www.wsj.com/articles/SB1016660095271132040.

Dumaine, Brian. "Warren Buffett's Mr. Fix-It (Full Version)." *Fortune*, August 2, 2010, accessed December 13, 2016, http://archive.fortune.com/2010/07/29/news/companies/buffets_mr_fixit_full.fortune/index.htm.

Editorial Board. "Bringing Justice to Justice: Sen. Chuck Grassley Wants Answers from DOJ on Prosecutorial Abuse." *The Wall Street Journal*, June 5, 2016, accessed October 27, 2016, http://www.wsj.com/articles/bringing-justice-to-justice-1465167217.

Elgin, Ben. "Managing Google's Idea Factory." *Bloomberg Businessweek*, October 2, 2005, accessed September 23, 2019, https://www.bloomberg.com/news/articles/2005-10-02/managing-googles-idea-factory.

Encyclopedia of American Cars, by the Auto Editors of Consumer Guide®, cited in How Stuff Works, accessed December 6, 2016, http://auto.how stuffworks.com/1971-1980-ford-pinto14.htm.

Farrago, Doug. "1000 Left Shoes." *Authentic Medicine Blog*, January 23, 2016, accessed November 1, 2018, https://authenticmedicine.com/save-more-with-aetna-and-sams-club-by-aaron-levine-md/.

Fleming, Jr., Horace W., et al. "Hilton Head Government: Analysis and Alternatives." Report Prepared for the Hilton Head Island Community Association, Inc. (1974).

Freeman, R. Edward. "Managing for Stakeholders." In *Ethical Theory in Business*, 8th ed., edited by Tom L. Beauchamp, Norman R. Bowie, and Denis G. Arnold. Upper Saddle River, NJ: Pearson Prentice Hall, 2007.

Friedman, Milton. "The Social Responsibility of Business Is to Increase Its Profits." *The New York Times Magazine*, September 13, 1970, accessed December 5, 2016, http://www.colorado.edu/studentgroups/libertarians/issues/friedman-soc-resp-business.html.

FTC Staff Report. "Self-Regulatory Principles for Online Behavioral Advertising: Tracking, Targeting, & Technology." Federal Trade Commission, February 2009, accessed December 24, 2018, https://www.ftc.gov/sites/default/files/documents/reports/federal-trade-commission-staff-report-self-regulatory-principles-online-behavioral-advertising/p085400behavad report.pdf.

Funding Universe. "Andersen History." Citing *International Directory of Company Histories*, Vol. 68. Detroit, MI: St. James Press, 2005. Accessed December 30, 2018, http://www.fundinguniverse.com/company-histories/andersen-history/.

Gandel, Stephen. "Warren Buffett Is Paying This Executive $41 million." *Fortune*, February 29, 2016, accessed December 13, 2016, http://fortune.com/2016/02/29/warren-buffett-berkshire-energy-greg-abel/.

Gandhi, Prashant, Somesh Khanna, and Sree Ramaswamy. "Which Industries Are the Most Digital (and Why)?" *Harvard Business Review*, April 1, 2016, accessed November 9, 2018, https://hbr.org/2016/04/a-chart-that-shows-which-industries-are-the-most-digital-and-why.

Gapper, John. "McKinsey Model Springs a Leak." *Financial Times*, March 9, 2011, accessed October 27, 2016, https://www.ft.com/content/144e6728-4a87-11e0-82ab-00144feab49a.

Gentile, Mary C. *Giving Voice to Values: How to Speak Your Mind When You Know What's Right*. New Haven, CT; and London: Yale University Press, 2010.

Gersch, Kathy. "5 Ways Mayer's Trying to Kick-Start the Yahoo! Culture." *Forbes*, July 18, 2013, accessed December 11, 2018, https://www.forbes.com/sites/johnkotter/2013/07/18/the-marissa-mayer-method-5-steps-to-kick-starting-the-yahoo-culture/#5d1de6c63dbc.

Gethin-Jones, Meredith and Susan Fleming. *Marissa Mayer at Google*. Charlottesville, VA: Darden Business Publishing, UV6474, 7, 2012.

Gilson, Ronald J. "Lawyers as Transaction Cost Engineers." In *The New Palgrave Dictionary of Economics and the Law*, edited by Peter Newman. New York: Stockton Press, 1998, 508–14.

Goldman, David. "Marissa Mayer's Payday: 4 Years, $219 Million." *CNN*, July 25, 2016, accessed April 24, 2017 http://money.cnn.com/2016/07/25/technology/marissa-mayer-pay/.

Golshan, Tara. "Ruth Bader Ginsburg Says Her 'Impossible Dream' Is for Citizens United to Be Overturned." *Vox*, July 11, 2016, accessed November 30, 2016, http://www.vox.com/2016/7/11/12148066/ruth-bader-ginsburg-citizens-united.

Google Dictionary, accessed September 23, 2019, https://www.google.com/search.

Green, Mark. "How Ralph Nader Changed America." *The Nation*, December 1, 2015, accessed December 7, 2016, https://www.thenation.com/article/how-ralph-nader-changed-america/.

Grimsley, Kirstin Downey. "Up in the Air with Andersen." *The Washington Post*, March 23, 2002, accessed December 30, 2018, https://www.washingtonpost.com/archive/business/2002/03/23/up-in-the-air-with-andersen/0518d1f1-99db-4e2d-85a9-4eb06f4bde18/.

Guthrie, Julian. "The Adventures of Marissa." *San Francisco Magazine*, February 8, 2018, accessed December 10, 2018, https://www.modernluxury.com/san-francisco/story/the-adventures-of-marissa.

Halberstam, David, reviewing. "The Vantage Point Perspectives of the Presidency 1963–1969." by Lyndon Baines Johnson, quoted in *The New York Times*, October 31, 1971, accessed December 31, 2018, https://www.nytimes.com/1971/10/31/archives/the-vantage-point-perspectives-of-the-presidency-19631969-by-lyndon.html.

Harris, Nicole. "Andersen to Pay $110 Million to Settle Sunbeam Accounting-Fraud Lawsuit." *The Wall Street Journal*, May 2, 2001, accessed December 19, 2016, http://www.wsj.com/articles/SB98875363447314931.

Hart Research Associates. "It Takes More Than a Major: Employer Priorities for College Learning and Student Success." *Liberal Education* 99, no 2

(Spring 2013), accessed May 24, 2017, https://www.aacu.org/publications-research/periodicals/it-takes-more-major-employer-priorities-college-learning-and.

Harvard Crimson Staff. "GM Settles Out of Court; to Award Nader $425,000'." *The Harvard Crimson*, August 14, 1970, accessed December 7, 2016, http://www.thecrimson.com/article/1970/8/14/gm-settles-out-of-court-to/.

Hay, Robert D., et al., eds. "BASF Corporation vs. The Hilton Head Island Developers." *Business and Society*. Cincinnati: Southwestern Publishing Co., 1984.

Heldman, Louis. "U.S. Fines Ford $7 Million for Emission Test Violations." *The Chicago Tribune*, February 14, 1973, Section 1, 2.

Hill, Andrew. "Inside McKinsey." *Financial Times*, November 25, 2011, accessed October 27, 2016, https://www.ft.com/content/0d506e0e-1583-11e1-b9b8-00144feabdc0.

Hobby Lobby homepage. "Our Story." Hobbylobby.com, accessed November 30, 2019, http://www.hobbylobby.com/about-us/our-story.

International Monetary Fund. "List of Countries by Projected GDP." The International Monetary Fund, accessed December 12, 2016, http://statisticstimes.com/economy/countries-by-projected-gdp.php.

Jaffee, Jay. "Roger Clemens, Arguably the Greatest Pitcher of All-Time, Is Trending toward Hall of Fame Induction." *Sports Illustrated*, December 13, 2017, accessed November 12, 2018, https://www.si.com/mlb/2017/12/13/roger-clemens-hall-fame-ballot-2018.

Jensen, Michael C. and William H. Meckling. "Theory of the Firm: Managerial Behavior, Agency Costs and Ownership Structure." *Journal of Financial Economics* 3 (1976): 305–60. http://ssrn.com/abstract=94043.

Jones, Del. "Some Firms' Fertile Soil Grows Crop of Future CEOs." *USA Today*, January 8, 2008, accessed October 25, 2016, http://usatoday30.usatoday.com/money/companies/management/2008-01-08-ceo-companies_N.htm.

Kant, Immanuel. *Groundwork of the Metaphysics of Morals*, 2nd ed. Translated by Mary Gregor and Jens Timmermans. Cambridge: Cambridge University Press, 2012.

Keller, Laura J. "Wells Fargo Board Claws Back $28 Million More from Ex-CEO Stumpf." *BNA Corporate Counsel Weekly* 32, no. 15 (2017): 113–5.

Kiechel, Walter. "The Tempting of Rajat Gupta." *Harvard Business Review Blogs*, hbr.org, March 24, 2011, accessed October 25, 2016, https://hbr.org/2011/03/the-tempting-of-rajat-gupta.

Kiersz, Andy. "Here's How Badly Warren Buffett Has Crushed the Market." *Business Insider*, May 4, 2017, accessed August 7, 2018, https://www.businessinsider.com/warren-buffett-vs-sp-500-2017-5.

Klein, Mike. "Google's AlphaZero Destroys Stockfish in 100-Game Match." Chess.com, December 17, 2017, accessed November 19, 2018, https://www.chess.com/news/view/google-s-alphazero-destroys-stockfish-in-100-game-match.

Klusmann, Steffen and Dirk Kurbjuweit. "Relotius Journalistic Fraud Case: Statement from DER SPIEGEL Editors-in-Chief." *Der Spiegel*, December 20, 2018, accessed December 24, 2018, http://www.spiegel.de/ international/zeitgeist/der-spiegel-statement-on-relotius-fraud-case-a-1244896.html.

Kundera, Milan. *The Unbearable Lightness of Being: A Novel*. Translated by Michael Henry Heim. New York: HarperCollins, 2005.

Laville, Sandra and Nels Pratley. "Brothers Who Sit at Blair's Right Hand: How McKinsey, the Secretive Global Consultancy Firm, Is Gaining Influence at the Heart of UK plc." *The Guardian*, June 14, 2005, accessed October 21, 2019, https://www.theguardian.com/uk/2005/jun/14/Whitehall.politics.

Lepro, Stan. "First Nine Banks Were Forced to Take Bailouts." *Associated Press*, accessed October 21, 2019, http://archive.boston.com/business/articles/ 2009/05/15/first_nine_banks_were_forced_to_take_bailouts/.

Little, Katie. "McDonald's Quietly Changes Its Quarter Pounder Size." *CNBC*, August 11, 2015, accessed November 7, 2018, https://www.cnbc. com/2015/08/11/mcdonalds-quietly-changes-its-burger-sizing.html.

Loomis, Carol. "Warren Buffett's Wild Ride at Salomon." *Fortune*, October 27, 1997, December 21, 2016, http://fortune.com/1997/10/27/warren-buffett-salomon/.

Loudenback, Tanza. "24 Mind-Blowing Facts about Warren Buffett and His $84.7 Billion Fortune." *Business Insider*, April 30, 2018, accessed August 7, 2018, https://www.businessinsider.com/facts-about-warren-buffett-2016-12.

Lubasch, Arnold H. "Shot by Shot, an Ex-Aide to Gotti Describes the Killing of Castellano." *The New York Times*, March 4, 1992, accessed December 12, 2016, http://www.nytimes.com/1992/03/04/nyregion/shot-by-shot-an-ex-aide-to-gotti-describes-the-killing-of-castellano.html.

Machiavelli, Niccolo. *The Prince,* 2nd ed. Translated by Harvey C. Mansfield. Chicago: University of Chicago Press, 1998.

Markopolos, Harry. *No One Would Listen: A True Financial Thriller*. Hoboken, New Jersey: John Wiley & Sons, 2010.

Martin, Andy. "A View from the Top: How 'Rogue Trader' Nick Leeson Made a Career out of Killing a Bank." *The Independent*, June 15, 2017, accessed November 13, 2017, http://www.independent.co.uk/news/business/ analysis-and-features/a-view-from-the-top-nick-leeson-barings-bank-debt-singapore-prison-sentence-a7791881.html.

Maslow, A. H. "A Theory of Human Motivation." *Psychological Review* 50, no. 4 (1943): 370–96.

Masterpiece Cakeshop, Ltd. v. Colorado Civil Rights Commission 584 U.S. ___ (2018).

Mayer, Marissa. "How to Avoid Burnout: Marissa Mayer." *Bloomberg Businessweek*, April 12, 2012, accessed December 11, 2018, https:// www.bloomberg.com/news/articles/2012-04-12/how-to-avoid-burnout-marissa-mayer.

McBride, Sarah. "Former Yahoo CEO Marissa Mayer Creates Tech Startup Incubator." *Bloomberg*, October 18, 2018, accessed October 30, 2019, https://www.bloomberg.com/news/articles/2018-04-19/former-yahoo-ceo-marissa-mayer-creates-tech-startup-incubator.

Merriam-Webster Online Dictionary, accessed September 23, 2019, http://www.merriam-webster.com/dictionary.

Mill, John Stuart. *Utilitarianism*, 2nd ed. Indianapolis, IN: Hackett, 2001.

Miranda v. Arizona, 384 US 436 (1966).

Moore, Mary and John Crampton. "Arthur Andersen: Challenging the Status Quo." *Journal of Business Leadership* 11, no. 3 (2000): 71–89, accessed September 23, 2019, http://citeseerx.ist.psu.edu/viewdoc/download.

Munk, Nina. "Steve Wynn's Biggest Gamble." *Vanity Fair*, June 2005, accessed December 6, 2018, https://www.vanityfair.com/news/2005/06/steve-wynn-las-vegas-resort.

Ng, Serena and Jean Eaglesham. "Ex-Protégé Criticizes Buffett over Exit." *The Wall Street Journal*, January 4, 2013, accessed December 13, 2016, http://www.wsj.com/articles/SB10001424127887323689604578222051534145538.

Ocrant, Michael. "Madoff Tops Charts; Skeptics Ask How." MAR/Hedge (RIP), No. 89, May 2001, accessed November 9, 2018, https://nakedshorts.typepad.com/files/madoff.pdf.

OECD, *G20/OECD Principles of Corporate Governance*. Paris: OECD Publishing, 2015, https://doi.org/10.1787/9789264236882-en.

Onion, Del Quentin. "New Clock Promises to Be World's Most Precise." *ABC News*, July 13, 2018, accessed November 15, 2018, https://abcnews.go.com/Technology/CuttingEdge/story.

Ovide, Shira. "Warren Buffett Lieutenant Resigns amid Stock Purchases." *The Wall Street Journal*, March 30, 2011, accessed December 13, 2016, http://blogs.wsj.com/deals/2011/03/30/warren-buffett-lieutenant-resigns-amid-stock-purchases-read-the-letter/.

Posner, Eric A. "There Are No Penalty Default Rules in Contract Law." *Florida State University Law Review* 33, no. 3 (2006): 564–87.

Quote Investigator. "A Lie Can Travel Halfway around the World while the Truth Is Putting on Its Shoes." Quoteinvestigator.com, accessed September 23, 2019, https://quoteinvestigator.com/2014/07/13/truth/.

R v. Dudley and Stephens [1884] 14 QBD 273 DC.

Raab, Selwyn. "John Gotti Running the Mob." *New York Times Magazine*, April 2, 1989, accessed December 13, 2016, http://www.nytimes.com/1989/04/02/magazine/john-gotti-running-the-mob.html.

Rakoff, The Hon. Jed S. "The Financial Crisis: Why Have No High-Level Executives Been Prosecuted?" *The New York Review of Books*, January 9, 2014, accessed October 27, 2017, http://www.nybooks.com/articles/2014/01/09/financial-crisis-why-no-executive-prosecutions/.

Rasche, Andreas and Dirk Ulrich Gilbert. "Cross-Disciplinary Ethics Education in MBA Programs: Rhetoric or Reality?" *Academy of Management*

Learning and Education 12, no. 1 (2013): 71–85, accessed May 24, 2017, https://www.researchgate.net/profile/Andreas_Rasche/publication/256030925_Cross-Disciplinary_Ethics_Education_in_MBA_Programs_Rhetoric_or_Reality/ links/5597716008ae793d137cc264.pdf.

Rawls, John. *A Theory of Justice*, 2nd ed. Cambridge, MA: Belknap Press, 1999.

Reference.com, accessed December 1, 2016, https://www.reference.com/business-finance/percentage-businesses-sole-proprietorships-731c60f3bd0 2b528#.

Rickover, Hyman G. "Doing a Job." Excerpt from a 1982 speech, accessed December 10, 2019, https://govleaders.org/rickover.htm.

Rickover, Hyman G. "Paper Reactors, Real Reactors" (5 June 1953), Published in AEC Authorizing Legislation: Hearings before the Joint Committee on Atomic Energy (1970), 1702, accessed December 11, 2018, http://ecolo.org/documents/documents_in_english/Rickover.pdf.

Rockwell, Theodore. *The Rickover Effect: How One Man Made a Difference.* Lincoln, Nebraska: iUniverse, 2002.

Sacco, Lisa N. "Drug Enforcement in the United States: History, Policy, and Trends." *Congressional Research Service*, October 2, 2014, accessed October 23, 2019, https://fas.org/sgp/crs/misc/R43749.pdf.

Sacks, Rabbi Lord Jonathan. "The Relevance of the Bible for Law and Ethics in Society Today." King's College London Lecture, March 3, 2014, at 13:02–15, accessed March 7, 2020, https://www.youtube.com/watch.

Sandel, Michael J. *Liberalism and the Limits of Justice*, 2nd ed. Cambridge: Cambridge University Press, 1998.

Schroeder, Michael. "SEC Fines Arthur Andersen $7 Million in Relation to Waste Management Audits." *The Wall Street Journal*, June 20, 2001, accessed December 19, 2016, http://www.wsj.com/articles/SB992971291203974783.

Seetharaman, Deepa. "Yahoo's Marissa Mayer to Reap $187 Million after Verizon Deal." *The Wall Street Journal,* April 25, 2017, accessed April 27, 2017, https://www.wsj.com/articles/yahoos-marissa-mayer-to-make-186-million-from-verizon-deal-1493103650.

Senator Warren Subscriber Channel. "Senator Elizabeth Warren Questions Wells Fargo CEO John Stumpf at Banking Committee Hearing." YouTube, accessed September 23, 2019, https://www.youtube.com/watch.

Shakespeare, William. *Henry V*. Open Source Shakespeare, accessed September 26, 2016, http://www.opensourceshakespeare.org/search/search-results.php.

Shewhart, Walter A. *Statistical Method from the Viewpoint of Quality Control.* Graduate School, Department of Agriculture, Washington, 1939; Dover, 1986.

Shiraki, Maki. "Exclusive: Takata Creditors Seek $30 billion, Far More Than It Can Pay—Court Filing." *Reuters*, November 8, 2017, accessed November 8, 2017, https://www.reuters.com/article/us-takata-bankruptcy-exclusive/

exclusive-takata-creditors-seek-30-billion-far-more-than-it-can-pay-court-filing-idUSKBN1D822X.

Sinclair Oil Corp. v. Levien, 280 A.2d 717, 720 (Del. 1971).

Singer, Sally. "From the Archives: Google's Marissa Mayer in Vogue." *Vogue*, March 28, 2012, accessed December 10, 2018, https://www.vogue.com/article/from-the-archives-marissa-mayer-machine-dreams.

Spencer, Alex. "Verizon to Shutter Yahoo and AOL Brands, Combining Both to Make Oath." *Mobile Marketing*, April 4, 2017, accessed April 19, 2017, http://mobilemarketingmagazine.com/verizon-yahoo-aol-acquisiton-oath-rebrand.

Stanford Encyclopedia of Philosophy. "Kant's Moral Philosophy." February 23, 2004 (revised July 7, 2016), accessed February 21, 2020, https://plato.stanford.edu/entries/kant-moral/.

Strobel, Lee Patrick. *Reckless Homicide?* South Bend, Indiana: And Books, 1980, 82.

Talmud, Sanhedrin 74a-b. Sefaria.org, accessed March 7, 2020, https://www.sefaria.org/.

Tax Policy Center. "Historical Highest Marginal Income Tax Rate." Taxpolicycenter.org, January 18, 2019, accessed October 28, 2019, https://www.taxpolicycenter.org/statistics/historical-highest-marginal-income-tax-rates.

Team Submarine Public Affairs Press Release. "PCU Hyman G. Rickover Celebrates Construction Milestone." Story Number: NNS180512–02. Release Date: 5/12/2018 10:46:00 AM, accessed December 11, 2018, https://www.navy.mil/submit/display.asp.

Twain, Mark. "Concerning the Jews." *Harper's New Monthly Magazine* 99 (New York & London: Harper & Brothers, June 1899–November 1899), accessed December 30, 2018, https://sourcebooks.fordham.edu/mod/1898twain-jews.asp.

U.S. Securities and Exchange Commission Office of Investigations. "Investigation of Failure of the SEC to Uncover Bernard Madoff's Ponzi Scheme—Public Version." August 31, 2009, Report No. OIG-509, accessed November 9, 2018, https://www.sec.gov/news/studies/2009/oig-509.pdf.

Uncommon Knowledge, Peter Robinson, Host, Parts I & II, Hoover Institution, July 25, 2014, accessed December 6, 2018, https://www.youtube.com/watch.

Untermyer, Samuel and J. P. Morgan. *Testimony of J.P. Morgan before the Bank and Currency Committee of the House of Representatives, at Washington, D.C., Appointed for the Purpose of Investigating an Alleged Money Trust in "Wall Street".* New York: Mail and Express Print. Co., 1912.

Verducci, Tom. "Roger Clemens' Recent Statements as Strange as Some Recent Contracts." *Sports Illustrated*, November 18, 2014, accessed

November 12, 2018, https://www.si.com/mlb/2014/11/18/roger-clemens-free-agency-james-shields-russell-martin.

Wall Street Journal Live podcast. "Part II: Steve Wynn Discusses the Future of His Business." At 12:17–12:26, accessed November 27, 29018, https://www.youtube.com/watch.

Wall Street Journal Live podcast. "Part II: Steve Wynn Discusses the Future of His Business." At 12:26–12:50, accessed November 27, 2018, https://www.youtube.com/watch.

Wall Street Journal Video. "Marissa Mayer on Being a Google 'Geek'." April 5, 2011, accessed December 10, 2018, https://www.wsj.com/video/marissa-mayer-on-being-a-google-geek/65DF05B0-1A28-41E8-8B0F-43E2F1196A04.html.

Warner, Charles Dudley. "Everybody Talks about the Weather, but Nobody Does Anything About It." Quote Investigator, accessed May 3, 2019, https://quoteinvestigator.com/2010/04/23/everybody-talks-about-the-weather/.

Wasserman, Elizabeth. "How to Structure a Partnership." *Inc.*, accessed December 1, 2016, http://www.inc.com/guides/structuring-partnerships.html.

Weil, Gotshal & Manges LLP. "Security Breach Notification Laws Data Privacy Survey 2014." Weil.com, accessed October 27, 2016, http://www.weil.com/~/media/files/pdfs/Weils_Security_Breach_Notification_Laws_Data_Privacy_Survey_2014.pdf.

Weil, Jonathan. "Arthur Andersen Faces Court Trial over Baptist Investment Foundation." *The Wall Street Journal*, February 19, 2002, accessed December 19, 2016, http://www.wsj.com/articles/SB1014067925637124880.

Weil, Jonathan. "Audits of Arthur Anderson Become Further Focus of Investigation by SEC." *The Wall Street Journal*, November 30, 2001, accessed September 23, 2019, https://www.wsj.com/articles/SB1007059096430725120.

Wieczner, Jan. "Wells Fargo's John Stumpf Beats Out Amazon's Jeff Bezos to Win CEO of the Year." *Fortune*, January 26, 2016, accessed October 27, 2016, http://fortune.com/2016/01/26/wells-fargo-amazon-ceo/.

Wilber, Del Quentin and Ann E. Marimow. "Roger Clemens Acquitted of All Charges." *The Washington Post*, June 18, 2012, accessed November 12, 2018, https://www.washingtonpost.com/local/crime/roger-clemens-trial-verdict-reached/2012/06/18/gJQAQxvzlV_story.html.

Wojdyla, Ben. "The Top Automotive Engineering Failures: The Ford Pinto Fuel Tanks." *Popular Mechanics*, May 20, 2011, accessed December 7, 2016, http://www.popularmechanics.com/cars/a6700/top-automotive-engineering-failures-ford-pinto-fuel-tanks/.

Wolfers, Justin. "Analyzing Roger Clemens: A Step-by-Step Guide." *Freakonomics* (blog), February 11, 2008, accessed November 12, 2018, http://freakonomics.com/2008/02/11/analyzing-roger-clemens-a-step-by-step-guide/.

Yahoo Finance. "Walmart Inc. (WMT)." Yahoo Finance, accessed December 12, 2016, https://finance.yahoo.com/quote/WMT,

Zafft, Robert. "Steer Clear of Political Crossfires." *The Corporate Board*, May/June 2017, 11–5, accessed September 26, 2019, https://www.greensfelder.com/media/publication/

Zafft, Robert. "Why Your Company Should Have Zero Tolerance for Zero Tolerance." *Corporate Compliance Insights* (blog), May 13, 2016, https://www.corporatecomplianceinsights.com/company-zero-tolerance-zero-tolerance/.

Index

■ ■ ■

Note: Page references for figures are italicized.

About the Author

■ ■ ■

Robert Zafft's introduction to business ethics came during Russia's wild 1990s, when bankers were getting blown up on Main Street at rush hour.

A Harvard Law graduate, Zafft has worked as a McKinsey & Company consultant, global-law-firm partner, private-equity principal, and public-policy expert. He has advised governments, international organizations, and Fortune Global 500 companies across North America, Europe, and Asia.

He teaches business ethics at Olin Business School, Washington University, in St. Louis.